Table of Contents

About the Author

Scott M. Schafer, MAI, MRICS, is a senior managing director of the Valuation and Advisory Group within Cushman & Wakefield Global Services Inc. Serving as the national quality control manager, his duties include developing listening systems to ensure that client needs are understood and met, implementing processes to align more closely with customer expectations, and coordinating quality control teams to enhance report content and improve effectiveness. These activities are performed in conjunction with a cadre of quality control professionals across the country.

As a member of the Appraisal Management Group, Mr. Schafer also orders and reviews appraisal reports for various clients nationwide. In this capacity, he reviews hundreds of appraisal reports on a wide variety of property types each year.

Prior to joining Cushman & Wakefield, Mr. Schafer spent 16 years at HSBC Bank USA. At HSBC, he helped establish the bank's appraisal and environmental services area and held various senior management positions within the Credit Division and Credit Risk Management Department. He began his career at Peter F. Korpacz & Associates, Inc.

Mr. Schafer received his bachelor of science degree in business management from Southampton College of Long Island University and holds the MAI designation. He has published several articles in appraisal, real estate, and banking periodicals and has served as guest speaker at various appraisal and real estate functions. Mr. Schafer has also served on several committees for his local chapter of the Appraisal Institute and holds the Six Sigma Green Belt certification.

Acknowledgments

Many individuals deserve recognition for supporting this publication. First, my undying thanks go to Peter Korpacz, mentor and friend, who gave me my start in the appraisal business and helped instill in me the importance of producing quality work and adhering to the highest ethical standards. These principles served me exceptionally well over the years, and I am grateful for having learned the trade from such a dedicated professional as Mr. Korpacz.

John Busi has also been instrumental in the publishing of this document. His unwavering commitment to continuous improvement and enthusiastic support of quality initiatives at Cushman & Wakefield helped establish some of the foundation of this book.

Thanks also go out to Richard Marchitelli for encouraging me to make the commitment to writing this book. His support of spreading the quality message to the appraisal industry helped make this publication a reality.

I am also fortunate to work with a dedicated group of Cushman & Wakefield quality control professionals across the country who offer guidance and support in our continuous efforts to improve. In particular, Gary Alexander, Steve Gragg, and Sid Womack are especially generous with their time and efforts as part of the National Quality Control Committee. Their friendship, humor, and dedication help make the quality challenge enjoyable.

Members of my "critique team" kindly donated their free time to read drafts and offer valuable insight and suggestions. Thanks go out to these generous people: Mark Borer, Leo Haggerty, and Tom Wurtz.

Last, but by no means least, thanks to Casey, Erin, and Eric for your love and support. The family time that was sacrificed so that this book could become a reality was regrettable, but you were inspirational and helped me get through the challenging–and ultimately rewarding–process.

Foreword

Internal quality control within appraisal firms is an increasingly important topic, especially in these times of heightened appraiser accountability. Appraisal firms that listen to clients, adjust their services to meet client needs, and implement effective quality control review processes have the opportunity to set themselves apart from their competition and secure client loyalty. The Appraisal Institute's newest publication, *Exceeding Expectations: Producing Appraisal Reports and Services That Delight Clients,* is designed to help appraisers do just that.

This publication presents an accessible overview of quality control principles and applies them to the appraisal industry. It provides tips for gathering client feedback and using it effectively. The details of an internal quality control review process are discussed along with such pertinent topics as verbal communication, active listening, and effective writing. Bringing these skills together can help ensure client and staff satisfaction as well as promote the creation of clear, concise appraisal reports.

Exceeding Expectations: Producing Appraisal Reports and Services That Delight Clients will certainly be a valuable addition to your library and will be instrumental in improving your appraisal firm's products and services.

Joseph C. Magdziarz, MAI, SRA
2011 President
Appraisal Institute

Preface

The term "delight" as applied to client satisfaction may make some cringe, thinking it to be a hokey and inappropriate use of the word. "Delight," however, is a common term in quality-management circles, and it is used to distinguish a customer experience that simply satisfies a consumer from one that *exceeds client expectations* and helps cement customer loyalty. This client devotion results in improved profitability for those firms that consistently deliver such products and services.

On the other hand, producing goods and services that do not meet client expectations or are defective can represent a significant cost to the company and to clients. The full cost of such defective goods is often sizable, and the true consequence is not recognized by many companies. An accurate accounting of the cost of defective goods, if it were properly analyzed, would likely grab the attention of owners and senior managers and provide ample incentive to correct the causes of the defective output.

Six Sigma and other quality-management approaches strive to reduce costs and consistently deliver a customer-pleasing experience. The application of quality principles received significant press beginning in the 1980s as a means to improve customer loyalty and increase profitability through customer focus and process streamlining. Despite its popularity in manufacturing industries, service businesses were late adopters of quality principles.

My first exposure to quality management came in the mid-1990s while I was working at HSBC Bank USA. The company committed to a quality program that was intended to be ingrained in virtually every aspect of the bank's business. Starting out as a skeptic who viewed this latest program as just another "flavor of the month" from the executive suite, I attended numerous training sessions that, to my surprise, proved to be thought provoking.

Still convinced that this new movement would be short-lived, I grudgingly assembled a team and undertook a quality improvement project for a service unit that I managed. Although the process was arduous (and frustrating at times), the results were stunning. Using quality-management principles, the team was able to turn this support unit with limited revenue-generating capacity into one that not only covered its costs but actually turned a profit.

Although the profit aspect was noteworthy to the bank, the institution's customers were pleased with the markedly reduced cycle time and the near elimination of errors resulting from the newly streamlined process. Turnaround times were significantly better than those of competitors, error rates were reduced, and overall customer satisfaction shot up. All of this was accomplished without major capital expenditures and using fewer employees. Six Sigma and quality-management techniques were applied, and similar results were realized several more times during my tenure at HSBC. I was sold!

Based on meetings, discussions, and surveys of appraisal clients nationwide, I have found that there is a sizable opportunity for appraisers to improve customer satisfaction levels as well as some distance to travel to achieve client "delight." In addition, many appraisers are unaware of the costs associated with producing reports that include errors or fail to meet the clients' needs. Principles used in Six Sigma and other quality-management programs focus on addressing these issues.

A few fairly simple techniques can be applied to elevate client satisfaction with appraisal reports and reduce costs resulting from "defective" reports. The effort starts with a thorough understanding of client needs and is followed by addressing those critical needs in the appraisal report and through other client service opportunities.

Various methods for obtaining customer feedback and ensuring that the final product consistently meets or exceeds client needs and desires are discussed in this book. In addition, some common criteria by which appraisal reports are judged during the client's review process are identified, as are mistakes frequently encountered by these consumers. Applying quality-management principles to these issues can help producers of appraisal reports and related services avoid common pitfalls.

Many of the examples used in this book involve narrative appraisal reports that are commonly performed by commercial appraisers. The fundamental quality-management principles applied, however, are fully pertinent to residential appraisers (and non-appraisers too). The universal concepts covered include:

- The importance of cultivating a client-centric attitude
- Techniques for obtaining customer feedback
- Interpreting and prioritizing client needs
- Building customer needs into products and services
- Using process standardization to ensure product/service consistency and reliability
- Applying technology to improve appraisal reports
- Implementing processes to check and continuously improve product quality

This book also identifies the general criteria by which clients judge appraisals and related services as well as specific items that clients often focus on when reviewing appraisal reports. These topics provide a clear idea of what clients consider to be of "good quality" from an appraisal vendor and serve as a road map for meeting and exceeding customer expectations.

The technical aspects of appraisal theory and techniques are not dealt with extensively in this book, since that topic is exceedingly broad and addressed by a library of existing publications from the Appraisal Institute and others. Rather, focus is directed on the issues of most concern to clients, allowing the reader to conduct further research on any technical aspects of these client concerns as needed.

As a practitioner who has dedicated over a quarter-century of my life to the profession, I am keenly aware of the various skills possessed by appraisers. Unfortunately, these talents are not always recognized by consumers of appraisal services, and our industry is sometimes viewed as a necessary evil in the lending and/or acquisition process. Appraisers often complain, with some validity, about a lack of respect for the profession.

There remains, however, a sizable opportunity to elevate the perception of the industry as a whole. Greater attention to client needs and continuous improvements to appraisal reports (our primary products) can lead to enhanced esteem from the clients we serve. Quality-management implementation is a significant step in the client-delight journey and can enable those who "build the better mousetrap" through its application to reap the consequent economic and social rewards.

1 Delighting Clients

Why Delight?

Businesses exist to maximize profit and shareholder value, and doing so requires that a firm provide products and services that consumers desire and are willing to pay for. Doing this consistently better than the competition enhances customer satisfaction and is a direct avenue to improving client loyalty and increasing profits as well as the company's value.

Conversely, firms that deliver inferior goods or services tend to lose customers and are often perceived poorly in the market. In fact, clients tell twice as many people about a negative business experience than they tell about a positive one, which increases the offending company's exposure to client loss and revenue deterioration.[1]

The impact of substandard products and services on the consumer can be seriously detrimental to a company's brand and even financially ruinous. This was the situation in the US auto industry in the 1970s and 1980s, when higher quality, competitively priced foreign goods began to erode the market share of Detroit's "Big Three" auto producers. The migration of customers to the foreign nameplates resulted in fiscal impairment of those manufacturers that persists today.

While there are numerous definitions of customer satisfaction, common themes include meeting customer expectations and desires and the extent to which those desires are met (or exceeded) by the provider. The price paid for the good or service is also a factor influencing the client's expectation for performance and his or her level of satisfaction.

Ensuring that products are aligned with consumer requirements begins with a thorough understanding of what features clients truly value in a product or service. Deriving this all-important customer

1. James R. Evans and William M. Lindsay, *The Management and Control of Quality* (Cincinnati: South-Western College Publishing, 1999), 174.

information can, however, be a challenge at many firms. Consider the traditional organization pyramid shown in Exhibit 1.1. In this structure, which remains typical for many companies, the senior managers at the top of the pyramid rely on customer feedback to filter up from front-line personnel (who have the most extensive client contact) to the middle managers and then on to the executives.

Given the layers in this communication chain, the potential for a distorted customer message is significantly increased. This problem is made worse by the fact that the front-line employees typically juggle the demands of day-to-day activities with relaying the customer feedback they receive clearly and accurately to their managers. Any compromising of client feedback clouds the understanding of consumer requirements and increases the probability of faulty decision-making. This traditional structure can also de-emphasize the significance of the customer when executive decisions are made.

Customer-focused organizations, however, take a view that is the inverse of the traditional top-down organization concept. This customer-centric view is often likened to an inverted pyramid, with the clients at the top and the frontline employees who serve them just below the clients in order of importance. Middle managers in this structure are required to support the front line by providing the tools and information necessary to maximize client happiness. Notably, senior managers, who typically maintain the least direct client contact, are at the bottom of the structure. This customer-centric concept is shown in Exhibit 1.2.

In addition, customer contact is extended to all tiers of the inverted pyramid through various means (although frontline staff remain the main client-facing group). In a truly customer-centric organization, all levels are focused on listening to and serving the clients. This

Exhibit 1.1 Traditional Organization Structure

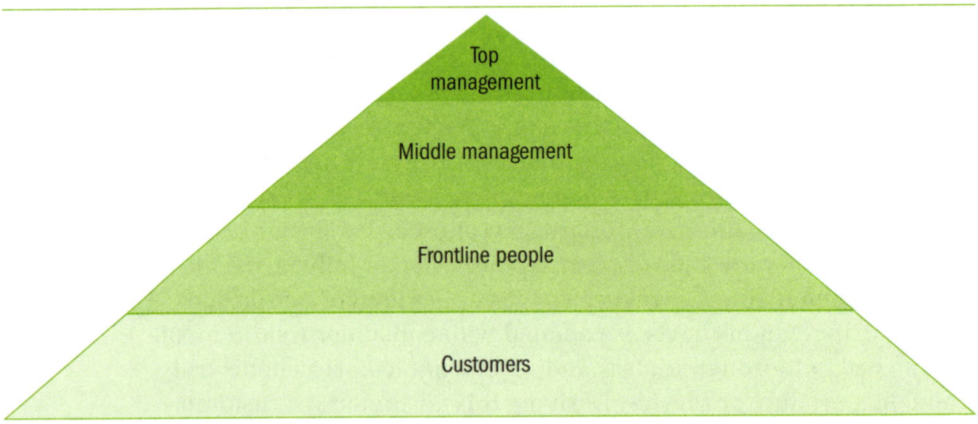

Source: Philip Kotler and Kevin Lane Keller, *Marketing Management*, 13th ed. (Upper Saddle River, NJ: Prentice Hall, 2009), 121. Reprinted with permission of Pearson Education, Inc.

Exhibit 1.2 Customer-Centric Organization Structure

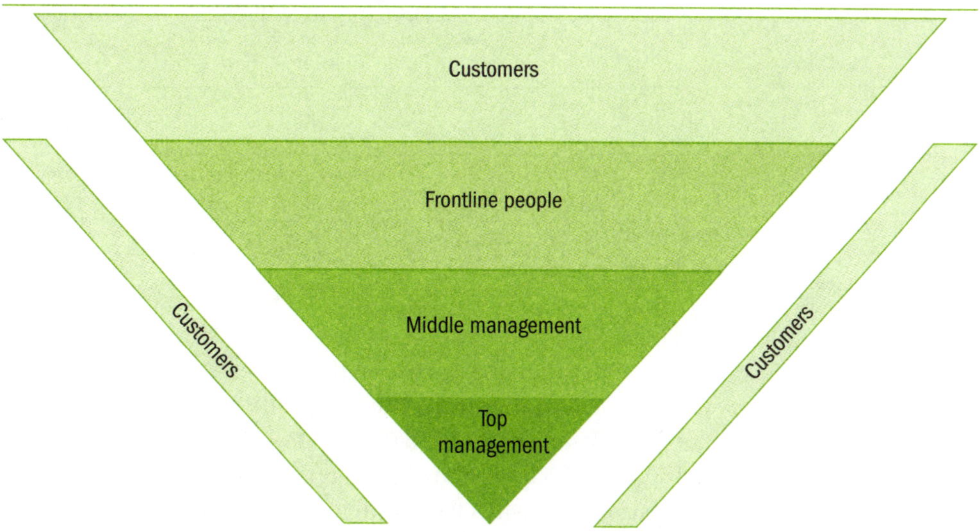

Source: Kotler and Keller, *Marketing Management*, 121. Reprinted with permission of Pearson Education, Inc.

modern alignment properly emphasizes customer significance and improves information flow, allowing the firm to make informed decisions on product and service adjustments.

There is often a significant challenge in shifting the mindset of a company from pleasing those at the top of the traditional organizational structure to identifying and satisfying the needs of the client. Such an effort involves a determined internal push by senior executives to achieve buy-in to the concept at all levels of the organization.

This customer-centric concept helps the entire firm to focus on the client, which is a key step in becoming attuned to customers' needs and desires. Determining how to truly satisfy clients and finding ways to do it regularly are challenges, but techniques developed through the modern process-quality movement can be applied to virtually any business to please clients and reap the resulting benefits.

Obviously, the client satisfaction delivered by individual firms within an industry depends on the level of customer focus to which each company is committed. The variation in client need fulfillment in any given field can be depicted as a normal distribution, with happiness levels ranging from dissatisfaction to extreme satisfaction (see Exhibit 1.3).

> "Don't try to tell the customer what he wants. If you want to be smart, be smart in the shower. Then get out, go to work, and serve the customer!"
> - Gene Buckley, Sikorsky Aircraft

The extreme satisfaction end of the chart is commonly referred to as "delight" in quality-management circles. Although it may appear a bit inappropriate to apply this

Exhibit 1.3 Customer Satisfaction Levels

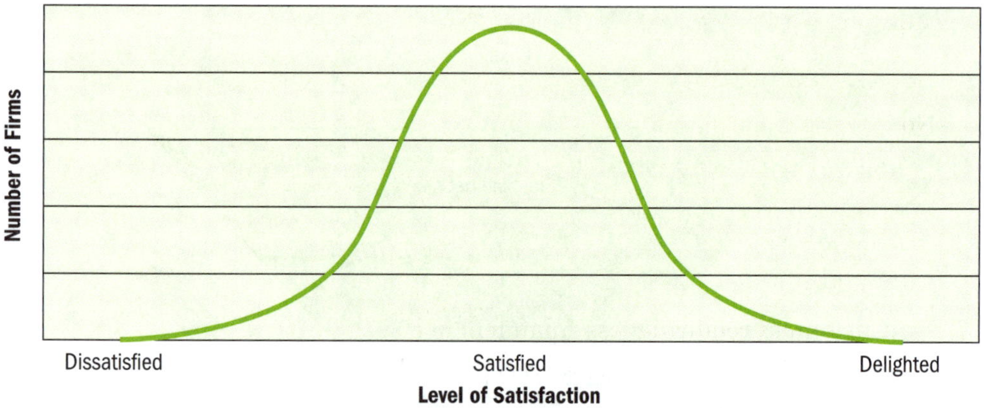

term in a business context, "delight" is used to distinguish a customer experience that simply satisfies from one that exceeds client expectations and helps cement customer loyalty. This concept is discussed in greater detail later in this chapter.

Obviously, companies that fail to regularly meet clients' base requirements (those that fall at the left end of the graph) perform poorly and are unlikely to remain in business if this lack of attention to customer needs is not corrected. The firms falling in the largest segment of the range (satisfaction) are simply meeting customers' expectations, although to varying degrees. These are viable competitors who often realize average customer turnover and financial results.

However, simply satisfying needs does not ensure customer retention. Studies have shown that 60%-85% of customers who switch to competing firms were "satisfied" with the product or service prior to the switch. This indicates that *merely meeting clients' expectations still exposes a company to customer turnover and its dilutive impact on profitability*. In fact, companies can increase profits by 100% by simply retaining 5% more of their customers than competing firms. Minimizing the loss of customers has a direct bottom-line impact, since it is much cheaper to maintain an existing customer base than it is to attract new clients. It actually costs, on average, five times more to attract a new customer than to keep an existing one.[2] Thus, there is clear incentive to do more than simply satisfy customer expectations.

By contrast, the extreme right end of the range includes those firms providing a truly exceptional customer experience. Providing a "delightful" initial transaction impresses a customer and markedly

2. Timothy L. Keiningham and Terry Vavra, *The Customer Delight Principle: Exceeding Customers' Expectations for Bottom-Line Success* (New York: McGraw-Hill, 2001), Preface; Evans and Lindsay, *Management and Control of Quality,* 51; Dale H. Besterfield, *Quality Control* (Upper Saddle River, NJ: Prentice Hall, 2001), 33.

increases the likelihood of another sale to that client. Consistently repeating such an experience breeds long-term customer loyalty, increasing direct revenue from that client and generating new business through referrals from that customer.

Not surprisingly, companies that consistently delight their clients realize superior financial results due to the following factors:

- Consumers who buy more frequently and in greater quantities
- Clients who are more prone to cross-buying other products offered by the firm
- Customers requiring less "maintenance"
- A customer base who is less receptive to overtures from competitors
- Increased sales from referrals
- Reduced marketing costs and price discounting

This superior client experience leads to improved retention and profitability, with one study indicating that a 2.4% increase in return on investment is realized with every 1% increase in customer satisfaction.[3] Companies that reside at the right end of the graph typically lead the industry in pricing and establish service expectations for the client that the competition is usually forced to follow. The incentive to provide more than simple satisfaction is obvious.

The "Delight Principle"

Realizing the benefits of high customer retention and enhanced profits is as simple as regularly delighting clients. The difficulty lies in figuring out *how* to do this and doing so consistently.

One approach to ensuring a delightful customer experience was developed by Noriaki Kano and involves identifying and categorizing customer-defined attributes. Kano, a quality management lecturer, writer, and consultant, reasoned that clients place different weightings on various attributes of a product or service, and certain features create higher levels of client satisfaction. The Kano model identifies three basic types of attributes:

- **Basic "must-have" attributes**
  Basic "must-have" attributes are expected by customers and are the minimum standards required for a firm to remain in business. Failure to include these attributes makes the

> "What it takes to win is simple, but it isn't easy."
> - NFL Hall of Fame coach Marv Levy

3. Keiningham and Vavra, *Customer Delight Principle,* 1, 23.

product or service unacceptable and excludes it from purchase consideration. An example of a "must-have" deficiency is a rental car company whose fleet is made up of vehicles that are in poor condition and/or are not reliable.

- **Linear satisfier attributes**
  Linear satisfier attributes include features that, when included in greater quantity, result in higher satisfaction. A wide selection of car models within a rental car company's fleet could be a linear satisfier.
- **Delighter attributes**
  Delighter attributes are not expected by the client, and their exclusion from the product or service does not result in dissatisfaction. The existence of these expectation-exceeding attributes, however, can have the greatest impact on customer satisfaction (the "wow" factor). A rental company that also includes roadside assistance, free pickup and delivery, and other features that its competitors do not offer would likely qualify as a delighter.[4]

In general, to be successful and not compromise profitability, a firm has to include all "must-have" attributes in its products or services and be in line with the competition relative to the linear satisfiers. Including delighters, however, is critical to differentiating a firm from its competitors.

These three types of attributes can only be identified with the help of focused consumer research and feedback. Since products tend to improve over time, customer expectations rise with these changes. As clients become used to them, delighters become the norm and often evolve into "must haves." As a result, customer feedback must be regularly solicited to keep in step with client and industry trends.

Methods of identifying the various features and their importance to clients are discussed later in this book. It is important, however, to ingrain the concept of delight within each individual in an organization. Unless each staff member internalizes the concept of customer delight, it will not become embedded in the company's culture, and the goal of extraordinary customer satisfaction will be jeopardized.[5]

Various techniques can help make sure that the customer's perspective is constantly considered. Some companies go so far as to require employees to complete self-assessment checklists that track their own shortcomings relative to desired results in customer-relat-

4. Noriaki Kano, Nobuhiku Seraku, Fumio Takahashi, and Shinichi Tsuji, "Attractive Quality and Must-Be Quality," *Journal of the Japanese Society for Quality* 14 (2): 39-48.
5. Evans and Lindsay, *Management and Control of Quality,* 23.

ed activities. Others include client satisfaction/feedback criteria in annual performance goals and evaluations.

While checklists and other formal approaches can be effective, success can also be realized by simply citing examples of exceeding customer expectations and challenging the staff to relate these examples to their own interactions with customers. This is often accomplished through training programs aimed at improving customer service.

The training approach is successful because employees and managers can often quickly recollect incidents in which a service or product he or she received exceeded original expectations. This is useful in helping create a common attitude and set of values within an organization. These positive experiences are often contrasted with negative experiences to highlight the consequences of different customer-service approaches.

Imagine the improvement in shoppers' experiences if all retailers (and all companies) doggedly followed Wal-Mart's customer-oriented philosophy (described below). Unfortunately, many firms and entire

Personalizing Customer Delight

I vividly recall searching for a part for my gas grill at a "big box" home improvement store. Having shopped there regularly, I found the selection, prices, and service acceptable and was a regular customer of the store. Unable to locate a service associate, I eventually found the right section on my own and discovered that the piece was out of stock. Feeling a bit frustrated about the wasted effort, I decided to check out a Wal-Mart store located within the same shopping center.

Previously, I had only rarely shopped at Wal-Mart, as there was another discount merchandiser closer to my home with which I was comfortable. Upon walking into the store, I was greeted at the door by an employee who immediately directed me to the gas grill area. To my surprise, the store not only had the part, but it was nearly 20% cheaper than the identical part at the home improvement store.

The combination of offering the right product, quick delivery, and an attractive price resulted in a "delightful" experience that I had not encountered at comparable high-volume merchandisers. Similar incidents were repeated several times since, and Wal-Mart won me over as a customer. I now stop there for many of my purchases before looking at other stores and have related this story to numerous friends and family members who are now potential "converts."

As a loyal customer, it did not surprise me to read a quote from Wal-Mart Chairman S. Robson Walton speaking at a *Forbes* magazine business conference. Discussing leadership, Walton said that leaders must "listen to the customer, listen to the customer, listen to the customer" to ingrain the proper service attitude for a company.[6] This customer-centered mantra helped build the firm into the world's largest retailer and string together consistently solid earnings and increases in shareholder value.

6. Rich Karlgaard, "Four Styles of Leadership," *Forbes* (November 2, 2009): 23.

industries are far from customer-focused and prone to poor quality goods or services. Airlines, for instance, are often cited for their inconsistent service and apparent indifference to customers, but the list is by no means limited to that industry.

It is noteworthy, however, that even in maligned fields like the airline industry, exceptional service providers exist. Southwest Airlines is renowned for its consistently high customer satisfaction rankings relative to its peers. This customer focus undoubtedly influenced the company's string of positive earnings that is unmatched in the business.

By ingraining the concept of a personal delight experience throughout the organization, empathy for the customer is improved and a superior client experience can result. Relating this concept to a firm's own products and services (including the Kano attributes of those products) through formal training is an effective way to guarantee consistent and widespread delivery of the message.

The Cost of Poor Quality

Customers choose one company's goods or services over another's based on perceived value, which is often some combination of price, speed of delivery, and the fitness of the good or service to meet the consumer's needs (overall quality). Quality is the key to proper value perception, with studies showing that product quality leads to a myriad of benefits for the company, including greater market share, premium pricing, lower costs, and overall enhanced profitability.[7]

While delighting customers with high quality has a clear and quantifiable impact on revenues, the lost sales resulting from substandard products reaching the consumer (referred to as "external failures") are much more difficult to gauge. Firms producing goods and services that contain defects as perceived by the client not only impair their revenues through lost customers but also significantly add to their own costs as well as the client's costs.

The concept of "quality cost" existed for decades in manufacturing industries and was typically limited to the direct expenses associated with inspection and testing, with many other expenses lumped in with overhead (discounts, returns, and so forth). As the concept evolved over time, however, additional costs that are not directly related to the manufacturing process (customer service, accounting, and so forth) have been identified.

Through more accurate analyses, it became apparent that other, less obvious consequences resulted from poor quality, such as lost future business and litigation defense. When added to other expenses,

7. Evans and Lindsay, *Management and Control of Quality,* 22.

these costs as a percentage of sales were found to be sizable. Managers also recognized that these costs resulting from poor quality were largely avoidable.

Despite the significance of the costs of poor quality, many companies are still not aware of the full consequences of producing defective goods and services and largely ignore some or all of these expenses, which are identified in Exhibit 1.4. In fact, *such expenses typically fall between 15%–25% of total sales for many companies.*[8] Given the magnitude of these costs, as outlined in Exhibit 1.4, there is clear economic incentive to improve quality standards for virtually every business.

Exhibit 1.4 Costs of Poor Quality

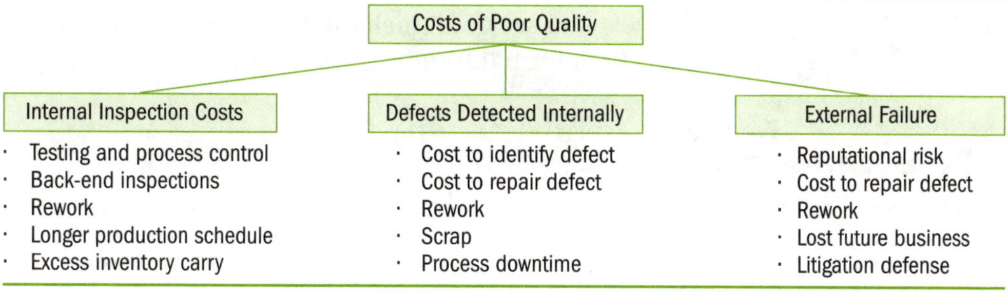

Poor-quality costs are further detailed as follows:

- **Internal inspection costs**
  Internal inspection costs are those associated with testing and controlling the process to ensure that products conform to their intended specifications. In environments with high failure rates, the amount of time (and resources) allocated to testing and altering the process is necessarily increased. In addition, production time lost to correcting problems (rework) and the requisite increase in inventories needed due to high scrap amounts markedly increase costs.
- **Defects detected internally**
  Internally detected defects are related to the back-end quality control (QC) process of identifying potential problems and correcting them before they reach the client. In this phase, the product may need to be discarded or sold at a deep discount (as a "second"), and resulting scrap costs can be sizable.
- **External failure**
  External failures are problems realized after the product reaches the customer; these can be among the most costly

8. J.M. Juran, *Juran's Quality Control Handbook* (New York: McGraw-Hill, 1999), 8.10-8.16; Mikel Harry, PhD, and Richard Schroeder, *Six Sigma: The Breakthrough Management Strategy Revolutionizing the World's Top Corporations* (New York: Doubleday, 2000), 28.

to a company. Depending on the severity and frequency of external failure, such defects can drastically damage reputation and brand image. In addition to the costs of repairing the problem (raw materials, labor, and so forth) and other direct expenses, future repeat business can be compromised. Finally, product liability can result if regulations and/or laws are violated by the product failure.[9]

External failure outlays can be significant and are typically a high multiple of what the cost would have been had the defect been corrected prior to delivery. For example, Toyota's widespread vehicle recalls in 2009 and 2010 were expected to

Toyota: A Dented Quality Icon

Toyota was recognized for decades as a leader in product quality in the auto industry, consistently ranking above nearly every other manufacturer in J.D. Power and Associates' customer studies. This perceived quality was historically a primary underpinning for the company's positive brand image and rising worldwide market share.

Toyota's grip on the top spot in quality perception was seriously shaken in 2009, however, by the recognition that sudden acceleration problems existed in some of its models. The recall of over nine million autos potentially affected by sudden acceleration in late 2009 was followed by the recall of Toyota's Tundra and Lexus sport utility vehicles due to road stability concerns in April of 2010. Several recalls of other models for differing defects followed.

This immense vehicle recall was expected to result in massive direct costs, possibly exceeding $5 billion. In addition to the direct costs, the company faced serious damage to its brand image (with customer quality scores expected to decrease by double digits) as well as regulatory scrutiny and widespread litigation. Toyota desperately fought back with a spike in advertising and buyer incentives aimed at preserving sales, but serious damage was already done.

While the legal and regulatory battle raged, Toyota was also forced to determine the cause of these serious product defects. Some, including Akio Toyoda, the company's president, were convinced that the root cause was focusing on profits over quality. This sentiment was echoed by Jim Press, Toyota's former top US executive, who maintained that the firm had lost sight of its traditional customer-first focus.

Some pin blame on the introduction of the company's "2005 Vision" plan in 1996. The plan's aim was to increase profitability and market share, among other desired outcomes. Fundamental concepts of the plan included:

- Simplifying product design
- Using cheaper materials
- Combining functions into fewer systems and parts
- Decreasing the number of parts used in vehicles by 50%

The program resulted in improved profits and increased market share, culminating in Toyota overtaking General Motors as the world's largest automobile seller in 2008. Mostly overshadowed by the positive financial news, however, was a marked increase in recalls

9. Evans and Lindsay, *Management and Control of Quality,* 23.

and the fact that competitors had largely closed the quality gap. To the company's chagrin, the quality issue was highlighted for the world to see with the widely publicized acceleration problems and the numerous quality issues that surfaced as a result.

The relationship of the company's growth-and-profitability drive to quality problems will be debated for some time, but the damage to the former icon's quality image is undeniable. In response to the missteps, the company established powerful committees to oversee operations, make sure that customer service is improved, and accelerate complaint responses. Time will tell if Toyota is successful in reversing the damage to its brand image by refocusing on its customers.

While quality has an important profitability component, the balance between cost and product reliability must be maintained. It is clear from this vivid example that external defects can severely damage a company's brand and financial well-being. The urgency to prevent such failures cannot be understated in a company's quality efforts.[10]

result in massive direct costs, litigation, and regulatory action (see the accompanying Toyota Case Study). The incentive to prevent such failures is clear.

Poor-Quality Costs in Appraisals

While poor-quality costs are typically related to manufacturing, most are applicable to service industries as well. However, the "production process" for services is highly labor-intensive and typically relies on human interaction. As a result, service businesses tend to rely more on back-end QC for detection rather than inspection during the production process. In addition, the lead time for many services is low, thus there is a greater propensity for external failure in many service industries (for example, medical services).

For an appraisal practice, a typical example of a poor-quality cost is receiving a call or e-mail about a report from a client who identified mistakes or has questions about the appraisal due to perceived inadequacies within the report. Another clear example is having a fine imposed by the client for an appraisal submitted past the promised delivery date.

Although a fine is an easily quantifiable cost, the expense of addressing an external defect in a report is less clear-cut. The amount of time spent retrieving the report, reviewing the issue, formulating a response (or multiple responses), correcting the report, and redelivering it can be significant. In addition, such an incident can damage

10. Much of the information in this example has been gathered from the following *Wall Street Journal* articles:
    - Daisuke Aisuke, Mariko Sanchanata, and Yoshio Takahashi, "Toyota Faces Fallout Over Recall" (February 1, 2010).
    - Mariko Sanchanata and Yoshio Takahashi, "Toyota's Recall May Top $5 Billion" (March 10, 2010): B2.
    - Norihiko Shirouzu, "Inside Toyota, Executives Trade Blame Over Debacle" (April 14, 2010): A1, A18.
    - Yoshio Takahashi, "Toyota Apologizes to Holders" (June 25, 2010): B2.

the appraiser or firm's reputation, particularly if it occurs regularly. These and other "hidden" costs of poor-quality appraisals are summarized in Exhibit 1.5. Unfortunately, many appraisal practices fail to consider these expenses, which can be sizable. Recognition of such costs could result in a heightened sense of urgency to reduce or eliminate defects before they reach the client.

Despite the associated costs, defective products can actually benefit a client-focused company by highlighting problems that need to be addressed. By carefully examining the process to identify the causes of defective products (commonly referred to as "root causes"), improvements in how the item is designed and produced can be introduced. This in turn reduces rework, scrap, inspection costs, and the whole gamut of poor quality–related expenses.

The key is that principals, senior managers, and all employees within an organization must be aware of poor-quality costs and be diligent in identifying opportunities for improvement. The resulting cost savings, when combined with improved revenues, can significantly influence profitability. The savings (or a portion thereof) can be passed along to the consumers, adding to their delight and further cementing the relationship.

Quality-management/process-quality programs, such as Six Sigma, are proven approaches for wringing defects and inefficiencies from processes using client-defined product requirements. Employing these programs is effective at identifying cost savings through efficiency gains and instilling a pervasive "quality" attitude throughout a company. These quality-management principles have been implemented with great success by such American quality pioneers as Motorola, AlliedSignal, and General Electric, and they will be discussed in more detail later in this book.

Exhibit 1.5 Poor-Quality Costs in Appraisals

Apparent Costs:

- Discounts for lack of quality
- Late penalties
- Defending legal/regulatory actions

Hidden Costs:

- Costs to retrieve reports (appraisers, administrative, delivery services)
- Manager's time handling issues
- Rework to change report
- Foregone bidding opportunities
- More bids lost to competitors
- Removal from approved vendor lists
- Negative word of mouth

The Need for Quality Focus in Appraisals

It is critical to understand customer needs for sustained success as a business. Once client needs have been identified, products that meet those needs must be turned out by aligning the appropriate processes, people, and other resources. Quality-management programs provide a very effective structure for improving processes and products in alignment with client needs. In fact, firms that adopt quality programs such as Six Sigma

- Earn 8% greater profits when significant gains in quality are realized
- Are three times more profitable than those with inferior quality levels
- Gain a 4% market share every year[11]

A small sampling of specific success stories is included in later chapters of this book. However, the inventory of such examples is vast, and readers can find a wide range of inspiring examples through a simple Internet search. The common thread among all of these cases, however, is that each firm evolved from the traditional business model to a more modern client-centric model.

Despite the clear financial benefits associated with quality-management programs, many companies remain entrenched in traditional top-down business models that prevent them from maximizing profitability and shareholder return. Many rationalize that their businesses are "different" and implementing quality programs would yield little or no benefit. American companies, overall, have lagged behind competitors in other countries (notably Japan and Germany) in forming their products and services around customer requirements. The slow adoption of quality practices was particularly acute in service businesses, which began introducing such practices several years after they were applied in manufacturing. The lack of international competition and the perceived challenge of implementing such programs in less standardized processes helped dissuade many service companies from embracing quality-management principles.[12]

Appraisal firms are no exception to this line of rationalization within service industries. In addition to the sometimes intimidating challenge posed by quality management, many appraisal professionals brush off the need for such changes by simply taking comfort that complying with the Uniform Standards of Professional Appraisal Practice (USPAP), government regulations, and other standards translates to a quality appraisal. Others are simply unaware of the benefits that result from quality management. This complacency can ignore client needs and run counter to the philosophy of high-performing organizations.

---

11. Harry and Schroeder, *Six Sigma*, 37.
12. Evans and Lindsay, *Management and Control of Quality*, 16, 50.

Appraisal reports are the primary products for most appraisal practices, and they serve as critical marketing tools in addition to conveying value estimates. Furthermore, reports are often the primary (and sometimes the only) exposure that a client has to many appraisers, so producing a professional document that addresses customer needs is critical to improving client satisfaction and, ultimately, delight.

Client feedback indicates that delivering a well-supported and reliable value estimate clearly and professionally in a report that is primarily free of errors is vital to meeting their expectations. This, when combined with consistent on-time delivery and speedy problem resolution, helps solidify the perception that an individual or firm is worthy of patronage and increases repeat business.

By conveying ideas clearly and with minimal errors, the number of follow-up calls and revisions to reports is diminished, which cuts rework costs for the appraiser and the customer. When clients perceive that a firm consistently produces trouble-free services, additional bidding opportunities and increased revenues result.

However, discussions with a broad sampling of appraisal managers and reviewers at financial institutions indicate that firms and individuals often do not meet basic consumer quality expectations (the "must-have" attributes). In fact, clients regularly encounter a wide range of errors in appraisal reports, including:

- Errors of judgment, carelessness, and other factors that impact the value estimate
- Formatting and appearance problems
- Grammar and typographical errors
- Inclusion of stale or inappropriate boilerplate
- Unprofessional writing style and compromised "readability"

These items create a negative impression of the individual and firm producing the appraisal and result in additional work (and expense) for the appraiser and others. Although it is unlikely that any professional wants to generate a defective report, the production cost and disruptions that such appraisals cause may not be adequately recognized. An appreciation for the consequences can increase focus and heighten the sense of urgency for the firm to minimize errors. Consider the steps displayed in the flow chart in Exhibit 1.6.

The sheer number of additional steps caused by a problematic report is obvious in Exhibit 1.6. The amount of time taken up by each item that results from the defect depends on the complexity of the problem(s), but it is clear that significant additional work results.

Exhibit 1.6 Consequences of a Defective Appraisal vs. a Problem-Free Appraisal

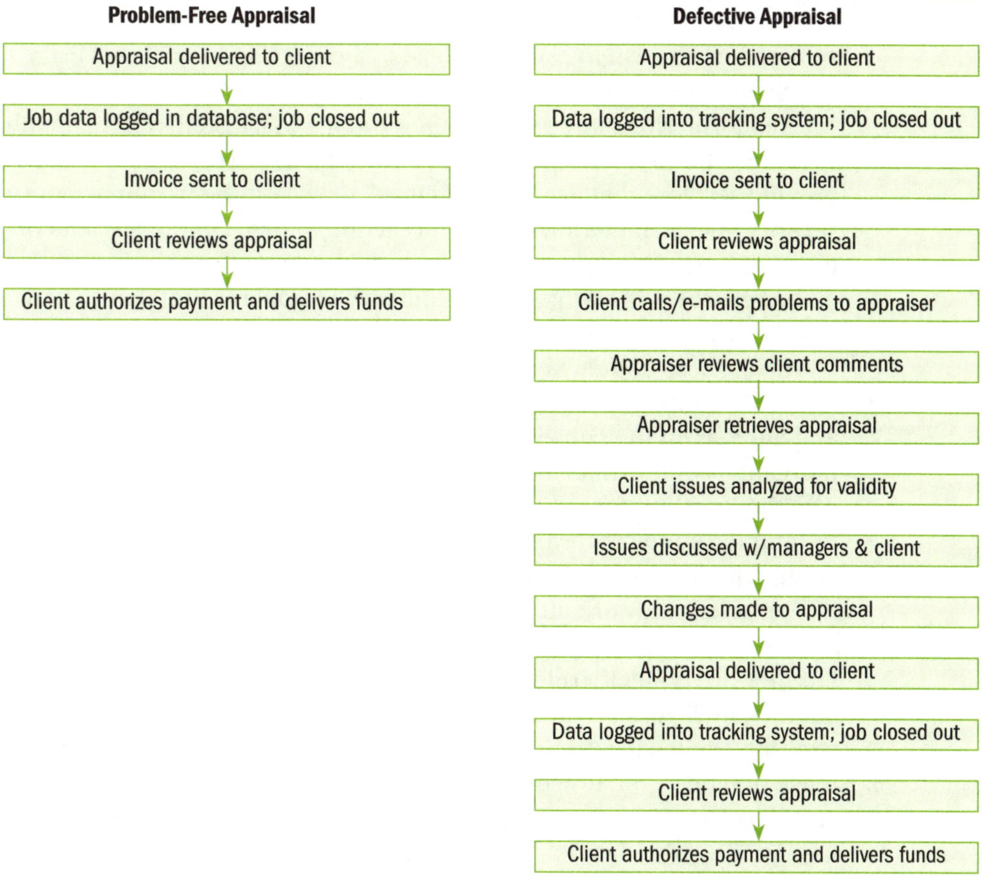

Addressing the defect also involves multiple parties, including the appraiser and administrative personnel. Depending on the firm size, the nature of the problem, and the characteristics of the client relationship, various levels of management time may also be consumed in the process.

More significantly, additional work is required of the client as well. Appraisers can fail to appreciate that reviewers have production responsibilities and addressing problem reports disrupts their workflow. Customers dislike interruptions in their process and the associated amount of time required to deal with these problems. One client put it very succinctly by stating the following:

> "We want to read the appraisal, be able to agree with it, and get on to our next job without the need for follow-up."
> - a financial institution client

Clients nearly universally indicate that they prefer to direct business to those practices that make their jobs easier. Very often, significant and/or consistent problems lead to a reduction in business from the client, if not outright removal from the client's approved vendor list.

Vendor performance is also often rated and tracked systematically to ensure that work is channeled to those firms perceived to regularly provide services that are low in defects. Based on the frequency and severity of external failures, client reaction to firms at the low end of the service spectrum can range from mild annoyance to submission of the report for investigation by industry or governmental authorities (not unlike the previously-cited Toyota recall example).

Regardless of the client's reaction, appraisers who fail to regularly meet "must-have" attributes are obviously far from delighters and fail to reap the consequent benefits. It stands to reason that these individuals and firms would, over time, cease to exist, yet clients indicate that they are forced to continue to use them. The need to guarantee ample vendor coverage given geographic or property-type constraints helps sustain the existence of these low-quality producers.

Although they are often the vendors of last resort, low-quality operators continue to receive business despite their poor quality, but they are typically relegated to non-complex assignments. Consequently, their fees are at or near the bottom of the market, aligning with the client's perception of the product quality. Fortunately for those practices, the low price is in line with the customers' perceived value, allowing them to survive in the business. These low-cost, low-quality providers exist in most industries and can serve a useful niche despite obvious quality deficiencies.[13]

Surprisingly, quality issues are not limited to a small group of low-quality appraisers. On the contrary, client discussions indicate that the quality problem is pervasive in the industry, with a relative handful of firms recognized as consistently delivering "must-have" and linear satisfying appraisal reports in any given market.

The imperative for improved quality in the appraisal industry based on this client feedback is clear. While it is highly unlikely that a typical narrative appraisal report can be issued completely free of errors, various process-quality methodologies and common-sense principles can be applied to allow practitioners to regularly deliver reports that meet or exceed their clients' expectations.

To address these issues, many appraisal firms have established some type of peer-review process, or "second reading" of appraisal reports. By applying concepts from the quality management phi-

13. Peter Murley, *Handbook of Customer Service* (Cheltenham, UK: Gower Publishing Limited, 1997), 36.

losophy, the effectiveness of these inspections can be significantly improved to more consistently detect errors and enhance the appeal of the report for the reader. This is achieved through a well-designed QC review process that includes a defined scope and guidelines to define a reasonable level of due diligence.

Focusing on client-defined quality parameters through effective listening practices and building these critical factors into the firm's report standards and processes also results in reduced defects. When combined with top-notch service provided by a motivated staff, customer loyalty and improved reputation through client delight are the end result.

Designing and Implementing Quality Standards

Quality-management processes can reduce defects and improve the efficiency of virtually any process. It is difficult, however, to spot every problem that exists within an appraisal report, even after quality tools are applied. In fact, research indicates that errors can remain despite reviews by several experienced appraisers. It is critical, however, that major issues are identified and corrected prior to client delivery, thus preventing serious external failure. Examples of such major problems in appraisal reports include:

- Any factors that significantly impact value
- Standards violations
- Obvious formatting and appearance problems
- Grammar errors
- Any writing that is not in line with the firm's standards of readability and branding (the process of promoting the features that set your firm apart from the competition)

Conversations with clients and quality control reviewers nationwide helped identify common problems and specific sections of the report that must be reviewed in detail to make sure that major issues are eliminated. These will be discussed in more detail later in this book. These major problems form the basis around which an effective quality program should be constructed.

Owners and managers of appraisal firms have a responsibility to define and implement a quality policy designed to minimize error and enhance customer satisfaction. Based on extensive client feedback and quality management principles, a quality assurance program in an appraisal practice can be achieved through the application of several "pillars" that are summarized in Exhibit 1.7.

Before launching a quality-management approach, common sense dictates that the business must first thoroughly understand its

Exhibit 1.7 Pillars of Quality in Appraisal

clients and their definition of quality relative to the product or service being offered. These factors must then be translated into the company's products. From an appraisal perspective, this means designing reports and the production process around client needs while adhering to industry and regulatory standards.

As will be discussed in a later chapter, a QC inspection of the final product is not typically relied upon in most quality-management methodologies. Given the non-standard nature of appraisal (particularly for "unique" narrative reports), an effective QC process is, however, critical to checking adherence to report standards and preventing defective reports from reaching the client.

This QC inspection is supported by an audit process that helps ensure product consistency, a major client imperative. The corrective action mechanism provides a means of addressing any fundamental causes for defects and deviation from report and QC standards. These steps must be delivered by a happy, motivated, educated, and empowered frontline staff to maximize effectiveness.

To properly implement these pillars within an appraisal practice, a background in the history and theories of the quality-management movement is necessary. The roots and modern applications of Six Sigma and other quality programs are summarized in Chapter 2 of this book to assist in addressing each appraisal quality pillar. Though not focused directly on the appraisal industry, the concepts and techniques inherent in quality management can be applied in appraisal to help consistently exceed client expectations.

2

Understanding the Quality Movement and Six Sigma

Defining "Quality"

It is virtually impossible in today's marketing-barraged society to avoid hearing or seeing the terms "quality" and "satisfaction" relating to product or service claims of advertisers. Count the number of times in a week that you hear companies proclaim that they have superior products, better service, and friendly staff waiting to help you. While many firms boast of high quality and guarantee customer satisfaction, these claims are often more rhetorical than fact based.

Actually providing quality products is important to achieving a competitive advantage and is key to regularly delighting customers. "Quality" goods and services that include better performance, desirable features, and higher reliability have more worth to the consumer and result in improved market share and the opportunity to command premium pricing. These increased revenues more than offset the costs of researching and designing a better product.[1]

Quality, however, is a challenging concept to define due to the different criteria applied by the variety of potential customers for any product or service. Dictionaries list numerous meanings for the term "quality," and there is no single or even widely accepted definition for the term within a business context. Many commerce-focused interpretations involve the concept of "suitability for use" as determined by the consumers of the product or service. Popular definitions of "quality" from the quality-management movement include those in the following list (all sources referenced are listed in the Bibliography at the end of this book):

- "Fitness for use" (from J.M. Juran's *Juran on Leadership for Quality*).

1. James R. Evans and William M. Lindsay, *The Management and Control of Quality* (Cincinnati: South-Western College Publishing, 1999), 22.

- "A predictable degree of uniformity and dependability at low cost and suited to the market" (from W. E. Deming's *Quality, Productivity, and Competitive Position*).
- "A product or service that suits customers' requirements (i.e., needs and desires) and is of fair price and quality" (from Kaoru Ishikawa's *Introduction to Quality Control*).
- "A state in which value entitlement is realized for the customer and the provider in every aspect of the business relationship. Entitlement means that companies have a rightful expectation to produce quality products at the highest level of profits, while customers have a rightful expectation to buy high-quality products at the lowest possible cost" (From Mikel Harry, PhD, and Richard Schroeder's *Six Sigma: The Breakthrough Management Strategy Revolutionizing the World's Top Corporations*).

As previously discussed, customer satisfaction is achieved by regularly addressing client needs. A popular definition of "quality" used in some service businesses and in quality-management circles that addresses these criteria and is easily applied to a multitude of situations is "consistently meeting or exceeding the customer's expectations." A key word in this definition is *consistently*. A company will never truly be recognized as high-quality if the customer cannot reasonably assume that its expectations will be met with every purchase. Significantly, these products must at least meet what clients define as quality and, preferably, exceed those standards to ensure maximum customer retention.

Regardless of the definition selected, it is obvious that the client must be the center of any efforts related to quality. As a result, it is critical in business to obtain a thorough understanding of what quality means to the buyers of the product or service. Identifying client preferences is addressed in a later chapter.

Quality, even as related specifically to the ability of a product to meet certain standards, means different things to different people. The meaning of quality depends on a person's perspective and the industry in question. Consider the different industries and criteria that can translate to a customer's perception of quality listed in Exhibit 2.1.

The common themes among the examples listed in Exhibit 2.1 are fitness for use, timely delivery, and product cost, or to put it simply: good, fast, and cheap. As a practical matter, it is unlikely that all three factors can always be achieved, so it is important to determine what qualities are most valued by the target customers. The determination of these "critical-to-quality"

quality. Consistently meeting or exceeding the customer's expectations.

- Popular definition used in quality-management circles and some service businesses

Exhibit 2.1 Perceptions of Quality

Industry	Criteria
Airlines	· On time · Low cost · No flight cancellations
Consumer goods	· No defects · Reasonable cost · Satisfies intended use
Insurance	· Prompt · Hassle-free payout · Low cost
Automobiles	· Reliable · Acceptable driving performance · Appealing design
Medical care	· Proper care/treatment · Minimal wait time · Friendly, empathetic delivery

factors is fundamental to ensuring wide product acceptance and, ultimately, delighted customers.

Consumers typically judge a firm's products and services based on the following general factors:

- **Quality**
  The client examines how well the product or service meets the perception of fitness for use based on lack of defects, performance expectations, duty cycle, ease of ordering, and other factors.
- **Timing**
  Timing relates to the client's opinion of how quickly the product was delivered and whether the promised delivery time or date was met.
- **Service**
  Customers also typically consider whether the proper item was delivered and if warranties were honored promptly and without hassle. The level of presale support and quick follow-up on questions before and after delivery are also service considerations.
- **Value**
  The cost of the good or service relative to the perceived value received is a major consideration. Often this decision is made based on comparisons to competitors' offerings.[2]

Clients compare the overall package in their perception of quality, so a thorough understanding of the competitive landscape is

2. Thomas Pyzdek, *The Six Sigma Handbook* (New York: McGraw-Hill, 2003), 66.

critical. If a competitor offers a product that is ostensibly the same as yours but at a lower price, the customer's choice is obvious. Thus, efficiency must be maintained in production to enable competitive (or preferably lower) pricing, and care must be taken to include only those features that customers deem valuable.

For example, a firm can produce a product or service using top-of-the-line materials and complicated production processes aimed at addressing client needs. If the customer is unwilling or unable to pay for the enhanced quality, however, sales (and profits) will suffer. Including excess features that are not deemed significant by the customer is known as "overprocessing" in quality parlance, and it must be avoided.

A person looking to buy a computer, for instance, may recognize that the top-of-the-line laptop with massive memory, enhanced processing speeds, the latest professional software, and sleek styling includes superior features to the common consumer version. However, at several thousand dollars versus several hundred, most consumers may not be willing to pay extra for those features that do not match his or her needs. Conversely, the consumer is not likely to buy a unit with a processor speed and memory that do not meet minimum requirements, regardless of how inexpensive it is.

In an appraisal context, it would be ineffective to expend a disproportionate amount of time researching and developing a section of an appraisal that is of relative low priority to the client. Efforts are better allocated to items that clients highly value, such as thorough analysis and presentation of comparable data.

Discussions with clients across the country and a review of client survey data reveal general client expectations and highlight numerous areas of deficiency for appraisal firms. These items are discussed in greater detail later in this book. The means for individual appraisers and companies to better identify those desires and how they can be addressed in production processes are also highlighted.

History of the Quality Movement

Early Quality Approaches

Although the quality movement received widespread interest in the late twentieth century, the concept of quality has existed since mankind began trading goods and services. Prior to the eighteenth century and the Industrial Revolution, consumers relied on craftsmen who had undergone apprenticeships under trade guilds. These organizations identified and established quality standards. Master craftsmen, who were loathe to lose a customer due to substandard work by an apprentice, strictly enforced the standards.

The Industrial Revolution and its mass-produced merchandise offered items of sufficient quality at a price that could not be matched by the craftsmen, thus eventually ushering them out of existence. This new method of producing goods eventually brought with it advancements in production standards, including:

- Specifications for materials, processes, finished goods, and product testing
- Customized measuring instruments and test laboratories
- Advancements in standardization[3]

As manufacturing processes evolved late in the nineteenth century, production began to be emphasized over craftsmanship and product defects increased markedly. The factory process relied on division of tasks, thus allowing defects to occur often unbeknownst to the employee, who typically never saw the finished product. This in turn gave rise to inspection departments charged with making sure that goods adhered to specific product standards. Significantly, the inspection occurred *after* the part or product was completed, with companies relying on detection rather than prevention as a means of eliminating defective goods. This inspection approach to quality prevailed through World War II.

After the war, the Japanese adopted a policy of regaining economic health through international trade. This effort, however, was held back by the country's widespread reputation at that time for producing low-cost, high-defect goods. Recognizing this deficiency, Japan's manufacturing and political leaders sought information on how other countries approached quality.

In 1950, the Union of Japanese Scientists and Engineers (JUSE), a group formed by the government to advance the country's industrial capabilities, invited an American named W. Edwards Deming to lecture on the concept known as statistical process control (SPC). Dr. Deming–a statistician, consultant, and professor–had dedicated much of his life to studying manufacturing processes and refined the SPC approach.

SPC stresses the elimination of variables within the manufacturing process as well as the need for employees to share in the design and revising of this process. The underlying philosophy is improving quality while cutting costs (primarily through elimination of waste), reducing staff attrition, and improving customer loyalty. Significantly, this approach sought to enhance quality through client-driven processes and considerable employee engagement, rather than relying solely on post-production inspection.

3. J. M. Juran, *Juran on Leadership for Quality* (New York: The Free Press, 1989), 3.

Deming spent much of his time prior to and during the war training engineers and factory workers in the United States in quality. Unfortunately, his efforts to spread the word to managers at large corporations in the United States were largely unsuccessful.[4] The 30-day seminar that he developed for the Japanese, however, was very well received. Deming returned to Japan frequently over the years and trained hundreds of executives, engineers, managers, and employees. The JUSE, in turn, trained thousands of engineers and managers on SPC, and the methodology spread throughout the Japanese manufacturing industry. Deming became so revered in Japan that the country began awarding the Deming Prize in his honor. The award recognizes companies that demonstrate a commitment to and success in quality management and is highly regarded in business circles.

Deming's philosophy reasons that quality is improved by reducing uncertainty and variability in the design and production process. Variation is a major contributor to low quality, and this inconsistency is a primary source of client dissatisfaction that can damage a firm's reputation[5] (see the accompanying case study on wine ratings). To address the problem and react to continuously changing consumer demands, companies must adopt a perpetual cycle of designing, testing, and follow up, as illustrated in Exhibit 2.2.

Deming's continuous improvement cycle, if properly implemented, leads to lower costs through fewer mistakes, a reduced number of defects that require employee rework, decreased needs for product inspection, and the more efficient focus of resources on customer-critical features. These lower costs can then be passed along to the consumer, thus increasing customer satisfaction with the now high-quality product.

Exhibit 2.2 The Deming Cycle

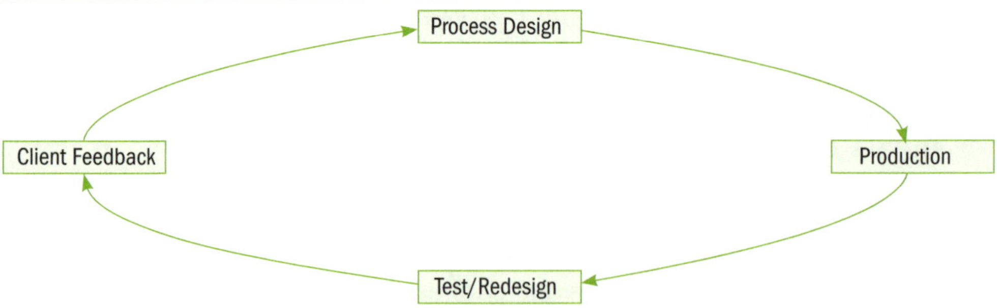

4. Evans and Lindsay, *Management and Control of Quality,* 72, 566.
5. Ibid., 72-73.

Standardization and Wine Ratings

What do the topics of standardization and wine ratings have in common? According to a study performed by a vintner, they have very little in common. The concept of standardization is espoused by W. Edwards Deming, J.M. Juran, and other quality experts as a prerequisite for providing an end product that consistently meets the needs of the consumer. It is also applied to reduce costs and defects associated with a given process. The challenge of standardization can be heightened, however, in processes that are largely manual in nature and subject to human interpretation and error.

An extreme example of human fallibility relates to the rating of wines. As many are aware, wines are often rated on a 100-point scale that gauges the quality of the product based on the opinion of "expert" tasters. The system is relied upon by many consumers, and it can have a major impact on the prices charged by wineries.

It turns out, however, that such ratings are highly inconsistent and quite unreliable. A disgruntled vintner named Robert Hodgson, who marveled at how the same wine could be a gold medal winner in one competition and roundly panned in another, decided to study wine tasting and became a member of a well-known wine judging board.

After considerable arm-twisting, Hodgson's colleagues on the board agreed to allow him to conduct a scientific study on the judging results to test for consistency. The winery owner found that the ratings are not much more reliable than random chance across certain categories of wine. This result occurred despite the extensive training and experience apparently possessed by the judges. (Note that numerous wine "colleges" offer varying levels of training and certification, replete with standard forms and information on the art of wine tasting. This can serve as the basic training for aspiring wine experts.)

While some wine critics were quick to dismiss the findings, wine makers supported the results based on their uneven experiences with the system. The implication for consumers is clear: selecting wines based on ratings and/or medals awarded at tasting events is highly fallible. One wine critic opined that variation is to be expected since wine experts are not robots.[6] This fact should not be lost on process observers, and it is the primary cause for the lack of end-result reliability

This example highlights the challenge of a manual-based process to which little empirical calibration can be applied. As discussed throughout this book, the human element prevalent in most service businesses is a major impediment to achieving consistent quality, and variation in results can yield unhappy consumers. Consider this example on your next trip to the wine store for a prized cabernet; it could save you lots of money.

The Japanese fully embraced Deming's philosophy as well as those of J. M. Juran and other early quality pioneers. After the widespread integration of quality management in Japanese manufacturers, goods

6. Leonard Mlodinow, "A Hint of Hype, A Taste of Illusion," *The Wall Street Journal* (November 14-15, 2010): W1-W2.

produced in Japan became widely regarded as the best in the world, leading to dominance in consumer products such as electronics and automobiles and helping Japan rise to economic powerhouse status.

Japan's success was largely rooted in:

- Recognition by senior managers of the urgent need for quality improvement and personal involvement in and commitment to the quality movement
- Robust training in quality management for employees at all levels of the organization
- Commitment to rapid and continuous improvement[7]

Adoption of these principles was also the key to breaking with the archaic top-down management philosophy that previously existed in Japan and virtually every other country. Under this philosophy, efforts to understand the customers and their needs were limited, and managers directed workers and processes with no input from the people actually performing the function. Managers and workers expected and tolerated mistakes and waste, with limited focus on getting the job done right the first time.

Japan's radical break from a traditional business philosophy included:

- **Unwavering customer focus**
  The customer is the ultimate arbiter of quality. Japanese firms focused their efforts on understanding what attributes the customers value and how the products are used, and then designed products and services to meet or exceed those standards.
- **Workforce engagement and teamwork**
  Leveraging all of a firm's human assets rather than just a handful of managers or specialists increases creativity and fosters improvement. Including employees in decisions about their jobs and customer-related processes markedly improves results and can help speed up the pace of change. This workforce participation, when combined with the empowerment to make customer satisfaction decisions, also builds trust and job satisfaction for the employee.
- **Commitment to continuous improvement and learning**
  Although the concept of identifying ways to improve products and processes has existed since the Industrial Revolution, the commitment to continually improve was not consistently fol-

7. J.M. Juran, "Managing for Quality," *Journal for Quality and Participation* 11, no. 1 (January/February 1988): 8-12.

> lowed, placing many firms in a reactive mode relative to their competitors. Improving products and services to keep pace with client and market changes is critical for any business.[8]

The ascendance of Japanese manufacturing power, largely at the expense of American corporations, grabbed the attention of some American companies as sales slid and customers migrated to higher-quality, competitively priced imported goods. This issue was highlighted in a 1980 NBC documentary entitled "If Japan Can, Why Can't We?" that examined Japan's exporting prowess and the work of Deming.

The Birth of Six Sigma

American companies started to recognize the value of quality management and eventually became highly motivated to duplicate Japan's success. Firms began adopting SPC, total quality management (TQM), just-in-time inventory management, and other quality programs in the early 1980s.

The need for change was first highlighted for Motorola in the late 1970s, when a Japanese company took control of an American television plant and soon produced televisions with significantly less defects than the Motorola sets at a lower cost. This was accomplished using the same work force, technology, and designs that Motorola employed.[9] Similar incidents were identified over the next several years.

The television plant episode and other quality issues caught the attention of Motorola's CEO, Bob Galvin, who focused the company's resources on improving processes and enhancing efficiency. Building on the foundations of SPC, TQM, and other early efforts, Motorola devised a methodology that measures defects in a product and systematically redesigns the production process using proven quality principles and techniques to reduce those errors.

In the quality-movement context, a *defect* is defined as anything that does not meet a customer-defined specification.[10] Motorola measured these deviations from customer specifications statistically using the Greek symbol sigma (σ) to represent one standard deviation from the mean in a normal distribution.[11]

The Six Sigma distribution chart in Exhibit 2.3 displays the population of a hypothetical product. The largest concentration of results is

8. Evans and Lindsay, *Management and Control of Quality,* 72-73.
9. Pyzdek, *Six Sigma Handbook,* 4.
10. George Eckes, *The Six Sigma Revolution* (New York: John Wiley & Sons, 2001), 5.
11. Author's note: Although a concerted effort was made to reduce the dry arithmetic nature of describing the workings of Six Sigma, statistics are, unfortunately, integral to the approach. For statistically averse readers, this may be an opportune time to open the previously mentioned prize cabernet before proceeding.

Exhibit 2.3 Six Sigma Distribution Chart

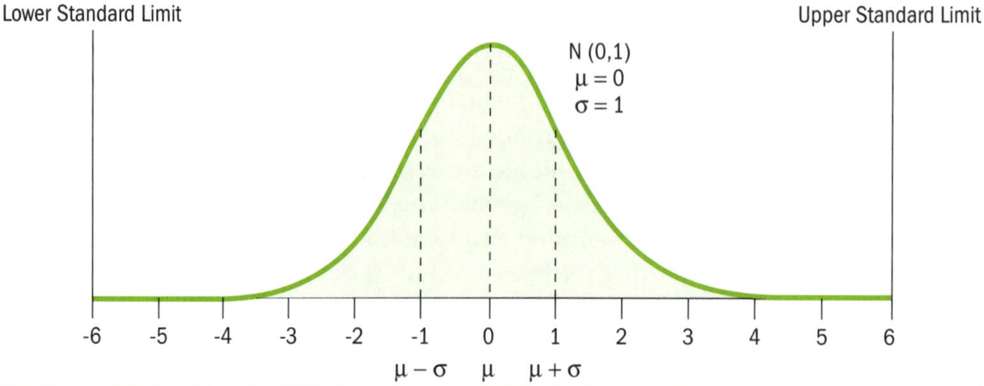

centered around the mean (μ), and the numbers drop precipitously as distance from the mean increases. The lines at the right (upper standard limit) and left (lower standard limit) margins of the graph represent the upper and lower limits of tolerance specified by the customer. Hence, the more results that fall within those customer-defined limits of acceptability (lower defect incidence), the greater the sigma value.

As displayed in Exhibit 2.3, Six Sigma equates to the population that exists within plus or minus six standard deviations of the process outputs and translates to only 3.4 defects per million opportunities (which is essentially no defects). Defects per million opportunities (DPMO) at different sigma levels are shown as follows:

- One sigma = 690,000 DPMO (31% defect-free)
- Two sigma = 308,000 DPMO (69.2% defect-free)
- Three sigma = 66,800 DPMO (93.32% defect-free)
- Four sigma = 6,210 DPMO (99.379% defect-free)
- Five sigma = 230 DPMO (99.977% defect-free)
- Six sigma = 3.4 DPMO (99.9997% defect-free)

Based on these figures, a "six sigma product" is one that includes 3.4 defects per million *opportunities*. This should not be interpreted to mean that 3.4 of the products out of 1 million will include a flaw. Rather, a *defect opportunity* is the number of times that a deficiency could reasonably occur in a given product.[12] Therefore, the greater the complexity of the product, the greater the prospect of a defect. For example, a hammer manufacturer realizes fewer chances of defects than an electric drill manufacturer over a production run of the same

12. Mary A. Williams, Thomas Bertels, and Harvey Dreshin, *Six Sigma Pocket Guide* (Lexington, MA: Rath & Strong, 2004), 90.

size, due to the larger number of parts and higher complexity of a drill relative to a hammer.

Historically, manufacturers have accepted variance equating to three to four sigma, and many businesses still operate at those levels or worse. This tolerance, though small on a percentage basis, results in roughly 6,200 to 67,000 defects per million opportunities. For some, the relatively small percentage of defects may seem inconsequential, effectively eliminating the desire to migrate to a higher sigma level.

However, consider a fast food chain that serves one million meals per day and operates at a three-sigma level. (While it is unlikely that most restaurants of this type operate close to this level, this provides a useful example.) At three sigma, that chain would serve 66,800 defective meals (wrong drink, cold burger, limp fries, and so forth) every day, which equates to nearly 67,000 opportunities to lose a customer to a competitor *every day*.

The prospect of that many dissatisfied customers is unacceptable to quality-minded firms in highly competitive industries. This is particularly true for high-volume producers and those in the health care (especially surgery and acute care) and human safety fields, where the consequences of errors can be severe. Due to competitive pressures, liability potential, and elevated customer expectations, many businesses in industries like these strive for near-perfect quality levels.[13]

Motorola pioneered the goal of achieving a level of six sigma for its products, and this term became applied to the design and management effort associated with achieving that level of reliability. Although the Six Sigma approach shares similarities with earlier quality programs, Six Sigma's significant contribution is the publicity it garnered and the resulting focus on it and other quality approaches by American industry.

In an early Six Sigma success, a team was assembled at Motorola to design the new "Bandit" pager. Using customer specifications and borrowing best practices from across the company and the industry, the project team redesigned the pager and the associated manufacturing process. They introduced a product that could be customized to each customer's individual specifications and produced within 72 hours with a life expectancy of 150 years.

The pager's flexibility and sturdiness were obviously very popular with customers. In addition, end-product quality was so high that quality control testing for the Bandit was eventually eliminated, since it was more cost effective to simply replace any defective pagers than spend time testing this essentially defect-free item. As the Six Sigma philosophy spread throughout the company, increased product quality and

13. Pyzdek, *Six Sigma Handbook*, 60.

lowered manufacturing costs as well as increased customer satisfaction were pervasive. Within four years, Motorola achieved an estimated savings of $2.2 billion as a result of its quality management effort.

Word of Motorola's success with this approach spread quickly after the company won the Malcolm Baldrige National Quality Award in 1988. Soon other companies began to adopt this methodology. Corporations such as AlliedSignal and Texas Instruments followed with their own Six Sigma programs, resulting in sizable sales gains while improving productivity and profitability.[14]

By 1995, Jack Welch, the celebrated CEO of General Electric (GE), learned of the successes realized by some of his peers. After researching Sig Sigma extensively, he was taken with its potential and quickly moved to implement the program at GE. The company's Six Sigma program was responsible for such achievements as:

- A 160% increase in transactions in the commercial finance division
- Improved customer retention and $60 million in new business from a single customer in the mortgage insurance business
- A 62% reduction in turnaround time for railcar repairs
- A 50% reduction in the cycle time of railcar leasing
- A 50% reduction in border delays for imported parts to the GE aircraft engines operation in Canada[15]

These examples are a small sampling of the successes wrought from Six Sigma at GE. During Jack Welch's tenure, the company's market value increased from $12 billion in 1981 to $280 billion by 1998, with Welch crediting the company's quality effort as one of the major driving forces behind this value appreciation.

The media-savvy CEO promoted these benefits, including the billions of dollars in enhanced profitability that Six Sigma yielded, at every opportunity. Its use spread and began to be adopted outside of the manufacturing realm. Today, this methodology is applied by service companies ranging from banks to medical service providers and even some government bodies.

Six Sigma Methodology Overview

So how did Six Sigma help GE and others realize these impressive gains? At its essence, Six Sigma and other quality programs seek to

14. Mikel Harry, PhD, and Richard Schroeder, *Six Sigma: The Breakthrough Management Strategy Revolutionizing the World's Top Corporations* (New York: Doubleday, 2000), 11; Eckes, *Six Sigma Revolution,* 6.
15. Harry and Schroeder, *Six Sigma: The Breakthrough Management Strategy,* 5, 48.

identify and understand customer requirements and streamline processes to reduce variation, prevent defects, shorten production cycle time, and lower costs. This is distinct from the traditional efficiency approaches that preceded the quality movement. These efficiency efforts were simple cost-cutting programs that also often resulted in lowered product quality.[16]

Six Sigma and other quality-management approaches differ from post–Industrial Revolution efforts that relied on *detecting and correcting* defects after the product is completed rather than *preventing* mistakes from occurring. Although it does not necessarily eliminate the need for quality control checks on the finished product (particularly in service businesses), Six Sigma can greatly reduce reliance on back-end checking for defects.

The objective of this section is not to provide detailed instruction on Six Sigma but to introduce the quality management concept and summarize the steps used in quality approaches such as Six Sigma. Essentially, this methodology is applied to evaluate a process and identify how that activity can be improved using a relatively simple system known as DMAIC. DMAIC is an acronym for the following steps:

- **Define**
  Delineate opportunities for improvement, including an understanding of the existing process and detailed knowledge of what is important to the customers.
- **Measure**
  Gauge the appropriate quality attributes in the current process, including identifying the type and frequency of defects relative to customer-defined standards.
- **Analyze**
  Scrutinize the data to identify why, when, and where the problems occur, as well as the root cause of the problem(s). A key to this phase is to be vigilant in identifying wasted steps and situations in which manual activities can be properly automated to reduce the potential for human error.
- **Improve**
  Enhance process performance by applying solutions that address the root cause of the problem(s). Think "outside the box" to identify new methods of doing things better, cheaper, and/or faster. The identification and use of best practices from within the company, the industry, or other disciplines is important in this phase.

16. Pyzdek, *Six Sigma Handbook,* 5.

- **Control**
  Manage the outcome by standardizing the process and monitoring results, and strive for continuous improvement.

First, a team that includes appropriate representation from within and sometimes outside of the company is identified. It is lead by a trained Six Sigma professional (green belt, black belt, and so forth). The assembled group follows the DMAIC steps and applies such tools as flow charts, fishbone diagrams, run charts, Pareto graphs, cause/effect diagrams, and other tools to better identify and understand the critical issues. After the appropriate study period (ranging from weeks to months), the recommendations are issued and the changes are implemented.

Significantly, the objective of any process improvement effort is *not* to produce the highest quality product possible. It is to guarantee that the end product meets or (preferably) exceeds customer needs at a profit level acceptable to the company. In other words, Six Sigma and other quality approaches seek to produce the maximum value to the customer while using the minimum amount of business resources.

As previously mentioned, the concept of including features in a product that customers do not need or are unwilling to pay for is termed *overprocessing*.[17] Overprocessing is a form of waste, and it is best avoided by maintaining a thorough and continuously updated understanding of client needs. One way to visualize this concept is the "goalpost view," where the uprights of a football goalpost symbolize customer needs. In general, as long as a product falls within the upper and lower specification limits, it is considered acceptable. Any products outside of these specifications incur some form of loss for the company.[18]

For example, assume that client listening systems applied by a hypothetical coffee chain identified that customers deemed it critical that the product be served within a specific temperature range. Serve the drink too cold, and the flavor is perceived as substandard, while too-hot coffee results in painful consumption.

The original process graph in Exhibit 2.4 displays the goalpost concept associated with the fictitious coffee retailer's existing operations. Within the sample, the tails of the bell curve that fall outside of the upper and lower limits represent output that did not meet the specifications and were defective (coffee that is too cold or too hot), while the remaining observations were within tolerance.

17. Michael L. George, *Lean Six Sigma for Service* (New York, NY: McGraw-Hill, 2003), 259.
18. Howard S. Gitlow, PhD, David M. Levine, PhD, and Edward A. Popovich, PhD, *Design for Six Sigma for Green Belts and Champions* (Upper Saddle River, NJ: Prentice Hall, 2006), 11.

A quality-improvement team was assembled to study the existing process in detail and identified several opportunities for improvement. The group streamlined the process and devised a simpler method of ensuring that the product is consistently served within the client-defined parameters. As shown in Exhibit 2.5, the variance in output is greatly reduced (the steeper curve indicates a smaller standard deviation within the sample), thereby improving overall performance.

Ideally, the improved process should be achieved by cutting steps and other forms of waste while delivering improved product performance. The fundamental concept is that the cost of implementing a quality-management program is more than offset by the savings realized from eliminating defects in the end products. In assessing savings, it is critical to consider the cost of goodwill and sales lost due to delivering products that fail to meet the customers' expectations. The increase in client satisfaction is sure to help retain clients and increase brand reputation.

Exhibit 2.4 Original Process

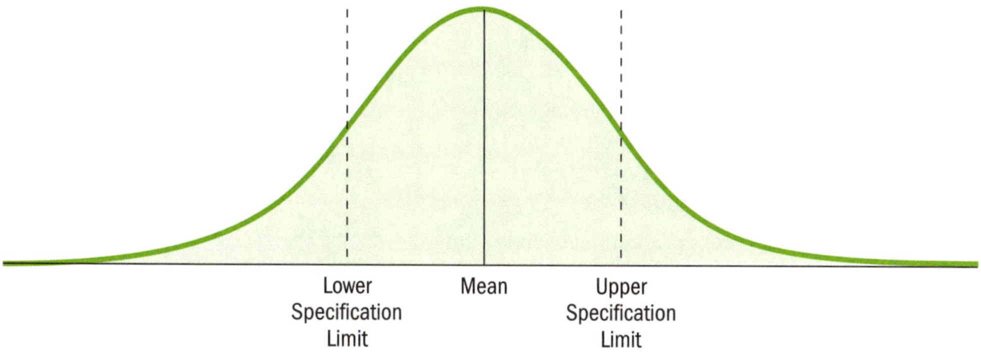

Exhibit 2.5 Improved Process

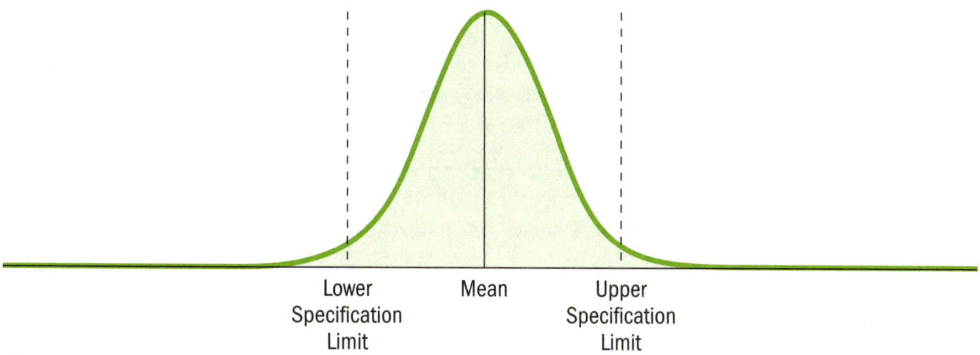

Actual Process Improvement Example for Flood Hazard Certification

Massive property losses were incurred due to severe flooding in the Midwestern section of the United States in the early- and mid-1990s. In response, federal banking regulators mandated that banks could no longer originate mortgages on properties that lie within flood zones without flood hazard insurance. In addition, these institutions were required to monitor the flood-zone status of each property over the life of the loan.[19]

Financial institutions were forced to hurriedly establish processes aimed at complying with the new regulations. At one major regional US bank, compliance with the new regulation was achieved in short order, in part by using a nationwide vendor to perform the actual flood zone determination and lifetime monitoring. The task was assigned to an existing service unit, which developed a process around the vendor capabilities.

The original process that was implemented, while functional, sometimes resulted in errors and loan-closing delays. Cycle time (the period from request to order fulfillment) also sometimes lagged behind client expectations. When client feedback systems indicated dissatisfaction from loan officers and external customers, a team was constructed to examine the process and identify ways to improve client satisfaction. In keeping with Six Sigma mandates, the group initially assembled was composed of employees from various disciplines and included:

- Experienced operators of the process
- A supervisor from the department
- Loan officers (internal clients)
- A trained Six Sigma advisor

In the *define* segment of the quality improvement process, the team set out to understand the existing process with the knowledge that clients desired faster turnaround and a reduction in errors. The first step was to develop a flow chart detailing each step used to produce the required flood certification itself. In addition, certain supplementary documents (primarily additional instructions for the requester) had to be delivered if the property fell within a flood hazard zone. These occasionally required steps were examined as well.

Moving on to the *measure* stage of the process, the team held discussions with various clients to better gauge their expectations on turnaround time and quality of the output (clarity of instructions, accuracy, follow-up service, and so forth). Their opinions on the type and frequency of defects realized and possible sources of the problem were solicited as well. Examples of defective service outputs were also collected and analyzed, and an examination of competitors' service levels was undertaken.

The substandard outputs were studied in the *analyze* segment to identify why, when, and where the problems occurred. Root causes (or suspected root causes) of each problem were collected and categorized. Several process steps that added no value from the customer's perspective were highlighted, and opportunities for human error were noted.

In the *improve* phase, it became apparent that unnecessary steps existed and technological solutions could be applied to eliminate many of the defects embedded in the process. As a result, the team was expanded to include a representative from the bank's information technology area and a technician from the flood certification vendor who was

19. *Loans in Areas Having Special Flood Hazards,* 61 Code of Federal Regulations (CFR), Federal Deposit Insurance Corporation, 1996.

familiar with the software's full capabilities. The expanded group identified several best practices from other departments and industry competitors. Specifications for a markedly streamlined process were developed by the expanded team.

Various prototypes were developed and extensive end-user tests were conducted in the control phase. The aim was to ensure that the changes implemented performed as planned and that client issues were adequately addressed. Several adjustments were made prior to and following implementation of the changes.

The team's study and efforts identified the following problems with the original process:

- The process was almost entirely manual, heavily paper-based, and subject to human variation and error.
- The request was handled by too many individuals during order fulfillment.
- Fairly standard computer software and technology could be applied to supplant several manual activities.
- The vendor software could be better leveraged to automate certain steps.
- The cost to develop a tracking system program to be added to an existing order entry/tracking system was relatively small and well below annual direct labor cost savings alone (without even considering other direct cost savings and client satisfaction gains).

The streamlining results are summarized in the flow charts in Exhibit 2.6. The process was now mostly free of "loops" that run counter to a streamlined system. Loops are decision points in the process that represent opportunities for errors and delays in product completion. Quality-management principles require that the number of "branches," or processes within processes, be eliminated or at least minimized to ensure simplicity and decrease the opportunity for error and non-value-added activities. They should be avoided in process planning and can sometimes be eliminated through automation or intelligent design.

The number of steps required to produce the flood certification and related documents decreased from a maximum of 24 to a maximum of nine. In addition, virtually all of the steps eliminated were manual, thus translating to direct labor savings. This also significantly decreased the opportunity for variation in the output and the incidence of human error.

Significantly, several steps were eliminated that added no value from the customer's perspective. For example, the client was not concerned that resources were expended making an extra copy for a file to provide an audit trail for regulators and others. This fact made the step a candidate for removal, and the team identified a work-around (maintaining an electronic copy in the system) that eliminated the need for the manual copy. Wringing such costs from a process is a key to streamlining any operation.

Perhaps most importantly, cycle time was reduced from days to a matter of hours in most instances. In fact, responses could have been completed almost immediately, if it were financially viable to have an operator available to respond as requests were submitted. Discussions with the clients indicated, however, that such a rapid response was unnecessary and well in excess of their needs (an example of potential overprocessing). It was important, though, to be capable of completing the rare "emergency" requests in such a fashion, and the revised procedure could more readily accommodate these.

The virtual elimination of operator errors, combined with the significantly reduced turnaround time, transformed the string of customer complaints into client praise for the marked improvement in performance. Of course, the compliments were short-lived, as the clients became accustomed to the new higher service standard and competitors raised their performance levels.

This is only one of countless examples of the power of quality-management tools like Six Sigma. The success of this and other projects lies in the proper composition of the process-improvement team and including the individuals who perform the task daily, as well as those from other disciplines (such as information technology) who can offer a fresh perspective on the issue. The proper empowerment for radical change from management is also critical.

Exhibit 2.6 Flood Certification Process Improvement

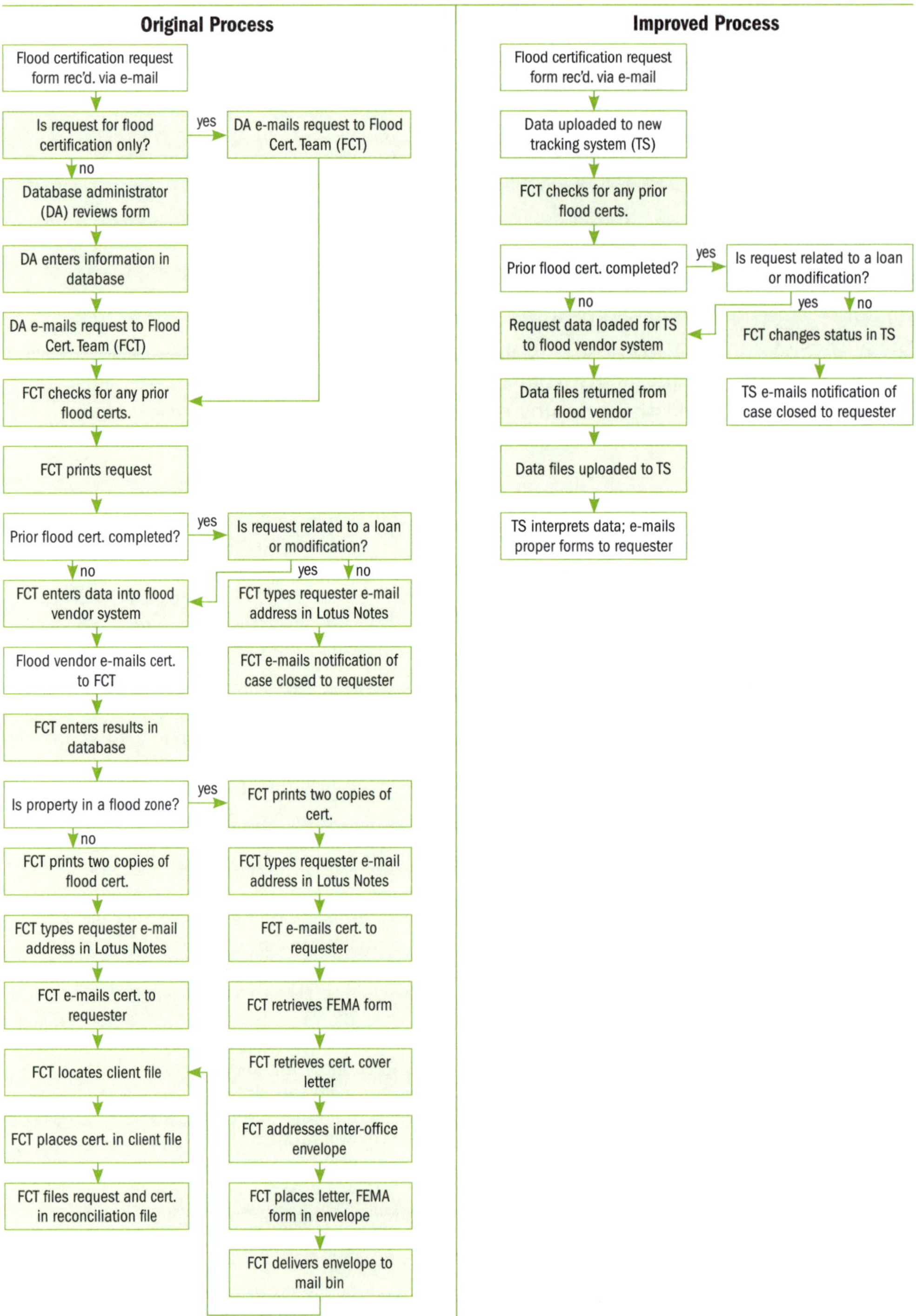

Note: Shaded boxes denote manual steps.

Quality Management and Appraisal

Quality Management Challenges in Service Businesses

Most service industries, including appraisal, operate well below the Six Sigma level. Consider, for example, the number of errors that can be identified in reports produced within your firm and compare it to the total number of defect opportunities in those appraisals. If your error rate is 3.4 per million or less (and you're doing it profitably), you're undoubtedly reading this book for pure amusement.

For those firms aspiring to decrease product defects and elevate customer satisfaction, it seems almost irresponsible not to apply the principles of a quality program such as Six Sigma. The methodology, however, is not without its drawbacks. For example, quality-management efforts can be costly to deploy and results can take months or years to be fully realized.

In addition, quality management methodologies like Six Sigma are readily applicable to manufacturing, where a high volume of homogeneous parts or products are churned out through a highly explicit process using standardized, specifically-calibrated machinery. In service industries, standardization and other quality tenets can be challenging to achieve due to the following factors:

- **Identifying and measuring client needs can be difficult.** Since the customer is not simply purchasing a product, each service transaction can require customization. Restaurants, for example, must cater to a wide array of tastes over a diverse customer base.

  For example, Burger King's "Special Orders Don't Upset Us" campaign in the 1970s sought to distance itself from the assembly-line perception of its competitors' food. This campaign was a result of customers providing feedback that their preferences were not being met (consider the myriad combinations associated with serving a hamburger). The drive was highly successful in promoting the chain's willingness to meet the needs of each individual consumer and forced the competition to follow with their own individualization campaigns. Although the customization approach resulted in higher consumer satisfaction (and likely higher sales), the move away from product uniformity drove up costs. Presumably, the expenses associated with catering to individual needs were more than offset by revenue gains.
- **Output can be intangible.** Whereas manufactured items can be measured against specific predetermined standards or tolerances, the measure-

ment for services is more challenging. With legal services, for instance, there is no standard product for the client to compare with competing goods. A defective product can be replaced, but a service is often a one-shot endeavor. This increases the urgency of leaving the customer with a favorable memory of the interaction.

- **Services are produced and consumed simultaneously.** Unlike manufacturing, where goods can be produced in advance and inventoried, services are often performed with the consumer present. In these situations, employees must be properly trained and the process must be as refined as possible to ensure a positive consumer experience. Medical services are a good example, wherein patients expect to see the physician on short notice and still receive proper treatment.
- **Services are labor intensive.**
While manufacturers rely heavily on machinery, service businesses are dependent on employees to produce their products. Employees are critical to a positive customer experience, and they must be properly trained and sensitive to the client's needs. An uncooperative or unpleasant airline ticket agent can ruin a customer experience, particularly if that customer has already been inconvenienced by a delayed or cancelled flight.[20]

Given these challenges, the need to customize outputs, adequately train and motivate staff, and provide an exceptional customer experience at every opportunity is apparent. This tends to be a labor-intensive effort that drives up costs, often resulting in a trade-off between quality and productivity (cost).

Quality is not, however, an all-or-nothing proposition. Within any industry, there is typically room for both high-touch, high-price, and low-cost mass-market business models. The key, of course, is to understand your customers' expectations and how to address their needs.

In retail, the Aldi food chain is a prime example of offering rock-bottom prices but limited selection and service in a warehouse-like atmosphere. Aldi's approach of stocking relatively few products, offering restricted hours and no baggers, and using cut-open cases in place of handsome displays is diametrically opposed to the model followed by most supermarkets. Despite this difference, both approaches are successful. The key is to fully comprehend the target market and the features that they deem important and to build those features into your service.

20. Evans and Lindsay, *Management and Control of Quality,* 52-53.

Given the lack of mechanization and the additional variables associated with the disparate capabilities and service commitment of the individuals involved, it may appear that the quality methodology is not well suited to service industries. On the contrary, numerous service firms, including all of the service functions within GE, have achieved dramatic results using quality management programs. Even service businesses with extreme variability, like health care, have realized success.

Not every company has the means or business model to apply quality-management principles on the same scale as GE or Motorola. However, the goal of profitably producing defect-free services can still be realized despite resource limitations. Such basic and relatively inexpensive steps as listening carefully to clients, improving process design, documenting procedures, and inspecting outputs can be applied to noticeably enhance services.

Quality Management Challenges within the Appraisal Industry

Some of the tenets of the quality movement are indeed difficult to apply to labor-intensive service businesses like appraisal, wherein the human element can significantly increase end-product variation. In addition, appraisal is an opinion-based business, sometimes likened to an art rather than a science. Given the wide variation in personalities, backgrounds, and other factors, the breadth of opinions makes standardization in the industry a challenge.

The varying opinions, levels of expertise, and motivations of clients who hire appraisers further clouds standardization. The challenge of addressing the sometimes irrational or emotional client reaction to appraisal results (especially value conclusions) is an issue that is not uncommon in service businesses. Given the lack of standardization apparent on each side of the transaction, it is impressive that the appraisal process functions as well as it does.

The predominance of small companies in the appraisal industry can act as a further impediment to rapid and widespread process improvement. Small firms with relatively limited human and financial resources often have a lower capacity for process examination and innovation.

Exceptional variation in the end product, due to flexibility in terms of scope of work performed as well as the different reporting options available, presents an additional roadblock. Factor in the widely diverse property types and geographic areas, and the variance in product type is nearly mind numbing. This can result in an almost "one-of-a-kind" product for each assignment.

Progress Realized to Date

It appears that we've now gone from espousing the world-beating qualities of Six Sigma and the quality-management movement to explaining why it won't work for an appraisal business. This is far from the truth, however. Regardless of size and resources, any appraisal firm can apply quality tenets by taking such actions as:

- Listening to the client and translating that feedback into the product
- Designing efficient process and report standards
- Establishing proper testing (QC reviews and audits)
- Implementing an effective corrective action/best practice process
- Properly training and motivating staff

As a firm or industry begins to focus on improving quality and streamlining processes, new technology is often applied and automation is used to reduce the potential for variation and human error. Although they are probably not widely recognized, the appraisal industry has already deployed some quality principles to enhance the end product and increase customer satisfaction as well as profitability despite the previously noted challenges. Great strides in process standardization have been realized through leveraging improvements in software and using data that is available electronically from vendors and other sources.

Perhaps the clearest evidence of this improvement emanates from the residential side of the industry, where standard forms (initially completed manually and later using form-filling software) provided immense improvements in report standardization. Residential appraisers, in particular, have vendor-developed, report-writing software options that include error-trapping features to markedly decrease manual report defects. In addition, reduced variation in format and content and relatively homogeneous subject matter helped spawn statistical "checks" for residential appraisals that test for anomalies. This also helps identify potential defects prior to delivery.

Both residential and commercial appraisers have ridden the wave of computing and software innovation over time. The simple implementation of word processing software and spreadsheets (eliminating typewriters, manual calculations, and data tables) was a significant step forward. Anyone who entered the field after the early 1980s would find the "old" appraisal report production process that typically involved typewriters, correction tape, calculators, paste, and adhesive tape archaic and laughable.

More recent innovations that have greatly enhanced the finished product and improved appraiser efficiency include

- **Digital photographs**
  Appraisers were early adopters of this technology after recognizing the process efficiency and costs savings that could result. Digital photos (and improvements in word processing software that accommodated their use) eliminated trips to the photo store, manual pasting of pictures into reports, and other "efficiency killers." In addition, report appearance was markedly enhanced and tape and paste failures became a thing of the past.
- **Electronic databases**
  The introduction of user-friendly database software greatly facilitated the reuse and updating of comparable data and eliminated redundant manual data entry. The eventual ability to embed digital photos within databases further improved software functionality.
- **Comparable data service vendors**
  The multiple listing service (MLS) originated the concept of a central repository for comparable data. Eventually vendors adapted the concept to commercial use and began to offer reliable leads and fully developed sale write-ups at reasonable prices. The ability to access both the MLS and commercial transactions online and drop the information into a practice's databases greatly enhanced productivity and standardization.
- **Electronic economic and demographic data**
  The capability to define markets and neighborhoods specifically and access economic and demographic information also improved appraisal content. Enhanced graphics and presentation flexibility improved the look of the reports, and the capacity to download the data directly into the document facilitated its use.
- **Graphics software**
  Advancements in sketching and mapping software as well as the development of online aerial and street-level property photos enabled the embedding of such high-quality graphics within the report. Improved ease of use eliminated much of the manual effort as well.
- **Online public records**
  The proliferation of property records, tax information, zoning codes, and other public information on the Internet signifi-

cantly enhanced search and identification capabilities and eliminated trips to town and county government facilities for most information.

These products, which were introduced and enhanced over the last 20 years or so, markedly streamlined the appraisal production process and the appraisal report. The resulting efficiencies allowed practitioners to maintain (or lower) fees, yet remain profitable. Given the competitive environment and demands of a production-compensation structure, appraisers are compelled to continue to seek process efficiencies through the application of new technology and by other means.

More innovations will undoubtedly occur over time. A hot topic in the industry today, for example, is open data standards. This effort seeks to eliminate the redundant manual rekeying of data that occurs throughout each phase of every real estate transaction. The effort of organizations such as MISMO and the Open Standards Consortium for Real Estate (OSCRE) to leverage extensible markup language (XML) technology in tagging and reusing data will yield efficiency gains and significantly reduce errors. While the timing of widespread adoption is uncertain, Fannie Mae began accepting appraisals using the MISMO XML standard in March 2010.

The goal of improved standardization and data quality was pushed further along with the announcement by the Federal Housing Finance Agency (a conservator of Fannie Mae and Freddie Mac) that it would launch the Uniform Mortgage Data Program. Under this effort, the standardization of key elements from appraisals would be combined with system-to-system interfaces to eliminate re-keying and provide more consistent data. The program will better streamline the process and improve risk management.[21]

On the commercial front, the lack of homogeneity of properties and report formats is a particular challenge in streamlining appraisals. In response, vendors have developed report-writing packages that help reduce variation and improve error trapping. Some large firms have also developed proprietary systems to standardize appearance and reduce human error in their reports.

These systems typically include standard templates in word processing software to which data and analyses can be fed from spreadsheets, databases, and lease-by-lease discounted cash flow packages. More sophisticated systems can upload comparable data and demographic reports directly from other platforms. The reduction or outright

21. Mark R. Linné and John Cirincione, "Open Data Standards: Why You Should Care," *Valuation* (Fourth Quarter 2009): 11-13; "GSEs to Enhance Appraisal Data Collection," *Appraiser News Online* 11, no. 9/10 (May 26, 2010), http://www.appraisalinstitute.org/ano/current.aspx?volume=11&numbr=9/10/.

elimination of rekeying data and manually inserting information greatly decreases opportunities for errors and enhances report standardization.

Even basic word processing and spreadsheet software can be leveraged to reduce inconsistency. Many appraisers have effectively applied macros and other tools and integrated spreadsheet data with word processing. In addition, the use of templates and boilerplate has been refined over time, largely through improved software capabilities. These innovations have resulted in significantly streamlined report-production processes and less errors.

Whether a proprietary or vendor package is used, templates and software should be leveraged to improve standardization whenever possible. The risk in using such templates, however, is neglecting to properly update and/or tailor the text to the subject appraisal problem. Failure to do so undermines the benefits of the standardization effort and can actually result in greater client dissatisfaction.

In addition, templates must be crafted to avoid sounding and appearing like boilerplate. The standardization provided by templates is important, but relying too heavily on these formats does not relieve an appraiser of the responsibility of tailoring the report to the assignment nuances and particular client needs.

Templates are also a key ingredient in improving the QC review process. A carefully crafted template gives the reviewer confidence that certain sections of the report have been properly done, thus reducing the time spent reviewing those sections. The QC professional is then freed to focus on other nonstandard sections of the appraisal and/or those deemed critical by clients.

Gains have also been realized in the allocation of human resources. Many firms have nonappraiser staff members who specialize in certain sections of the appraisal. This resource distribution is particularly applicable to portions of the report where appraisal expertise is not specifically required (such as economic and demographic analysis or researching and developing certain comparable data). Such an approach frees the appraiser to focus more closely on technical aspects of the report and improves standardization through the specialization of duties.

Vendors have also spotted the opportunity for specialization. Some firms concentrate on entering comparable data into databases, while others specialize in entering lease data and other information into discounted cash flow software. Such services relieve the appraisal professional of nontechnical tasks, allowing more time for exercising professional judgment.

Employing nonappraisers to complete certain sections of the report is an effective means of freeing the appraiser to concentrate more fully on items that require appraisal expertise. However, the appraiser remains responsible for making sure that the information prepared by others is accurate and that it is properly reflected in the assumptions applied in deriving the value conclusion.

The appraisal industry overall has made great strides in increasing efficiency in researching and completing appraisals. This progress was prompted largely by the ongoing and urgent need for efficiency in maximizing production (and profit), and it is likely to continue. The consequent decrease in manual errors has improved appraisal reports and enhanced client satisfaction as well.

Although process efficiencies have largely been realized with the introduction of new technology, opportunities remain for improving customer satisfaction. Improved listening practices, effective QC processes, corrective action procedures, and employee education and motivation represent notable opportunities for appraisers to move toward the "delight" end of the quality spectrum. These topics are a main area of focus in the rest of this book.

3 Customers and Their Needs

Listening to the Customer

Understanding customers' needs and applying those concepts to a company's products and strategic vision are of paramount importance. The idea that successful companies are those whose products and services are customer driven is fundamental to quality management. According to feedback from consumers of appraisal services nationwide, there is a sizable opportunity for improvement in this respect in the appraisal field.

It is easy for appraisers to assume that quality is high as long as products and services adhere to USPAP and other regulatory pronouncements. In addition, concern over inviting client pressure or undue influence can be a deterrent to some appraisers actively seeking input on appraisal content, quality, and other issues. Such a view, however, short-circuits the opportunity for improved products and services. In fact, successful firms regularly seek out client input.

A primary purpose of listening to the customer is to identify the items that customers deem to be critical to quality. Using this information, processes can then be streamlined to remove non-value-added features, *which can account for up to 50% of the total cost of producing the item.*[1] In addition, the improved end product more closely aligns with the customers' expectations, thus improving overall satisfaction.

Recall the flood certification process-streamlining example in Chapter 2. Sizable cost reduction resulted from the elimination of nonproductive steps (such as making a copy of each flood certification for auditors) as well as avoiding overprocessing (for example, designating an operator to stand by waiting for flood certification

1. Michael L. George, *Lean Six Sigma for Service* (New York: McGraw-Hill, 2003), 3.

requests to come in). Nonproductive steps and overprocessing are costly and do not result in an increase in client satisfaction. Their removal reduces expenses without decreasing customer satisfaction.

Various methodologies have been developed over the years to assist with developing an understanding of customer needs. The techniques differ in terms of sophistication and cost. One school of thought, for instance, suggests that simply tracking sales trends from each customer is a reliable measure of a company's performance in the client's eyes. This is particularly true if it can be determined that the firm's "share of wallet" with each client is increasing or decreasing. Such information, however, can be difficult to obtain.

Exhibit 3.1 outlines the steps for listening to the customer in a typical quality-management approach.

Identifying and Grouping Customers

In the first step, a comprehensive list of the company's customers is developed and the list is classified into appropriate groups. One common classification method is segregating the clients into the "vital few" and the "useful many," with the vital few composed of the firm's largest and/or most important customers. The remaining set includes the relatively large number of customers who are of less significance.[2]

The variance in client expectations can be (and typically is) wide, and firms generally cannot be all things to all customers. Some clients or industries may be targeted to enhance a company's potential for penetration into a particular field or advance brand image in a certain area, and specific product requirements must be identified to increase the probability of success.

Exhibit 3.1

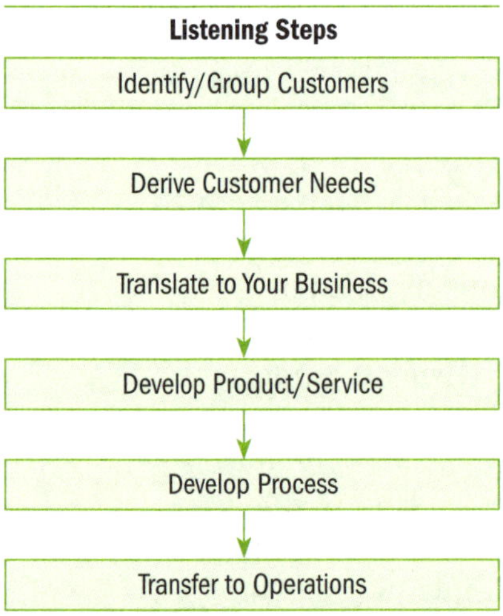

Source: J. M. Juran, *Juran on Leadership for Quality* (New York: The Free Press, 1989), 88.

Classifying customers helps prioritize the product changes that should be made (or new products that should be developed) given existing resource limitations associated with the process or product. Obviously, needs of the firm's vital few customers are likely to be included in the top tier, but it is also important to identify those clients who present the opportunity to generate additional business and consider placing those firms in this category as well.

2. J. M. Juran, *Juran on Leadership for Quality* (New York: The Free Press, 1989), 90.

It is also important to consider which customers are the source of future profits and the competitive dynamics faced in establishing, maintaining, or expanding relationships with them. The customer list serves as the basis for setting priorities and applying client-listening systems.

In appraisal, the needs of litigation clients can be distinct from those of financial institutions that, in turn, differ from those of customers who require valuation for financial reporting. Given this variance, it is often useful to group customers into categories and prioritize those who are targeted for retention and/or increased sales. This step ensures that top-tier customers' needs can be prioritized should conflicts arise among the different groups.

The customer-classification exercise is also an opportunity to identify customers who should be "fired." Although this may seem to be a contradiction to quality principles, some clients demand product or service features that cannot be produced profitably by the firm or require excessive support and follow up. Also, some customers' philosophies and attitudes may not be aligned with those of the firm. An example is a client of appraisal services who consistently hammers for value increases with a clear bias to inflate values and no valid reasoning. The classification process can weed out such customers.

Deriving Customer Needs

Deriving customer needs directly from the end user can be accomplished in several ways using a combination of time-tested tools, including:

- Client interviews
- Focus groups
- Unsolicited client feedback (complaints, compliments, monitoring online chat room and industry forums, and so forth)
- Surveys
- Review of clients' vendor rating systems/criteria

These tools will be discussed in more detail later in this chapter.

Research should be conducted with the appropriate population of customers and with the most in-depth study focused on the "vital few" to make sure that their needs are most clearly understood. If possible, deriving data from former clients and prospective new clients is also useful. The investigation should procure information from each customer as to what benefits the customer hoped for in buying the product and why the product was chosen over competing options.[3]

3. Ibid., 96.

There are a number of techniques for categorizing customer responses. Most revolve around listing the issues under major headings with the specific component parts of the major topics attached to the main heading. For example, appraisal clients often cite timing as an important issue, so timing could qualify as a major heading and a component issue could be meeting the report deadline. It is useful to have a solid understanding of what competitors are doing relative to each issue and how your firm's capabilities compare. Opportunities to identify and implement best practices from others in the industry should be leveraged in this phase. Competitive knowledge can also help gauge the consequences of not implementing a particular feature.

One approach used in prioritizing such findings entails placing each item into a matrix with four categories. The features are classified based on their respective client impact, and the perceived performance of the company's product or service relative to each item is rated. Based on this analysis, priority should be placed on improving those aspects that clients deem to be "high impact" with resources being allocated to those areas that need improvement.[4] A sample matrix is shown in Exhibit 3.2.

Exhibit 3.2 Prioritization Matrix

Low Client Impact but Strong Performance (Maintain or reduce resources allocated to feature)	**High Client Impact but Strong Performance** (Maintain resources; protect competitive advantage)
Low Client Impact and Weak Performance (Reallocate or reduce resources)	**High Client Impact but Weak Performance** (Allocate resources to improve feature)

The major category features that fall on the right side of the matrix are items deemed to be critical to quality (CTQ) and form the basis of quality requirements for the firm's products and services. Exhibit 3.3 shows what a list of CTQs for real estate lending clients in the "timing" category might look like.

The CTQs are then prioritized using the matrix. While it is obviously preferable to meet all of the CTQs identified, resource constraints often prevent this. In keeping with the quality methodology, profitability must also be considered in prioritizing the CTQs.

For example, it might be a "delighter" if an appraisal company could assign an individual to shepherd each assignment through every step of the process and provide regular updates on its status, thus effectively addressing each of the CTQs. This would, however, likely be inefficient and prohibitively expensive for the firm.

4. Michael D. Johnson and Anders Gustafsson, *Improving Customer Satisfaction, Loyalty, and Profit* (San Francisco: Jossey-Bass, 2000), 13.

Exhibit 3.3 Critical-to-Quality (CTQ) List

Major Heading	CTQs
Timing	Realistic/achievable turnaround quote
	Request property data shortly after engagement
	Early and frequent communication on data delays
	Communicating data receipt problems in writing
	Meeting the report deadline

Alternatives for *profitably* achieving as many of the CTQs as possible should be examined. Viable options may include implementing rules specifying when an appraiser must contact the client (e.g., at various milestones) or establishing at web-based tracking system that the customer could access to view report progress.

Translating to Business

Translating involves converting responses from the terminology used by the customer into the language of the business or industry and ensuring a thorough understanding of the issue. This step is most important for businesses that produce a variety of products or services wherein the lack of standardized terminology can complicate the understanding of customer issues. The appraisal industry is fortunate to have specific standards and jargon that are universally understood. Despite this homogeneity, an adequate understanding of the client's meaning of each CTQ is critical.

Under the timing category, for example, the need for requesting data shortly after engagement may appear odd to the appraisal vendor. From his or her perspective, the assignment is in the queue and it may be several days or longer before the job can even be started. Taking the time to contact the property owner for information and to set up an inspection may seem to be inefficient at such an early stage in the appraisal process.

Discussions with various financial institution clients nationwide, however, indicate that prospective borrowers and the banks' relationship managers (the client's own clients) frequently request follow-up if appraiser contact is not made shortly after engagement. This, in turn, causes numerous e-mails and/or phone calls to the various parties and creates unnecessary work for the client. The prospective borrower's unease over what is perceived to be a delay in the process is also an undesirable outcome for the banker. Enhanced understanding of these consequences helps the appraiser appreciate the client's point of view, which results in greater empathy for the client's plight and increases the sense of urgency to build "defect" prevention into the appraiser's process for this and the other CTQs.

Whatever CTQs are selected for inclusion in the product or service design, care must be taken to guarantee that each feature

- Directly correlates to client-defined needs
- Is clearly defined and easily understandable by operators of the process
- Is quantifiable, thus allowing measurement to guarantee that the CTQ is being met[5]

Given the desire for early contact in the process, a solution could be to require that the appraiser assigned to each job calls or e-mails the property owner within 48 hours of approval to proceed with the assignment. Such a mandate directly addresses the CTQ, is easily comprehended by the process operator, and is measurable, which allows for performance testing. This aligns properly with translating to the business's product or service. Notably, this does not add cost; it simply moves the timing of the contact to align with customer expectations. (Client satisfaction improves at no cost!)

Developing the Product or Service

After defining the clients' CTQs and gaining a full understanding of those needs, the next step is to design or modify the product or service to make sure that the CTQs are being addressed. In manufacturing operations and some service businesses, this phase can be quite complex and time consuming.

Ample time must be allocated to this design phase to guarantee smooth execution when the product is actually introduced. Depending on the complexity of the item, it is also useful to structure this stage, which may include the use of such tools as diagrams, cause-effect analyses, or checklists. The development phase typically involves a cross-functional team that ensures that the proposed product or modification

- Actually meets the clients' needs
- Is aligned with company goals and requirements
- Meets or beats the competition
- Minimizes costs for the company and the clients[6]

When the end product is an appraisal report, product development is limited to a degree by the parameters prescribed by USPAP and oth-

5. George, *Lean Six Sigma for Service,* 369.
6. Juran, *Leadership for Quality,* 111.

er standards. The "fit and feel" of the appraisal, the manner in which it is delivered, and the service surrounding the appraisal, however, are open to interpretation. Therein lies the opportunity for a firm to differentiate itself from the competition by building in "delight" attributes as well as making sure that linear satisfiers are adequately addressed.

As with other facets of customer listening, this step is best accomplished using a team that includes managers, producers, client-contact personnel, and possibly others. The team is charged with translating the CTQs into product features that are implemented to meet customer needs while maintaining profitability.

The timing issue is one of several main categories of satisfaction for clients, and it must be included along with other facets (and their related CTQs) in designing "delightful" appraisal services. Other priorities identified by clients are discussed later in this chapter. One such feature that can be used to illustrate proper report development is appraisal report formatting and appearance.

Clients identify report formatting and appearance as a common problem with appraisals. To address report appearance, the team should draw upon specific examples proffered by the clients and extract best practices from the appraisal industry and other disciplines. Some firms, for instance, engage professional technical writers to assist with report design. The report's format and features should be developed and refined using feedback from the team and client input.

As the report and supporting service are being developed, however, it is important to bear in mind that quality must be improved profitably and with the buy-in of the staff producing the product. It would not be appropriate, for example, to design appraisal reports that contain copious data and analyses but are exceptionally laborious to produce and must endure excessive QC review. The resulting lowered revenues from reduced production capacity and fatigue of the producers due to the overly rigorous process do not adhere to quality objectives.

Developing the Process

The process development phase results in procedures and parameters to be used in producing the end product while addressing the clients' primary needs, including CTQs. To make sure that the final product *consistently* adheres to the client design, the process must be engineered with reproducibility and standardization in mind.

Close attention to input from those involved in actually producing the good or service is critical here. This also means leveraging technology to standardize the process and minimize human error. Even the most diligent and engaged employee will make errors; an effective process reduces the opportunity for such mistakes. In addition to technology, consideration must be given to ways to reduce task monotony, improve error-trapping, and provide proper training. Another key to process engineering is reducing the number of steps and any activities in a process that add no value from the customer's perspective.

The flood certification process-improvement example cited in the previous chapter highlights the benefits of simplification and technology use. In that example, clients' CTQs on turnaround time and error rates were the drivers behind the streamlined process, which actually exceeded client expectations once the changes were implemented.

In an appraisal context, process development entails applying templates and standardized software as much as possible. The use of minimum report standards with boilerplate, standardized (and properly debugged) spreadsheets, and other automation tools are keys to maximizing standardization and including CTQs in the appraisal process.

Transferring to Operations

Once the process is designed, the handoff from the quality-planning team to the operators begins. Adoption by the producers and their managers will be compromised if the new process is prone to failure, does not achieve an improved result, or is perceived to be a step back from the legacy approach.

It is, therefore, critical that the design team adequately test the process with the operators and ensure that the operators thoroughly understand it. Techniques for realizing this goal include:

1. **Test runs**
   In a test run, the new procedure is performed, often using the actual operators, but the end product is not sent to the customer. Instead, the result is compared to the product specified in the design phase, and necessary adjustments are made.
2. **Simulation**
   Simulation involves testing the process under "laboratory" conditions, ideally involving actual process operators.
3. **Acceptance tests**
   An acceptance test is a highly structured exercise in which various conditions are set that are designed to stress test the process to help identify weaknesses and risks.[7]

Once the requisite testing is complete, it is often preferable to roll out the changes on a limited basis or for a narrow range of products to help reduce the risk of failure. During the rollout, the planning team and process operators must work closely to monitor the new

7. Ibid., 133-134.

procedure and the end result to make sure that it performs as intended and that the finished product meets the new specifications.

The requisite operator training and information must be provided along with a summary of the revised process and the new and improved features of the end product. It is also important to provide the rationale for implementing the new process (e.g., client demand) to help foster "buy in" from the staff and reinforce customer focus.

Using the appraisal report format example previously cited, changes may involve the rollout of new templates that incorporate the enhanced product design. The introduction to the templates should include highlighting significant new features and the client impetus behind those features. The quality team and anyone involved in quality control of the finished product should make sure that the templates are properly used in the process. Client feedback on the enhanced reports must also be solicited, with any adjustments that are identified promptly introduced.

Customer Feedback Tools

While most organizations claim to be customer driven, such status can only be achieved if systems are in place to measure customer satisfaction and acquire feedback. Various methods exist for listening to clients, and more than one should be applied to guarantee that a representative sample of opinions is obtained.

Customer feedback can be actively sought (through client surveys, focus groups, interviews, and so forth) or received without solicitation through customer calls and e-mails, complaints, website hits, referrals, and other means. Depending on the size of the company and the sophistication of the program, customer data collection can be performed by an individual, team, or dedicated department.

Regardless of the method by which it is received, this information is valuable for customer-focused companies. It can alert a firm about what it is doing wrong and provide information on competitors, the features and services that clients truly value, and where the firm is positioned in the clients' eyes.

The tools typically employed in mining customer data include:

- Client interviews
- Focus groups
- Unsolicited client feedback (complaints, compliments)
- Surveys
- Reviews of clients' vendor rating systems and criteria

Each tool has its own strengths and weaknesses, so it is important that multiple techniques are employed to maximize the depth and breadth of data received. In addition, seeking client feedback must be an ongoing process, but the frequency of application of some of the tools should be balanced.

Feedback solicitation frequency varies by company and depends on the type of clients and the stability or volatility of the product and the industry. While it is preferable to obtain as much input as possible, requests should never be considered bothersome by the client. This is a particular risk when the customer base is relatively small.[8] The criticality of client input, however, increases when new products are introduced or a disruption or significant change is occurring within the industry. Seeking client input should be a major priority in these situations.

Interviews

Client interviews can be conducted formally or informally. They may occur in person or over the telephone, although the personal touch is often preferred, particularly if familiarity with the client is low. The ability to better establish a rapport (leading to more open and honest communication) and to observe the client's body language are advantages to the face-to-face approach.

The client interview is most effective at getting detailed answers and "drilling down" to get more information on a topic. The downside is that such interviews are time consuming (costly) and often require involvement of a relatively senior staff member who is familiar with all aspects of the operation. Interviews are often best suited to companies with relatively small customer bases, where a high return can be realized for the amount of time invested in the interview.[9]

A specific set of questions identified prior to the meeting should be covered to ensure consistency among all interviews. Questions should be carefully selected to cover any previously identified CTQ issues and help uncover additional CTQs.

Questions should also be open-ended to prevent the respondent from simply answering "yes" or "no." For example, questions like, "Do our appraisal reports meet your needs?" should be restructured to elicit a thoughtful, detailed response. The question would be better phrased as, "Please give me examples of how our reports meet your needs." This could be followed by, "What features of our appraisals or services need improvement?"

To the extent possible, the interviewer should also find out who his or her most direct competitors are and how the services compare among the different firms. The interview is also a primary avenue to identify potential "delighter" attributes. These could be features

8. Johnson and Gustafsson, *Improving Customer Satisfaction, Loyalty, and Profit,* 42.
9. Ibid., 74.

offered by competitors or items that the client desires in the product that are currently not provided by anyone in the industry.

An important consideration in interviews (and all client interactions) is listening effectively. If the client's salient points are missed or misunderstood, the effort is wasted and any tangible benefits will be compromised. In fact, studies show that people remember a mere 25%-50% of what they hear. This leaves a sizable margin for error in verbal communication.

Tools and tips for improving listening skills are detailed in Appendix A at the end of this book. General themes to keep in mind when interviewing a client or conducting a focus group or any other verbal communication forum include the following:

- **Pay attention.**
  Don't allow personal thoughts or environmental factors to become distractions.
- **Show interest.**
  Use body language, including nodding, facial expressions, and proper posture.
- **Offer feedback to ensure understanding.**
  Periodically ask questions to clarify issues and summarize the speaker's thoughts.
- **Don't interrupt.**
  Interrupting a person prior to completion of his or her point can frustrate the speaker and compromise understanding of the concept being conveyed.
- **Respond with respect.**
  Providing your opinion is helpful to gain a fuller understanding of the interviewee's perspective, but it must be done with requisite etiquette to help guarantee continued open dialogue. Follow up with any questions after the client's point is made.[10]

Many of these items may seem obvious, but client feedback consistently indicates that their message is often not received by vendors. Following these guidelines will help ensure that the meaning is understood and interpreted as the interviewee intended. When active listening skills are properly applied, the interview subject is left feeling that his or her opinion is truly valued, which increases the likelihood of more and better feedback in the future.

It is also important to take notes so that the information can be accurately summarized, and the notes should be reviewed and

10. MindTools, "Active Listening," 2010, http://www.mindtools.com/CommSkll/ActiveListening.htm/.

supplemented (as needed) directly after the session. While recording conversations is useful, it typically requires the consent of the interviewee and can sometimes make the subject uncomfortable, possibly inhibiting his or her responses.

Regardless of the method chosen, the results of the interview must be summarized and entered into a database for analysis and reporting. Analysis is critical for spotting CTQs and plotting appropriate actions for improvement.

Focus Groups

A focus group is composed of a specific set of customers who are assembled to discuss services rendered and/or test new ideas. To ensure proper participation while still offering an ample variety of opinions, these groups should be limited to six to ten members and consist of individuals who are insightful and likely to offer honest feedback.[11]

Focus groups share many of the advantages of customer interviews (such as deriving detailed answers), and they can be useful in brainstorming ideas and examining different perspectives. The group setting can also stimulate conversation and idea generation. Given the similarities, the guidelines for this client feedback approach parallel those of the interview.

Focus groups can, however, be even more costly than interviews, since the sessions are typically longer, require significant planning, and may involve refreshments and other items to help entice attendees to the event. In addition, as with any group, there is a risk that a small number of participants can dominate the conversations or influence other participants.

To guarantee success, an experienced moderator should conduct these sessions. The facilitator must diligently guard against domineering participants while eliciting input from all members. Keeping conversations on topic and within allotted time frames and ensuring that proper energy is injected into the meeting are other challenges.

Like interviews, responses and issues identified must be tracked for future use. Identifying a scribe or recording the session are ways to make sure that the feedback is properly documented.

Unsolicited Feedback

Unsolicited client feedback consists of complaints as well as compliments, and a significant advantage is its low cost (it is basically free). In addition, this type of feedback is typically received shortly after the product or service is delivered, thus allowing for a response and

11. Carter McNamara, PhD, "Basics of Conducting Focus Groups," Authenticity Consultants, 2006, http://www.managementhelp.org/evaluatn/focusgrp.htm/.

investigation while the circumstances remain fresh in the minds of the various participants in the transaction.

The primary disadvantage of unsolicited client feedback is that relatively few people are inclined to complain, with typically only one out of 25 customers taking the time to lodge a criticism. Even fewer proffer compliments. Clients who provide this form of feedback typically are highly motivated by an exceptionally bad (or good) experience, one that may have also been encountered by other clients who are less inclined to take the time to complain.

Some companies ignore this form of feedback, avoiding the sometimes-confrontational nature of complaints and almost viewing the customer as the enemy. Such firms sweep the issue away by offering an apology and possibly some type of discount or refund, then filing the complaint without addressing the root cause of the problem. This does not address the source of the failure and can leave customers feeling that their problem was ignored or not properly resolved.[12] Failure to properly address the issue also exposes the company to repeat failures.

Quality management prescribes designing processes to "get it right the first time" and minimize defects through a streamlined production process. W. Edwards Deming believed, however, that companies who refuse to acknowledge that failures will occur would not succeed in their efforts over the long term. Given defect inevitability, firms should embrace this unsolicited client feedback as a significant learning tool to be applied in improving the process.

If a client takes the time to complain, it is safe to assume that he or she expressed this displeasure to others (including existing and potential clients). This increases reputational risk to the firm and negatively affects revenues. The proper handling and resolution of the issue is critical to retaining the customer and mitigating damage to the company's reputation.

Firms that are highly skilled at accepting and addressing customer complaints can actually enhance a client relationship, provided that the failure does not recur. This "recovery paradox" results when a timely response is provided along with an explanation of how the problem arose and a plan to guarantee that the problem will not be repeated. In fact, customers can actually be

> "Your most unhappy customers are your greatest source of learning."
> - Bill Gates

12. James R. Evans and William M. Lindsay, *The Management and Control of Quality* (Cincinnati: South-Western College Publishing, 1999), 189; Stefan Michel, David Bowen, and Robert Johnston, "Making the Most of Customer Complaints," *The Wall Street Journal* (September 22, 2008), http://online.wsj.com/article/SB122160026028144779.html?mod=todays_us_the_journal_r/.

more impressed with a skillful complaint response than a product or service that is free of defects from the outset.[13]

High-performing companies greatly value unsolicited feedback, regard it as a tool for continuous improvement, and make it as easy as possible for a client to initiate the contact. Toll-free hotlines, a prominent section on a company's website, and the inclusion of the customer service phone number and e-mail address affixed to the product are obvious avenues for facilitating comments.

When complaints are received, there are several issues to keep in mind to ensure proper handling and a positive outcome:

- Respond as quickly as possible. Allowing complaints to languish for several days reflects badly on any firm striving to be perceived as client-driven and can further agitate a customer who took the time to register the issue.
- Thank the person, no matter how harsh the tone of the complaint, and apologize for any inconvenience realized.
- Listen actively; do not be defensive or biased.
- Try to elicit specific problems and useful details. Simply hearing that "your work stinks" does not help identify root causes of the problem that will help eliminate future occurrences.
- Do not send a "canned" response or form letter.
- Acknowledge your understanding of the problem and show empathy for any inconvenience caused.
- Identify actions that you will take and provide an estimate of the expected amount of time required to investigate and resolve the issue.
- Adequately research the matter with any parties involved to get other perspectives.
- Respond to the client with the findings and specific actions that will be taken (assuming that the investigation indicates that a problem actually exists).
- Implement any changes to the process or the product as well as best practices identified in the investigation.
- While it is important to be empathetic, the complaint recipient should not be subjected to abuse (profanity, hostility, threats, and so forth). When this occurs, the communication should be terminated or forwarded to the appropriate level of management.

13. Peter Murley, *Handbook of Customer Service* (Cheltenham, UK: Gower Publishing Limited, 1997), 253-254; Michel, Bowen, and Johnston, "Making the Most of Customer Complaints."

Using a structured approach guarantees that complaints are handled consistently and also provides an effective vehicle for circulating feedback to the staff. All employees involved in the process should be aware of the quality characteristics that are identified through this channel; this helps build a pervasive focus on client needs and increases the firm's ability to eliminate future problems.

To ensure effectiveness and consistency, a specific party or parties must be designated as responsible for complaint handling and resolution. A department could be established for this purpose in larger firms, while the president or a senior staff member could be designated to handle these matters in smaller firms. The key to setting up the "complaint department" is making sure that it is staffed with experienced people who have the ear of senior management.

As part of the resolution process, use of a standard form can help ensure that all relevant issues are addressed consistently. A sample complaint investigation form for an appraisal firm is shown in Exhibit 3.4. Significant features of this document are important dates, a summary of the steps taken in the investigation, best practices identified, and conclusions. The form must be properly filed upon completion, should there be a need to refer to it in the future.

During the complaint investigation, it is critical that the background of the situation is understood and the appropriate parties involved with production of the good or service are consulted. A step-by-step analysis of the transaction is often required, particularly for service businesses, where the process or service is less standardized. In an appraisal context, this includes understanding the specifics of the engagement (such as scope, timing, and specific requests) and alerting the appraiser involved to the client criticism. For written complaints, it is useful to provide all internal parties with the actual document so that each specific point can be considered. A meeting or call with the appraiser and others is then necessary to determine the merits of the issues and chart a course of action.

Upon conclusion of the investigation, the client must be contacted and informed of the results. Any internal problems uncovered should be identified, along with how they will be addressed to prevent future breakdowns. Requisite tact must be applied when it is concluded that the issue is not really a problem or (worse) if the client had a hand in the failure.

Customer contact can be the most uncomfortable step in the process, but it is critical to making the client feel that his or her comment was properly addressed. A skillful response is the key to achieving the previously mentioned "recovery paradox" and ensuring client retention.

Exhibit 3.4 Client Complaint Investigation Summary

File ID Number: ____________________

Project Name: ____________________

Client Company: ____________________

Client Contact: ____________________

Primary Appraiser(s): ____________________

QC Reviewer: ____________________

Complaint Investigator(s): ____________________

Timing:

Date Notified of Issue: ____________ (via ____________)

Date of Initial Client Contact: ____________________

Date Appraiser(s) Contacted: ____________________

Date of Final Resolution: ____________________

Identified Client Issues (Be as specific as possible. Copy direct customer complaints and supplement with any additional information provided): ____________________

Investigation Summary (Identify names of parties contacted, dates, and the information obtained in each conversation): ____________________

Conclusions:

1. Was the report properly reviewed prior to delivery to the client? ____________________
2. Did the reviewer identify the problem(s) surfaced by the client? ____________________
3. Did the appraiser complete any changes identified in the review prior to submitting the appraisal to the client? ____________________
4. Does the client's criticism appear valid? ____________________
5. Was the complaint properly addressed? ____________________
6. Was the problem identified by the client within the typical scope of the QC review process? ____________________

Learning Points/Best Practices: ____________________

Compliments are another form of unsolicited feedback. The proper handling of compliments is addressed in the "Celebrate Successes" section of this chapter.

Surveys

Surveys are another effective tool for obtaining client input and can be conducted in an interview format or by directly sending forms to clients. Virtually everyone has taken surveys, and they can be very cost effective. Other advantages to surveys include their ability to receive pointed feedback on specific topics and their capacity to quantify the feedback using a ratings scale.

Survey questions should be targeted to issues that cannot be measured by other approaches. For instance, on-time performance has been identified as a CTQ and will be discussed later in this chapter. Rather than allocating precious survey response time to this topic, it may be more effective to analyze on-time performance empirically using data from an existing order tracking system. This provides detailed empirical information and frees the client to focus on topics that are more subjective.

Like other facets of the quality movement, development of client surveys is best accomplished using the team approach with the involvement of different functions within the organization. Clients should be consulted for their opinions on the survey whenever possible. Suggested steps in constructing a survey include:

1. Assemble a team that is familiar with the target group and understands the subject matter thoroughly.
2. Examine customer feedback on their needs (CTQs).
3. Categorize data into general issues.
4. Draft questions aimed at those issues.
5. Revise the draft using team input.
6. Send the draft to other stakeholders inside the organization for feedback.
7. Revise the draft.
8. Send the draft to select customers or a focus group for feedback.
9. Revise the draft.
10. Determine the best method to distribute the survey to clients.
11. Devise a process to collect, analyze, and report on the feedback received.
12. Implement the survey process.

To gauge client satisfaction with the areas covered in the survey questions, a rating system known as the Likert Scale is often used. This scale, named after the psychologist Rensis Likert, typically arrays responses on a scale of one to five accompanied by descriptive text. Respondents are asked to select the response that best matches his or her feelings. For example, ratings can be designed as shown in Exhibit 3.5.

While such a scale is critical for providing a quantitative measurement of performance, it is also useful to provide a qualitative component for each response. This is often achieved by including space for comments along with each question in addition to the ratings scale. By giving an option for the respondent to include contact information, the opportunity to obtain more detailed information is available when respondents agree to allow contact. A sample question format is shown in Exhibit 3.6.

Care must be taken to ensure ease of use for the client, so the survey should be limited in size to facilitate quick completion. In addition, requiring clients to input information not directly related to their satisfaction on each particular transaction (type of product, where purchased, and so forth) lessens the likelihood of completion. The use of serial numbers, job file numbers, and other forms of product identification can be applied to eliminate the need for such information in the survey while maintaining the ability to link the response to the proper transaction for internal analysis purposes.

Delivering the document by e-mail as an Internet link or as an attachment to another document (such as an appraisal report) is a fast and efficient alternative to mailed surveys. Electronic surveys also facilitate downloading of the response data without re-entering the data. Several inexpensive vendor software packages are available that provide fairly sophisticated and easy-to-use survey templates.

Communicating survey results to staff is also important to ensure an aligned

Exhibit 3.5 Likert Scale

- ❑ 1–Poor
- ❑ 2–Below Average
- ❑ 3–Average
- ❑ 4–Good
- ❑ 5–Excellent

Exhibit 3.6 Sample Survey Question Format

Please rate your overall satisfaction relative to cost, timing, and quality.

- ❑ 1–Poor
- ❑ 2–Below Average
- ❑ 3–Average
- ❑ 4–Good
- ❑ 5–Excellent

Comments: ______________________________

sense of purpose and stress the need for continuous attention to client satisfaction. The numerical responses can be compiled and analyzed to identify areas in need of attention. In addition, tracking and trending responses over time can identify progress on improving problem areas.

The graph in Exhibit 3.7 summarizes client survey responses for a hypothetical appraisal firm over a four-year period. The graph indicates that the firm's ratings for report support and overall satisfaction decreased in 2009. This suggests that research is needed to identify whether these changes are related. Direct contact with the respondents, interviews, and focus groups can be employed to help identify the root cause of the problem if it is not apparent through the survey responses themselves.

Follow-up on specific comments, low ratings, and other issues should be structured. The same investigation process and form used for unsolicited client feedback can be applied to survey responses that suggest further analysis is needed.

Review of Clients' Vendor Rating Systems

Many clients rate and track vendor performance based on specific criteria that they deem important. These criteria are discussed in greater detail in the next section of this book, but major themes are report quality, responsiveness, service, and timeliness. These rating systems have often been developed in response to regulatory pronouncements and/or the demands of the clients' own customers.

Exhibit 3.7 Client Survey Summary

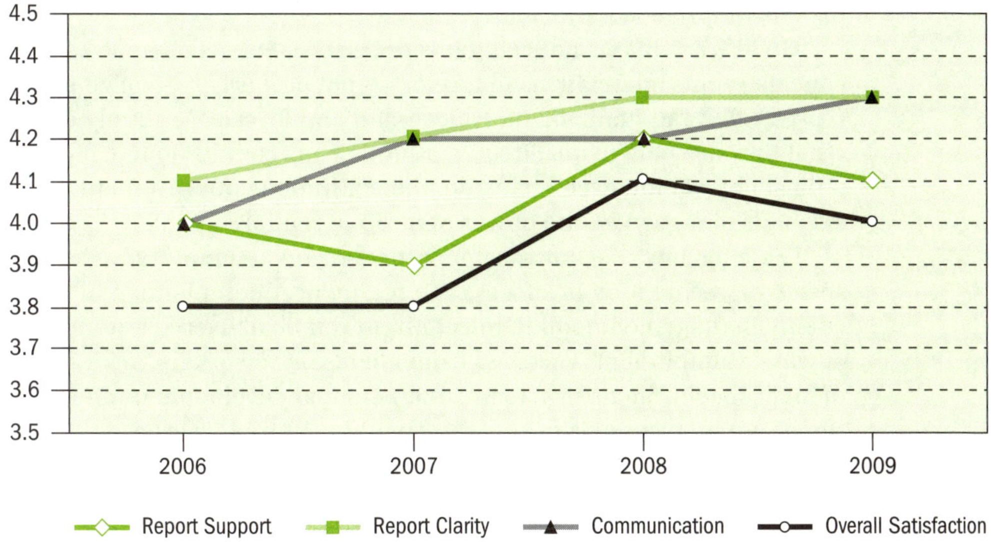

Understanding the parameters by which your products and services are judged is valuable information for aligning appraisal services with user expectations. Most clients are willing to share their general themes with vendors to help improve the service that they receive (and making their jobs easier in the process). Some clients also share their specific ratings with vendors. This is an important source of information that should not be overlooked.

Celebrate Successes

Consistently providing customer satisfaction also requires that employees with regular client contact be highly satisfied with their employer. Studies have shown that companies whose employees are committed to the employer deliver a 112% return to shareholders versus a 76% return for firms whose employees' commitment is average or below average.[14]

Some companies have found that a high level of satisfaction and motivation by their employees directly results in improved customer satisfaction. Analysis indicates, however, that the path to satisfied employees is complex and involves not only compensation but also such items as an appealing career path, benefits, and management attitudes.

A surprisingly significant item identified by employees, however, is the importance of the relationship with their managers and personal recognition received from these managers. In fact, a wide body of research suggests that simple recognition for a job well done is a reliable motivator. One study indicates that 78% of employees feel that it is "very" or "extremely" important that their managers recognize them for good performance.

Good work that is noticed tends to be repeated. As obvious as this concept seems, many firms ignore or do not properly recognize successes, often rationalizing that successful employees are simply doing what they are paid to do. Such an attitude runs counter to the quality philosophy of employee inclusion and continuous improvement. It also fails to recognize the power of positive reinforcement.

Given its low cost and sizable impact (from an employee's perspective), recognition of success is a highly useful implement in the quality management toolkit. Recognition can be delivered a number of ways. Compliments received from clients or coworkers, achievement of specific goals by a team, and personal development milestones are all examples of successes within an organization.

To maximize effectiveness, the celebration of success should be sincere, take place within a reasonable amount of time after the

14. Timothy L. Keiningham and Terry Vavra, *The Customer Delight Principle: Exceeding Customers' Expectations for Bottom-Line Success* (New York: McGraw-Hill, 2001), 86.

event occurred, and ideally be delivered by the appropriate manager or a person held in high esteem by the employee or employees.[15] Recognizing client and coworker praise and accomplishments in an in-house publication or broadcast e-mail are cost-effective means of encouraging appropriate behavior. Care must also be taken to guarantee that such celebrations are appropriate in number and that the events are of ample significance to prevent dilution of the effect.

From a quality and customer satisfaction perspective, such items as "top quality" awards combined with "advertising" stories of employees who were recognized by clients for a specific act are particularly useful in reinforcing a company's customer service focus. Monetary rewards for money-saving suggestions or business-building ideas are also useful for encouraging innovative thinking.

Analyzing and Applying Customer Feedback

Information obtained from customers via the previously discussed techniques is vital for a business to understand its clients' needs and its positioning within the competitive market. When feedback is received, it must be applied to improve the existing product or develop new products or services. This continuous improvement process is summarized in Exhibit 3.8.

First, a team is often assembled to compile and analyze the information received. As previously noted, effective means of analysis include grouping the issues identified into major categories and identifying common themes or characteristics of those issues.

When ambiguity poses a problem, the team may need to obtain specific examples to help better understand each issue so that the root cause is more easily identified and the problem properly correct-

Exhibit 3.8 Client Feedback Loop

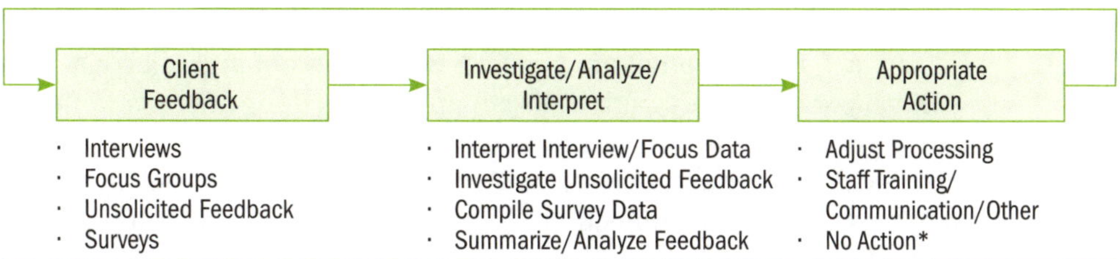

* In rare situations, it may be possible that no action is necessary. Inappropriate feedback or unfounded criticisms may occasionally be received. Faulty assumptions derived from such data can actually lower product quality.

15. Neville C. Tompkins, "Employee Satisfaction Leads to Customer Service—Employee Relations," *HR Magazine* (November 1992), http://findarticles.com/p/articles/mi_m3495/is_n11_v37/ai_13603614/; Bob Nelson, PhD, "Everything You Thought You Knew about Recognition is Wrong," *Workforce Management* (January 2004), http://www.workforce.com/archive/feature/23/61/87/index.php/.

ed. It is also necessary to gauge the relative importance that clients place on the identified feature. The team should also analyze competing products, taking into consideration features as well as pricing.

Once the suggestions are understood and properly prioritized, the team analyzes the change opportunities in the context of profitability and waste elimination. If the prospective alteration cannot be implemented profitably (after thoroughly analyzing the potential for increased sales, customer delight, reduced defects, expense reductions, and other criteria), then it is not a candidate for implementation under the quality-management philosophy.

In an appraisal practice, for instance, feedback may indicate that less effort is needed in economic and demographic analysis, since the client already operates within the subject area and is familiar with the information pertaining to it. Based on this knowledge, the firm could reduce the amount of time spent on those parts of the appraisal and instead allocate effort to other areas deemed more important by the client.

For those changes deemed worthy of adopting, it must be determined how the change can be best implemented. This may include altering the production process or training the staff. Following implementation, feedback should be monitored to ensure that the change had the desired impact on customer perceptions. Continuous monitoring also helps guarantee that any gains realized are held over time.

Defining Report Standards

The Need for Report Templates and Standards

A critical facet of quality management principles is translating client needs into the company's products and services. From an appraisal perspective, this means designing reports and the production process around client needs while adhering to industry and regulatory standards. A further challenge is making sure that the reports can be reproduced consistently.

In fact, a common client concern is that content and analysis can vary significantly with different appraisers in one firm, and this can be compounded for multiple-office practices. This shortcoming results largely from the inherent flexibility of industry reporting standards as well as the subjectivity associated with the profession. Considerable improvement in consistency is possible, however, through establishment of a standard report framework.

Defined report standards are the guideposts through which appraisals must be completed for any firm. They help make sure that CTQs and regulatory issues are properly addressed and improve product consistency. These guidelines include report templates and other standard instructional documents that identify the requisite guiding principles, definitions, and explanations to ensure clarity for the user.

Templates and supporting documents should be comprehensive enough to cover the vast majority of issues staff members are likely to encounter. This often entails maintaining multiple templates to address the various property types and other nuances that can arise within the practice. In addition, a template is often developed for each reporting type available (restricted, summary, and self-contained).

Form reports are the most basic type of templates, and the residential sector of the industry was an early adopter of this efficient means of presenting value opinions. Driven by the need for standardization and ease of use, Fannie Mae and Freddie Mac introduced the Uniform Residential Appraisal Report (URAR) in 1986. The URAR enhanced standardization and addressed clients' needs for improved efficiency in their high-volume review processes. The form also helps guarantee that no client-required data is omitted.

Despite its clarity and relative simplicity, instructions on the data and analysis required for each section of the report are, nonetheless, integral to the URAR. In fact, various instructional documents and seminars have been developed to aid proper user understanding of the report. *Using Residential Appraisal Report Forms: URAR, Form 2055, and the Market Conditions Form* is a recent book on this subject available from the Appraisal Institute.

Narrative reports are typically used for more complex commercial properties, and the lack of homogeneity of property types as well as the sheer complexity of some projects makes standardization challenging. Despite these variations, the Appraisal Institute identifies five common sections within a narrative appraisal report:

- **Introductory material**
  Title page, letter of transmittal, certification, etc.
- **Identification of the scope of work and the appraisal problem**
  Identification of the type of appraisal, the client, the intended use, general assumptions and limiting conditions, etc.
- **Presentation of data**
  Property description and history, market area data, assessment data, etc.
- **Analysis and conclusions**
  Highest and best use, valuation approaches, reconciliation, etc.
- **Addenda**
  Detailed subject/comparable descriptions, historical operating information, supporting cash flow forecast schedules, etc.

While the specific content under each heading varies according to the requirements of each assignment, this outline forms the basic framework of an appraisal report.

The main headings (or variations thereof) of this outline often serve as the basis for report templates, with "stock" language inserted in appropriate sections to guarantee that USPAP is addressed as a minimum starting point. Other sections are completed using the firm's standard boilerplate language, and users typically "fill in the blanks" as appropriate.

As with the URAR, however, it is usually not adequate to simply issue these standard documents and allow appraisers to use them as they see fit. Instructions providing the background and intended use and content of each section must be provided to help ensure consistent application and standardization of the end product.

Designing Report Templates

Since the appraisal report is a firm's most prominent and effective marketing tool, thoughtfully designed templates are critical to promoting the practice's brand image to the client base. Failure to deploy templates reduces standardization, and the resulting variation in content and format runs counter to establishing a consistently high-quality product. Creating individual reports "from scratch" is inefficient and can risk noncompliance with USPAP and other standards.

Report standards and templates must incorporate industry and regulatory requirements as well as CTQs uncovered through client listening systems. A team that includes staff from different levels and disciplines within the company should be formed to create or revise templates, thus maximizing idea-generation and evenly spreading the workload. Steps involved in the design process typically include:

1. **Define the elements to include for each format.**
   The design process begins with previously assembled industry, regulatory, CTQ, and other requirements. These elements should be included within the appropriate major sections in the report. The resulting consistency is a significant aid to clients in reviewing reports, since they will quickly learn where to look for specific information, thus saving them time and effort.

   Adherence to proper grammar, style, and formatting rules are critical to guarantee that the appearance of the document is proper and pleasing to the reader (another common client complaint). The effective use of spacing, margins, font type and size, colors, photos, graphics, and other factors optimizes the document's appearance. (Suggestions on grammar and style are included in Chapter 8 of this book.) It is important to use identified best practices from within the firm, other industry sources, and (for true innovation) sources outside of the appraisal discipline. Designing a winning report template presents the opportunity for a firm to differentiate itself from the competition, so effort must be expended to ensure that the best possible product results.

2. **Develop a prototype.**
   A prototype is created based on the design requirements, and it serves as the working document that the team uses to test ideas and innovations. The prototype typically starts out as a rough word-processing draft that is circulated to the design team and others to help check that the critical elements are properly addressed and to solicit suggestions on content and formatting. Numerous revisions of the draft are often required before proceeding to the next step; however, diligence with the prototype pays off in the later steps.
3. **Construct the template.**
   The prototype is then converted to the actual template using the report production process employed by the firm (such as the vendor report-writing package or in-house system). In this step, attention to detail is critical to identify any flaws within the document and to guarantee that the process can properly accommodate the new formats. Again, it is important to circulate the draft to the team and various stakeholders, and several rounds of revisions may be needed here as well. Involvement of clients for feedback on the product (or critical elements of it) is very helpful in this stage.
4. **Test, test, test.**
   The test phase applies the approved template through the actual assembly process to check for any problems in producing the report. Tests should occur with an appropriate cross-section of users, and feedback on strengths and weaknesses should be collected. Adjustments are then made based on the input received. Proper testing and revising helps limit errors once the document is introduced into the "live" environment.
5. **Place in production.**
   Prior to placing the documents into production, the requisite training and information must be provided to the appraisers, administrative staff, and other appropriate personnel. The new and improved features of the end product should also be highlighted and related back to the client input that helped prompt the

changes. Staff should also seek client feedback on the enhanced reports and convey that information to the project team.[16]

During the process, it is critical to keep in mind quality principles, including the need to reduce non-value-added content and steps and limit opportunities for human error. Reducing the chance of leaving stale or inappropriate information in the report is a key to preventing embarrassing mistakes from reaching the client. The use of blank spaces and pick lists can help in this effort.

Technology should also be leveraged as much as possible to limit human error and improve standardization. Downloading information directly from other sources (comparable sales/rental databases, economic and demographic data providers, discounted cash flow software, and so forth) eliminates data entry errors and improves efficiency. Statistical analysis can also be applied to cash flow forecasts and different sections of the report to spot anomalies, identifying potential errors prior to completion.

Finally, the templates and related explanatory documentation should be included as part of the firm's standard business practices and procedures. This, along with continuous reinforcement from senior management, ensures that the concepts are ingrained as the "rules" within the practice. Those tenets also become the criteria by which reports are produced and subsequently judged in the QC review process, resulting in a more consistent product.

Appraisal Client Feedback

Lenders and other appraisal clients gradually increased the sophistication of their appraisal operations over time in response to regulatory and capital market demands. As a result, many of the larger companies implemented their own quality programs that prompted their appraisal departments to track vendor performance.

Although it is not necessarily conveyed directly to the vendors, the appraisal departments at many banks and financial institutions now track various components of the appraisal and the level of service provided by the firm. A review of the criteria tracked by a handful of the financial institutions indicates a heavy focus on compliance with industry standards and timely performance.

The level of detail and sophistication of tracking, as well as rating procedures in particular, varies for each institution. However, common features that are considered and/or rated by some institutions are summarized in Exhibit 3.9.

16. Gabriel Powell, "Step-by-Step Guide to Designing InDesign Templates," *Adobe Press* (March 14, 2008), http://www.adobepress.com/articles/article.asp?p=1181454/.

Exhibit 3.9 General Client Rating Criteria

Report Quality	Responsiveness and Service	Timeliness
· USPAP adherence · Minimal errors · Proper approaches/analysis · Ample data used · High readability · Professional appearance	· Prompt return of calls/e-mails · Openness to discussion · Insightful/objective responses · Professional demeanor	· Number of days late · Frequency of late reports · Prompt return of corrections · Early notice on any delays

Despite differences in rating procedures, the criteria listed in Exhibit 3.9 form the basis of what most clients deem to be "quality" appraisal services. While the specific ratings of each review are not always shared with the vendor, the existence of the ratings process is widely known. The simple knowledge that these items are considered by a client should be ample impetus for appraisers to focus on them. In fact, the improved sophistication of these large clients has forced many appraisers to improve quality and timeliness by adhering to customer-dictated performance parameters.

Surveys, focus groups, interviews, and informal discussions were conducted with a wide array of clients nationwide to better understand client needs and obtain greater detail than the fairly broad criteria used in client rating systems. The results of this research suggest a need for improvement in consistency and client focus for the industry as a whole.

As is the case with any industry, better understanding of client requirements and challenges is critical to improving client satisfaction and enhancing profits for appraisers. In fact, it is apparent from the investigation that appraisal vendors often do not understand or appreciate the challenges faced by their clients.

As shown in the accompanying quote, many clients prefer to receive appraisals that are free of defects. Clients are busy, and addressing problem appraisals disrupts workflow and reduces productivity. The aversion to vendors who consistently produce defective work in favor of dependable suppliers is understandable.

> "Reviewers, contrary to what some might think, generally hate to find problems with an appraisal because they typically have to spend two or three times their normal effort to correct mistakes and straighten things out."
> - A reviewer at a financial institution

After applying the previously discussed listening tools (surveys, focus groups, interviews, and so forth), the following themes of client dissatisfaction emerged:

Unprofessional Final Product

Clients commonly cited a wide array of "careless" errors and lack of attention to appearance and presentation of the appraisal reports.

The prevailing attitude is that clients expect reports to arrive in pristine condition, although there is some flexibility when drafts are submitted or if a very tight turnaround time is required. Pervasive complaints include:

- Lack of professional formatting and overall report appearance
- Grammatical and typographical errors
- Unprofessional writing style and low level of "readability"
- Boilerplate from prior assignments left in reports
- Inconsistent quality among appraisers within a firm
- General lack of attention to detail
- Inadequate narrative explanations
- Conflicting statements and conclusions

Untimely Delivery

Clients indicate that lack of adherence to deadlines can create a wide array of problems for them internally, with some signifying that deadlines are "crucial" to their process. Others point out that severely delayed deliveries and/or consistent lateness are the surest way to be removed from the approved appraisal panel.

Missed deadlines cause disruption to the client's internal process and can affect closing dates and other events that impact relationship managers, borrowers, and others. This can result in a loss of credibility with the client's internal and external customers, so it is important to maintain communication when delays are unavoidable. Deadline problems identified by clients include:

- Poor on-time delivery performance
- Missing due dates without informing the client or providing advance notification
- Quoting unrealistic turnaround times that cannot be achieved
- Vendor frustration when late fees and other reprisals are levied, despite clear lack of adherence to deadlines
- Perceived delays (by the borrower and/or relationship manager) in requesting data and setting up the property inspection
- Conveying data receipt problems to the client at the last minute

Inadequate Communication and Follow Up

Lack of communication appears to be a root cause of many problems experienced by appraisal customers. The need to correspond throughout the process, particularly when problems arise, is a common issue cited by clients. Most indicate that vendor contact is limited or nonexistent, causing a chain reaction of excess work for them in contacting "nervous" borrowers and loan officers as well as the vendors themselves. Specific problems cited include:

- Communicating issues verbally rather than via e-mail (which fails to provide an audit trail or facilitate passing the information along to other stakeholders)
- Failing to return phone calls or e-mails promptly or at all
- Lack of courtesy and professionalism
- Lack of insightful responses to client questions
- Not completing corrections promptly, properly, or in conformance with what had been agreed
- Blindly defending the issue/conclusion rather than objectively considering another viewpoint
- Simply providing additional commentary in responses rather than addressing the specific issues raised

Technical Appraisal Issues

While the preceding complaint categories are related to service levels and report appearance, numerous issues have also been cited regarding the data, analyses, and conclusions within appraisals. Many of these issues impact the reliability of the "answer" that clients need and some can have USPAP violation implications. Specific items identified include:

- Errors of judgment, carelessness, and other problems that impact the value estimate
- Lack of current comparable data
- Poor analysis of comparable data (such as failing to derive capitalization and discount rates or to identify buyer/seller motivations)
- Not reflecting the terms of the engagement letter in the appraisal
- Too many errors, some very material ("death by a thousand cuts")
- Too many revisions needed to get the report right
- Inadequate primary market research (including discussions with investors, brokers, managers, etc.)
- Incorrect subject property information (land and building areas, lease data, etc.)

- Making a simple appraisal problem overly complicated
- Too much boilerplate and not enough analysis

While these concerns certainly do not apply to every appraisal by every firm, the common themes and frequency of recurrence suggest that the problems are widespread, if not universal. Although numerous other issues were identified by clients, those listed here have been found to be concerns with virtually all client types, and they represent clear CTQs for a wide swath of consumers of appraisal services.

It is interesting that cost was not identified as an issue, since it is one of the "big three" factors (along with time and quality) typically considered by any consumer of a product or service. It appears from discussions, however, that the multiple-bid process used by most clients helps to make sure that the price paid will be at market level for that property type at that point in time. Although a lower price is always desirable, appraisal clients appear to be fairly comfortable that fees charged are at least competitive for any given assignment.

In addition, most high-volume consumers of appraisal services maintain several lists of vendors that are used to match experience, skill, and any property-type specialties with the property and appraisal problem. Fees are connected to the characteristics of the property type and related scope of work, usually lessening fee disparity and better aligning with clients' expectations for each list.

Ideally, an appraisal will contain few of the issues cited by the clients and will sail through the review process without incident. Unfortunately, it is challenging to produce a report completely free of errors, particularly for narrative appraisals that involve complex properties and appraisal issues.

Clients indicate that a relatively low number of defects is expected and most reviewers are tolerant when the incidence is small. As the number of problems identified increases, however, reviewer frustration grows and confidence in the conclusion and the appraiser erodes. Careless errors appear to be particularly prone to shaking a client's faith in the appraisal.

Errors and other issues with an appraisal often result in heightened scrutiny of the report and cause additional work for the client. Reviewer aggravation increases if the nature and frequency of the problems requires follow-up with the vendor, resulting in a significantly increased amount of time allocated to that review.

Relative to the Kano Model of client satisfaction discussed in Chapter 1 (basic "must haves," linear satisfiers, and delighters), most of the attributes identified by clients are merely basic features that an appraisal must have to prevent unacceptability. Although it could be argued that performing exceptionally well in some or all of the categories would qualify these categories for linear satisfier status, the consequences for regularly failing to meet these basic attributes can be dire for a firm. The bar for appraisal practices must be set higher than meeting basic client needs, and this philosophy should be adopted by any appraiser in any firm to help promote the customer service attitude.

> "Help your client look good for having hired you. It is the surest way to get rehired, and often at a premium."
>
> - A former chief appraiser at a major lending institution

The need to minimize the occurrence of problems to enhance client satisfaction (or at least avoid customer aggravation) is clear. As previously discussed, however, the lack of standardization in the appraisal process complicates efforts to consistently avoid problems. Variability in reviewer experience and interpretation on the client side of the transaction further complicate the equation.

There is an element of subjectivity to many of the problems noted by clients, and even the most efficient process cannot always completely eliminate every problem, particularly if the appraiser is not adequately trained or fully committed to exceeding customer expectations. This suggests a need for a second set of eyes on the report prior to delivery.

4

Implementing a Quality Control Review Process

Quality Control Review Process Overview

The Need for Quality Control Review

The Industrial Revolution brought heavy reliance on product inspections as a means to prevent defective goods from reaching the customer. As implemented, however, these inspections typically did not improve the production process or provide better training to workers, and companies incurred continuing and unnecessary costs (such as costs related to ongoing defects, high inspection expenses, and so forth) as a result.

Deming and other quality pioneers discouraged reliance on final inspection as a sole means of quality control and argued that production efficiency must be maximized through a robust, continuous feedback loop aimed at process and worker improvement. The quality movement emphasizes the prevention of defects over their detection and is an important means of providing short-term control and long-term enhancements to any production environment.[1]

The introduction of modern tools and sophisticated computer controls over time markedly increased product quality in many manufacturing environments and greatly reduced reliance on inspections. This allowed many producers to replace 100% inspection with a simple sampling process without significantly increasing the rate of defects that reach the consumer.

While limiting post-production inspection is an important goal that helps reduce direct quality control expenses, it is best applied in a highly standardized manufacturing environment involving homogeneous products. Inspection sampling can expose a company to

1. James R. Evans and William M. Lindsay, *The Management and Control of Quality* (Cincinnati: South-Western College Publishing, 1999), 566.

increased external defects, however, when applied to low-volume, unique products, even after employing quality principles in the design and implementation of the production process.

In some environments, however, 100% inspection is critical in certain circumstances. Products and services in which human safety is involved, or the cost of defects reaching the end user is high, are clear examples of the need for the additional layer of comfort that high inspection rates provide. Final inspection is also needed for products that cannot be effectively tested until they are fully assembled.[2]

As discussed in prior chapters, the appraisal should result from a process designed to address all of the critical-to-quality (CTQ) items identified through the firm's customer listening systems. Quality management philosophies like Six Sigma also stress the need for efficiency in the design and production of a good or service aimed at meeting those CTQs.

The appraisal industry has realized sizable process-efficiency gains over the years, largely from leveraging software innovations. Despite these strides, the process remains heavily labor intensive and subject to differences in appraiser experience, ability, and motivation. These factors limit the effectiveness of process engineering.

The lack of standardization as well as the subjectivity and "one-of-a-kind" nature of appraisals suggests the need for quality control reviews to reduce defects and ensure high-quality reports. Given the variability of the process and the potential consequences of external failures, appraisals are likely candidates for relatively high-percentage inspections. This is particularly true for large narrative reports, where opportunities for variation are abundant.

Top-quality appraisal firms recognize that appraisal reports are their best marketing tool. When combined with consistent on-time delivery and responsive, empathetic customer service, regularly producing high-quality appraisals guarantees exceptional customer satisfaction and enhanced profits. These top companies often rely on a QC review process to improve appraisal reports through an independent review of appraisal drafts prior to delivery to the client.

QC reviews are typically conducted by qualified appraisers within the firm, although it is also possible to outsource the function to a vendor. The QC review function performed within an appraisal practice is similar to reviews completed by clients (financial institutions, for instance), but the in-house activity should be more detailed. It should ensure that not only industry and client requirements are met but also that the product adheres strictly to the firm's defined stan-

2. Kaoru Ishikawa, *Introduction to Quality Control* (Tokyo: 3A Corporation, 1989), 379.

dards. As will be discussed in later chapters, other nuances within the internal QC review process also exist.

The Quality Control Review Process

The quality control process is founded on defined report and QC review standards and is ideally supported and validated through an audit process designed to guarantee proper adherence to those standards, as illustrated in Exhibit 4.1.

Exhibit 4.1 QC Review Process

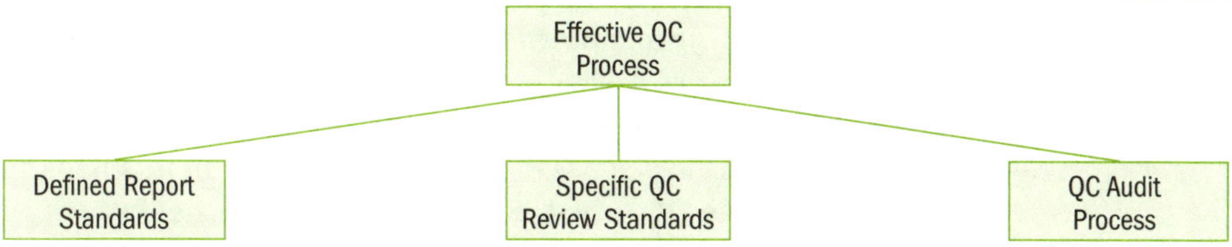

Report Standards

Defined report standards are the guideposts by which appraisals must be completed. These standards must be written and clearly understood by the production staff. As previously discussed, these guidelines may consist of report templates and other standard documents and should be comprehensive enough to cover all issues staff members are likely to encounter. This often requires having multiple templates on hand to address the various property types and appraisal issues that may arise in different assignments.

Quality Control Review Standards

Quality control standards provide a minimum scope for reviews by identifying common problems and significant sections of the report that must be reviewed in detail to make sure that the defects are spotted and corrected. It is critical that client-defined CTQs are addressed in the review standards, including the following issues previously identified by clients:

- Any factors that significantly impact value
- Standards violations
- Obvious formatting and appearance problems
- Grammar errors
- Any writing that is not in line with company standards of readability and branding

The QC standards guide establishes a minimum level of due diligence required of QC reviewers and is used in conjunction with minimum report standards and other guidelines. The minimum standards should be flexible to allow for differences in the experience, sophistication, and ability levels of the appraisers. In addition, the complexity of the property and the appraisal problem should be considered in the application of these guidelines.

Quality Control Audit Process

The third pillar of an effective QC process involves auditing. Despite well-conceived report standards, quality can suffer if those defined parameters are not followed. Inconsistency can occur from inadequate commitment to quality or misinterpretation of the standards by appraisers and QC reviewers. Periodic audits can reduce this variance by ensuring that defects are consistently identified and corrected by QC reviewers. This process is discussed in more detail later in this book.

The objective of the QC process is to help guarantee delivery of appraisals that consistently meet or exceed customers' expectations while adhering to industry standards and any applicable regulations. The process should be documented and clearly reference and incorporate the firm's report and QC standards. All appraisers, QC reviewers, and managers must read the related documents and embrace the concepts identified.

The QC review is necessarily the "last line of defense" to catch and correct any defects that may have slipped through during production. Such inspections, however, are far from infallible and are afforded much less prominence in many Six Sigma programs for the following reasons:

1. The inspection process is subjective and prone to human error and inconsistency. As a result, it is virtually impossible to detect all defects.
2. Inspectors can be viewed as excess manpower and additional costs to the organization.
3. Production staff can view the inspection team as a "crutch," feeling that the team relieves them of the responsibility to initially produce a quality product.
4. Data on defects derived from inspections are often not used as feedback to facilitate learning about how to make improvements. This eliminates a significant benefit of the QC inspection.
5. Even when defects are identified, it results in scrap and rework.

These are valid criticisms, and QC procedures should be designed with these pitfalls in mind. The process must also operate at maximum effectiveness to minimize the burden on the appraisers and ensure timeliness.

Human inspectors are far from perfect, and upwards of 30% of defects can be missed.[3] To help minimize slippage, QC reviewers should be well-qualified appraisers with extensive and wide-ranging appraisal and appraisal review experience as well as an eye for detail. Other attributes of effective reviewers that aid in process effectiveness are detailed in the section on QC reviewer qualifications that appears later in this chapter.

Assuming that the reviewers are not principals of the company or executives who are otherwise compensated for their efforts, QC reviewers should also be properly paid to review reports. Compensation helps guarantee that the requisite effort will be expended, and it can be given in the form of hourly rates, flat fees, a percentage of the appraisal fee, or other means.

The review process must be simple and allow for proper communication to facilitate a learning experience for the appraiser and production staff. Qualified reviewers check the appraisal against previously defined report and quality standards and communicate feedback to the appraiser as directly as possible.

Sample Review Process

A sample quality control review process is shown in the flow chart in Exhibit 4.2. The steps follow a logical progression and reflect the previously identified concepts aimed at maximizing problem identification while minimizing process burden. The process begins with timely submission of a draft report to allow for a proper review prior to the due date.

Note the lack of "looping" in this sample process. As discussed earlier in this book, quality management principles require that the number of branches be eliminated or at least minimized to ensure simplicity and limit the opportunity for error and non-value-added activities. A "straight-through" process also tends to be more time efficient than one fraught with decision points.

The draft appraisal should be delivered to the reviewer in client-ready form with minimal errors and an appealing appearance. "Client-ready" implies that the report is in an appropriate state to be delivered to the client and displays proper spelling, formatting, and graphics as well as inclusion of all addenda items. This helps prevent last-minute errors from slipping by that can occur in the rush to get the report completed and into the client's hands.

The QC professional completes the review and returns comments to the appraiser for correction. (Depth of review, response format, and other issues relating to the review will be discussed later.) De-

3. Ishikawa, *Introduction to Quality Control,* 14, 379.

Exhibit 4.2 Sample QC Review Process Overview

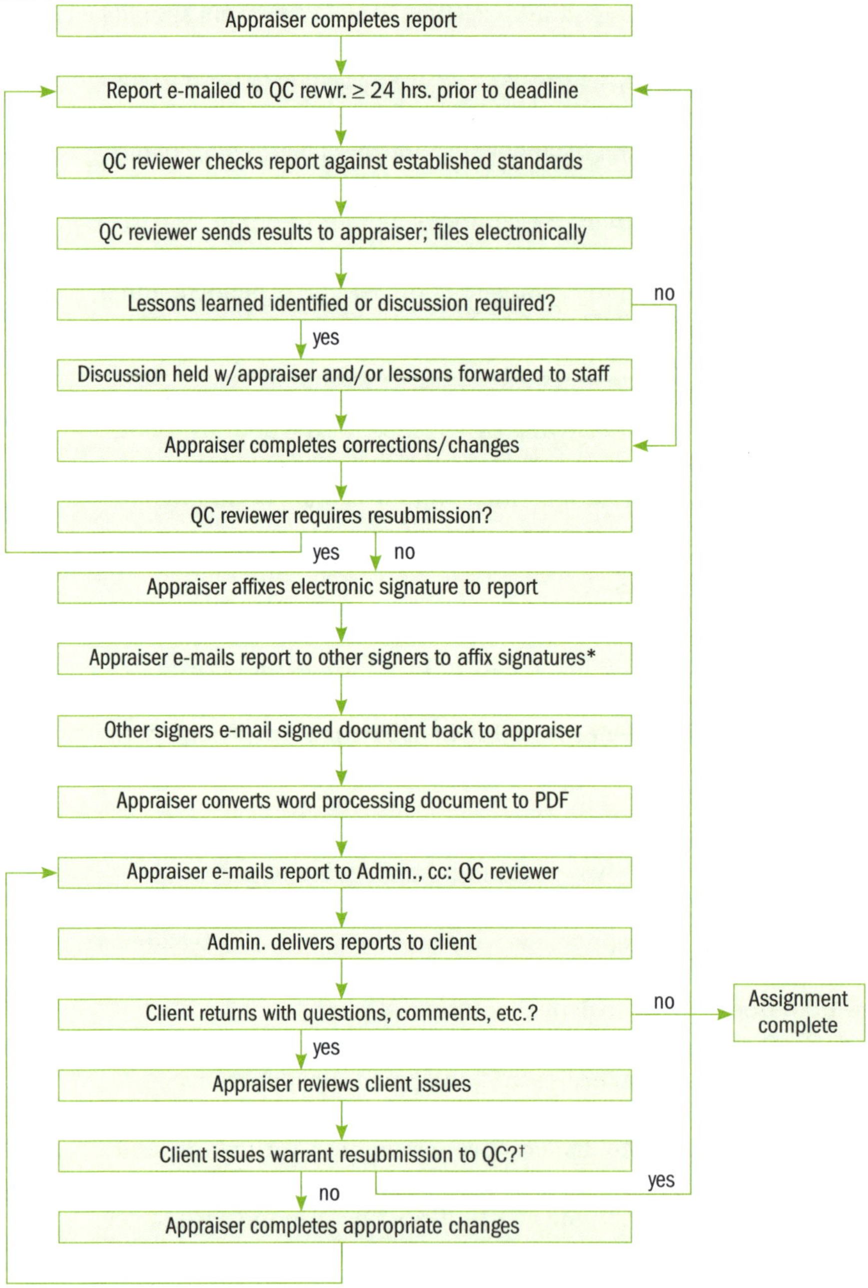

* The report must be sent in the format (draft versus signed final) that the client requested. If the client requests a draft, the signature is not affixed until approval is received to issue the final report. As discussed in this chapter, caution must be exercised when issuing a report in draft form.

† The nature/number of client issues may suggest that a new QC review is required. Items that impact value, assumptions, or opinions may suggest that a new QC review is needed.

pending on the number of occurrences and the significance of the issues identified, the reviewer may require that the corrected report be resubmitted for a second review.

A critical step in the process involves highlighting learning points for the appraiser. This includes noting any mistakes that indicate misunderstood concepts and introducing any applicable best practices. Once identified, time should be taken to discuss the issue or issues with the appraiser and other staff members, if appropriate. This helps guarantee proper understanding of the concepts and prevent recurring errors.

As will be discussed later in this chapter, care must be taken to make sure that signatures are properly controlled and affixed. Signatures should not be attached to the document until all defects identified in the review are properly corrected and all report signatories have reviewed the finished product.

Once the review is complete, the process varies depending on the setup of the company and the availability of administrative resources. It is usually preferable to channel reports through a central administrative function to guarantee proper processing (logging in and out of job tracking systems, invoice processing, and so forth). However, variation occurs based on firm size and the type and level of automation.

From time to time, feedback is received from the client after an appraisal is submitted. This commentary ranges from relatively minor questions or suggestions to significant issues related to assumptions and conclusions in the report. Upon receipt of these comments, the appraiser must determine if their significance warrants changes or if a discussion with the QC reviewer is necessary. When in doubt, it is best to forward the client feedback to the QC reviewer and then mutually decide on the merits of the issues and whether report revisions and a second review are necessary.

If the client-specified problems are valid, the QC reviewer and the appraiser should consider how the defects went undetected and what can be done to prevent such slippage in the future. Any solutions identified should be circulated to the remaining staff as a lesson learned.

Clients often request that a draft be submitted rather than a final appraisal; however, this is not cause for avoiding the QC review. In such instances, the report should be sent for QC review and the word “draft” must be inserted in appropriate sections of the appraisal. To avoid misleading the reader, the draft stamp should be applied to sections of the report that show the value conclusion.

Client feedback indicates that the use of watermarks noting “draft” on every page should be avoided. This seemingly minor issue evoked a strong response from clients during focus groups. The use of watermarks is a computer memory hog and is wasteful of ink toner for those sections of the report that are typically printed out. Watermarks can also reduce report legibility.

Quality Control Review Frequency and Special Exceptions

As the last line of prevention against external failure, consideration should be given to reviewing all final products in non-standardized processes such as appraisal production. The potential for, and magnitude of, defects likely to be included in a finished product must be determined and the consequences of those failures considered. Staff experience levels, differences in property type and geographic coverage, and other factors that influence variation in the process are all part of the analysis.

Obviously, 100% reviewing is the most conservative approach. This high rate of review is particularly relevant to narrative appraisals, especially those that are voluminous and involve complex properties or appraisal problems. Defect opportunities can abound for such products and erring on the cautious end of the inspection spectrum is advisable.

Sampling can, however, be applied in lieu of 100% inspections for form appraisals and less in-depth narrative formats like restricted reports. Given the more standardized nature, typically higher levels of automation, and limited amount of original writing in these reports, the risk of defects is reduced. Even for these reports, however, sampling should only be considered for experienced and reliable appraisers and for "standard" product types and locales.

Depending on the size and configuration of the practice, it may also be desirable for senior managers and/or specialists to perform second reviews on a sample of reports produced by the firm. This sample may include the highest-value properties or unique assignments. This best practice is critical for nonproduction staff to remain aware of product features and become engaged in the quality process, which is valuable for client meetings and responding to questions or complaints.

The review process is circumvented in some situations, such as when "emergency" submissions are requested by the client. In certain rare instances, the client is under extreme time pressure (sometimes due to events unforeseen at the time of engagement) and requests that the appraiser immediately send whatever portion of the report is completed. Clients indicate that accommodating this need is appreciated and that a less stringent review is applied, pending receipt of the final report.

From the appraiser's perspective, however, this type of unexpected "fire drill" often results in an elevated number of defects due to partial report completion and/or the lack of quality control. Given the increased riskiness of this type of situation, forwarding appraisals prior to review under rush circumstances should be an extraordinary exception.

To mitigate risk, the draft report should only be forwarded to the client with the approval of the proper level of management or designated QC reviewer. Approval should be given only after a discussion with the appraiser's manager about the property, the appraisal (including assumptions and general valuation parameters), and any particular risks associated with submitting an appraisal that lacks QC.

After approval is received from the manager, the document must be clearly marked as a draft prior to delivery to the client. When forwarding non-reviewed drafts, it is critical that the client is informed, in writing, that the report remains in draft form and that it did not undergo the company's required QC review process. It must also be noted that the report is subject to change as a result of the pending QC review.

The following language, or similar wording to the same effect, should be inserted with the document transmitting the draft:

> In response to your request that our preliminary findings be submitted, the attached draft report did *not* undergo our normal quality control review. As a result, the report format, assumptions, and conclusions are subject to change, and the report should *not* be viewed as a finalized document.

Although drafts are occasionally requested by clients, *caution must be exercised when issuing these types of appraisals.* The Appraisal Standards Board has been grappling with the question of draft reports for some time, and it is unclear whether draft reports are allowed under USPAP. Some state appraiser boards have taken the position that drafts are not allowed. Keep in mind that any report delivered to a client should comply with USPAP Standards 1 and 2. The report can be marked "draft" if the client so wishes, but if changes are needed, a corrected report should be issued with a new signature (report) date.

Signing the Appraisal

The signature on a report is evidence that the appraiser accepts responsibility for the content and conclusions of the report. This effectively "locks" the appraiser to the report, so care must be taken to guarantee that the best possible product exists prior to affixing the professional's signature. The signature also indicates to the client that the appraisal report is a final document that is fit for review and in compliance with all customer requirements.

According to USPAP, a signature is "personalized evidence indicating authentication of the work performed by the appraiser and the acceptance of the responsibility for content, analyses, and conclusions in the report."

With most appraisal firms, the appraiser's signature typically consists of an electronic image that is "pasted" into the word processing document and then converted to PDF format. While this is an efficient means of entering the signature into the report, it is vital that the appraiser maintain control of his or her signature's use.

To mitigate potential misuse, each staff member (appraiser, manager, QC reviewer, and so forth) signing the appraisal should apply his or her own signature. This can be accomplished by each report signatory attaching an image of the signature in the word processing document prior to being sent to the client.

As a contingency for times when a signatory is unavailable to sign the report, the signature should also be given to an administrator or another individual who is authorized to apply the image in the signer's absence. USPAP permits another individual to sign on the appraiser's behalf, as long as the appraiser provides specific authorization. Such authorization can only be delegated on an assignment-by-assignment basis.[4]

Quality Control Reviewer Qualifications

Quality control reviewers are responsible for helping ensure that the final report received by the client is accurate, well-written, free of errors, and aligned with industry and company standards. This review process is integral to delivering appraisal reports that consistently meet or exceed client expectations.

To properly perform the QC review function, each reviewer must have the requisite experience and attention to detail to identify and correct any issues in the reports submitted for review. Ideally, the reviewer will have previously served in a review capacity as a manager in a "fee" appraisal firm or in a review position at a bank, financial institution, or similar environment where exposure to a wide range of appraisal types and styles is prevalent. It is also desirable that the reviewer have experience with a wide array of property types and geographic areas.

It is imperative that the QC staff member has spent time or is currently in a production environment and has an established track record of high levels of performance in that capacity. Professional experience combined with these attributes is valuable in promoting and implementing best practices. Previous recognition for consistently producing a high-quality product (received from clients, peers, or managers) is vital, as is solid on-time delivery performance. These qualities indicate a high level of performance and a drive to guarantee customer satisfaction. Less tangible desired qualities include a passion for the business, a clear focus on client needs, and strong communication abilities.

4. The Appraisal Foundation, *Uniform Standards of Professional Appraisal Practice,* 2010-2011 ed. (Washington, DC: The Appraisal Foundation, 2010), U-4, F-101.

Based on feedback from QC reviewers nationwide, general parameters for selection as a QC reviewer may include:

- An MAI or similar designation
- Ten years of experience, including previous reviewing experience
- In-depth familiarity with USPAP and other industry standards
- Prior and consistent recognition for producing high-quality appraisal reports from clients, peers, managers, and others
- A solid on-time delivery track record
- Attention to detail
- Keen focus on customer satisfaction

The qualifications of each candidate should be reviewed against these criteria by the appropriate levels of management. For larger firms, a formal nomination and approval process may be desirable to ensure the consistent selection of properly qualified individuals.

As part of a "probationary" period, each new QC reviewer should have a sampling of his or her reviews examined by other QC reviewers and/or senior managers. This second look will help make sure that the new reviewer's interpretation of the firm's report and QC standards are properly aligned with those of the firm.

Turnaround Time Standards

Discussions with reviewers across the country indicate that drafts are often submitted at the last minute prior to the due date, forcing the reviewer to rush through the process. This can result in a higher incidence of overlooked defects and issues that would have otherwise received attention. Rushing the inspection of products reduces effectiveness and increases the probability of defects reaching the client.

To avoid such a compromised position, it is useful for the reviewer to be aware of the assignment pipeline and for the appraiser to be forthcoming with information about any upcoming jobs with tight deadlines. While such measures are effective, the quality control review program must include turnaround guidelines that are well known to all parties.

As a general rule, reports should be submitted for QC review as early as possible prior to the due date. This allows the reviewer to spend adequate time reading the report and also provides a time cushion should questions arise or serious problems be identified in the appraisal.

Many reviewers suggest that at least 48 hours is needed for a review assignment in order to allocate the requisite time given their typical work queues. Few firms have the luxury of full-time staff reviewers, but even full-timers have workload queues. QC reviewers acknowledge, however, that 48 hours is not always practical given the quick turnarounds and workloads that confront most appraisers. The consensus opinion is that reports should be delivered to the QC reviewer a minimum of 24 hours prior to the date that they are promised to the client.

While 24 hours is a reasonable standard minimum submission time, flexibility should be maintained, allowing this window to be increased to 48 hours for some individuals at the discretion of the QC reviewer. This expanded submission requirement may be appropriate for appraisers who consistently submit reports that require significant editing or changes and allows for ample time to complete corrections prior to the due date.

Communication is important to help the process run smoothly. The following best practices have been identified to help minimize glitches:

- Each appraiser should e-mail the QC reviewer to notify him or her about the anticipated workflow for the upcoming week.
- Appraisers should identify due dates, particularly if the review must be completed more quickly than the 24-hour standard.
- Appraisers should also alert the QC reviewer to any prior appraisals completed on the subject property, along with the change in value and any significant changes in assumptions relative to the last appraisal.
- Reviewers must inform the appraisers when they will be away from the office.
- QC professionals must also identify alternative reviewers when they are out of the office or when work "bottlenecks" are anticipated and they are unable to meet the 24-hour turnaround standard.

Because workloads may vary significantly and are difficult to control, occasions will arise when the minimum submission time cannot be met and the review must be performed in a compressed time frame. Such situations should occur rarely, since they usually disrupt workflow, lead to a rushed review, and increase the probability of errors going undetected.

If reviewers note that an appraiser frequently disregards the 24-hour standard (or whatever parameter is established by the firm), discussions should be held with the individual and should be escalated to the management as appropriate. Prolonged abuse should result in fee penalties or other corrective action to encourage the desired improvement.

5

Determining the Scope of the Quality Control Review

The Scope of the Review

Establishing the proper review scope can be tricky, considering the need to balance the identification of critical defects (CTQs) against the amount of time a reviewer should expend given the type of appraisal and the scope of the appraisal problem (as well as the fee). The appraiser's level of ability and attention to detail can also influence the scope, with the reviewer required to read more of the report in detail for less reliable professionals than those who meticulously address all details.

The intended use of the report is also a key driver of the quality control scope. It is advisable, for instance, to intensify the QC review for a report that is intended for court use rather than an appraisal that is likely to be less scrutinized.

Further complicating the challenge is the need to recognize and adjust for differences in job demands. Any type of workload stress tends to increase the opportunity for error. If a professional completes four narrative appraisals in a week when one is the norm, for instance, a heightened level of scrutiny may need to be applied, as carelessness can mount under such high-production circumstances.

Since quality-management principles have a profitability component, the review scope needs to be tailored to the client and report type. It would be fiscally unwise to apply the same rigorous inspection to both an appraisal of a simple property for which the analysis and value are reported using a restricted report and a complex appraisal presented in a voluminous self-contained report. Opportunities for error are much greater in self-contained appraisals. The appraisal fee (and related review fee) likely reflect the complexity of the task, providing adequate compensation for the reviewer to expand his or her level of focus.

While the QC review should be tailored to fit the type of appraisal, the property, and other factors, there are certain basic steps that must be completed to help ensure that the CTQs are addressed. These fundamental items must be identified and communicated to all parties involved in the report production.

In general, the appraisal fee is a reasonable indication of the complexity of the property and the appraisal assignment. The fee, however, is not the sole criterion for the scope and level of detail for the QC review, and a low fee does not absolve an appraiser or reviewer from adequate due diligence. In general, the QC review should be structured to check the appraisal against the CTQs that have been identified by clients. While the process will vary based on the practice's client base, previously summarized issues drawn from conversations with a cross section of appraisal clients suggest that the following minimum steps should usually be taken, regardless of the fee or report type:

1. Read the narrative in sufficient detail to spot errors in logic, data deficiencies, inadequate analysis of subject and comparable data, and any other issues that may result in an incorrect, unreliable, or poorly supported value estimate.
2. Identify improper grammar, formatting errors, and other issues that affect the appearance of the report and reflect negatively on the company and the appraiser or appraisers.
3. Review the summary information on the subject and comparable data. Depending on the type and scope of the report as well as the confidence level associated with the appraiser, it may also be advisable to review any detailed comparable data write-ups included in the report.
4. Apply general tests of reasonableness and diagnostics to any pro forma income estimates and cash flow forecasts. Depending on the results of these diagnostics, additional investigations (such as detailed auditing of any discounted cash flow modeling) may be warranted.
5. Examine the report addenda to make sure that proper supporting schedules and all items referenced in the narrative and other report sections are included.
6. Check that ample photos, maps, and other graphic materials are included to assist the reader in understanding the property, its surrounding area, and any other pertinent items affecting value.

The QC review *usually* doesn't include all of the following steps, although it certainly may include one or more of these items:

- Verify market analysis information and comparable data
- Inspect the property
- Read the statistical portions of the regional analysis and market analysis sections in detail
- Check math calculations
- Reconcile or conduct a detailed comparison of client rent roll, income statements, and other financial data with the appraiser's forecast

While the amount of detail applied in the review can be adjusted based on the experience, sophistication, and skill level of the primary appraiser, even the most experienced and diligent professionals are subject to making errors. In addition, experience is not necessarily an indication of the appraiser's commitment to producing a quality appraisal. As a result, attention to detail is required in all QC reviews, regardless of the appraiser's experience level.

Critical Items of Focus

The Pareto Principle

Using quality-management principles (and common sense), firms should concentrate resources on correcting those areas of a process that are responsible for the greatest share of product defects. Six Sigma and other quality programs refer to this methodology as the *Pareto principle* or the *80-20 rule.*

The Pareto principle gets its name from Vilfredo Pareto, a sociologist and economist who conducted studies on the distribution of wealth in Europe in the early 1900s. Pareto found that wealth was not evenly distributed in various countries, and prosperity was concentrated in a relatively small portion of the population.[1] He revealed that 80% of the wealth in Italy and other countries was concentrated among 20% of the population.

In the 1930s and 1940s, Joseph Juran similarly observed that this disproportionate distribution could be universally applied to many population samples and situations. Juran called this phenomenon the "vital few and useful many," and it was eventually referred to simply as the *Pareto principle.*

This principle is used to remind individuals and managers that, in almost any environment, a few items (20%) are vital while many

1. Dale H. Besterfield, *Quality Control* (Upper Saddle River, NJ: Prentice-Hall, 2001), 74.

(80%) are not. In business, companies often note that 80% of sales or profits come from 20% of their customers. From a quality perspective, Juran found that 20% of the defects in a product resulted in 80% of the product's problems. He reasoned that, since these few factors are responsible for the bulk of poor-quality costs, focusing resources on these contributors maximizes improvement results.[2]

The concept was eventually expressed as a graph that ranks the occurrences of each item in descending order from left to right, with the "vital few" represented on the left end of the horizontal axis. The vertical axis is typically expressed in dollars or number of occurrences, or as a percentage of total occurrences. A line is also often added to display the cumulative impact of each of the items being measured. Such a graph is useful to visually depict those items of greatest importance.

For example, assume that an appraisal firm tracking and categorizing client feedback notes that the incidence of complaints on poor appraisal report appearance is increasing. The reasons noted for the clients' opinions are tabulated and shown in the Pareto chart in Exhibit 5.1.

As indicated in Exhibit 5.1, issues relating to "typos/poor grammar" and "prior boilerplate used" represent 78% of the defects identified by clients and are the vital few characteristics associated with the problem. Given the diminishing returns associated with the remaining issues, management would be best served by focusing

Exhibit 5.1 **Pareto Chart: Poor Appearance of Appraisals**

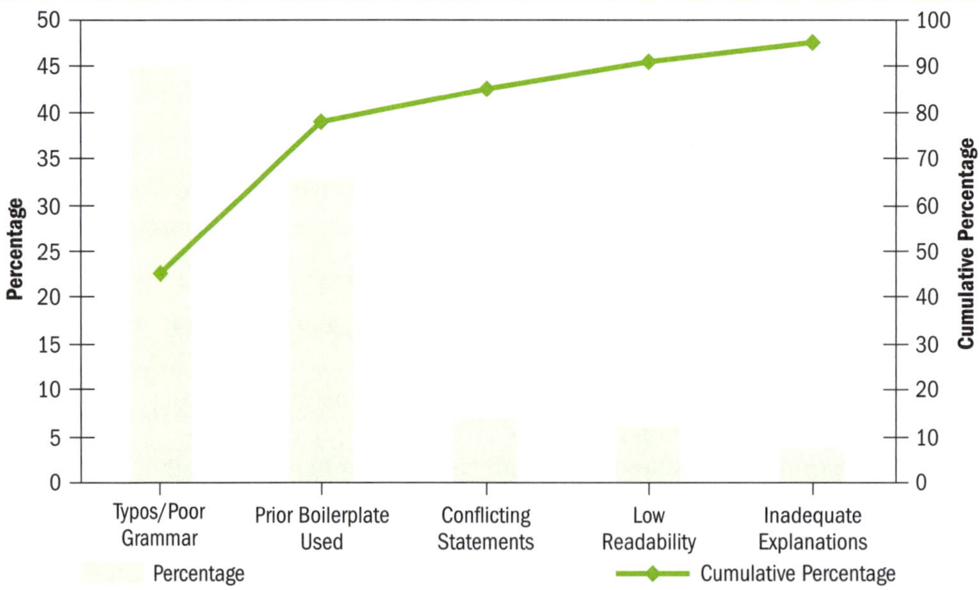

2. J. M. Juran, *Juran's Quality Control Handbook* (New York: McGraw-Hill, 1988), 6.20, 22.19.

quality improvement efforts on the vital few issues. This would likely involve reexamining the reports for which those issues were cited and identifying the root causes of those problems. Solutions can then be developed to address those causes.

Pareto analysis, as with all quality-driven approaches, is a continuous process. In this example, the problems relating to typos and boilerplate will slide down in the scale once they are adequately addressed, and a new set of vital problems will ascend in importance. These new issues must, in turn, be addressed if report appearance continues to be a problem cited by clients.

The "Vital Few"

While the Pareto principle can be applied to analyzing customer complaints, the principle is also useful in preventing problems through gaining a better understanding of what clients focus on in the end product. Like those producing the work, reviewers expend their limited time resources concentrating on certain sections of the appraisal that they consider to be the "vital few" and that are the keys to quality.

Recognizing that common problems exist within the industry, the Appraisal Institute produced a white paper that identifies frequent issues in appraisal reports. This document, "Common Errors and Issues in the Appraisal Report," is included in Appendix B in the back of this book.

Discussions with appraisal clients nationwide indicate that they almost always read certain portions of the appraisal in some detail. While there is variation among each institution or individual (that frustrating lack of process standardization again), common areas of focus exist. Sections of the report that are likely to receive scrutiny include (but are not limited to) comparable sale and rental write-ups, income and expense analyses, property descriptions, and discount and capitalization rate selections.

In addition, it is quite possible that the client reading the report is not familiar with the particular market and did not inspect the property. As a result, clients consistently indicate a need for ample descriptions, photos, maps, and other graphics of the property and neighborhood.

Significant Issues Found in Appraisal Reports

A detailed list of significant issues that are often found in appraisal reports follows. Although this list may appear to be exhaustive because of its sheer length, it actually touches on only the portions of an appraisal that have been deemed particularly significant by a nationwide sampling of clients and quality control reviewers. However, this list should not be interpreted to be the "vital few." Each firm is left to determine its own vital few through its specific customer feedback process. It is a safe bet, however, that any appraisal practice that properly addresses all of the items in the list can boast a highly satisfied client base.

Some of the items in the list may seem overly simplistic (such as applying the proper units of comparison in a sales comparison), but research indicates that such errors occur with regularity. Some of these items are also obviously more significant than others.

The following list of important areas to consider in appraisal reports is broken down by report section. For those appraisers who regularly construct discounted cash flow forecasts, a list of common cash flow modeling issues is included in Appendix C in the back of this book.

Letter of Transmittal

- The client, the client's professional title, the date(s) of value, the intended users, and the intended use should be properly identified. (It is helpful to have a copy of the engagement letter on hand to check these items.)
- Any unusual items or features regarding the property or significant issues or concerns (such as unpaid property taxes or lack of available utilities) should be noted.
- The client's job number should be included.

Extraordinary Assumptions and Hypothetical Conditions

Appraisers often mislabel or do not properly interpret the distinction between extraordinary assumptions and hypothetical conditions. Additional guidance on this topic is provided in Appendix B in the back of this book. The following issues can increase the risk of misleading the reader if extraordinary assumptions and hypothetical conditions are not properly applied:

- When estimating the "as is" value of a property, hypothetical conditions cannot be used.
- When an extended lease-up is forecast or a prospective value is estimated, an extraordinary assumption with language such as the following should be applied:

  > The prospective market value estimate is based on market conditions existing as of the ____ quarter, 200_. The appraiser cannot be held responsible for unforeseeable events that may alter the market conditions prior to the future effective date of the prospective market value opinion.

- When a retrospective value is estimated, an extraordinary assumption with language such as the following should be applied:

  > It is assumed that the subject property was in similar condition as of the retrospective date of value (____, 200_) as it

> was on the date of inspection (____, 200_). Every effort has been made to reflect income, expenses, and other items as of the retrospective value date.

- When the subject is proposed construction, extraordinary assumptions or hypothetical conditions with language similar to the following should be applied:

> This analysis specifically assumes that development of the subject property is completed in a timely manner, using quality materials and design in accordance with the plans and specifications provided to the appraiser. Any undue delay in the subject's construction timeline or change in the construction quality or design could materially impact the value conclusion reported herein.

Note that this statement is classified as an extraordinary assumption when the date of value is a future date and the improvements are expected to be completed prior to that future date. It is a hypothetical condition when the date of value is the current date and the property is being appraised as if the improvements exist today.

- When a new or proposed lease is used in the analysis, an extraordinary assumption with language similar to the following should be applied:

> This analysis assumes that the tenant lease with _______ is implemented according to the terms provided. The commitment of this tenant to the property is an integral part of the analysis herein.

Summary of Significant Facts

- Data must be placed in all standard fields.
- Significant factors must be properly identified.
- Sales history and leasing comments should identify significant incidents affecting the property.

Introduction

- The scope of work should match the appraisal problem and the work actually performed.
- The sales history/disposition section must adequately identify any sales or significant recent changes at the property (such as renovation or leasing status changes).
- If a recent sale occurred, a sale contract exists, or the property is listed for sale, it must be *analyzed* and related to the value conclusion.

Regional Analysis

Clients often do not focus on the regional analysis section in great detail, particularly if the reader is already familiar with the subject property's market area. Data in this section should be up to date, and the conclusion should be current and match the data in the tables.

Local Area Analysis

The local area analysis section is typically completed in the appraiser's original writing, so it should be read carefully to check for typos and grammatical errors and to confirm factual accuracy.

- This analysis should tie in all relevant information pertaining to the subject property.
- Demographics, new developments, competing developments, access, major properties, special or adverse hazards, and any changes in the area should be discussed.

Market Analysis

- The market analysis conclusion should be logical and supported by market data.
- All relevant information pertaining to the subject property should be tied in.
- The subject's submarket should be identified within the first or second paragraph.
- The subject's position within the market or submarket should be explained, and marketability and/or feasibility should be discussed.

Site Description

- The site's suitability (in terms of size, physical attributes, etc.) for the existing or proposed use should be discussed.
- Physical factors (such as visibility and topography) should be identified.
- There should not be any redundant data.
- Street frontage information should be included.

Description of the Improvements

- Significant historical factors (such as sales, listings, tenancy changes, and renovations) must be identified.
- Any capital expenditures or deferred maintenance issues must be discussed and tied in with the approaches to value.

- The building layout description must paint a clear picture for the reader.
- The effective age and the actual age must be logical and flow through to the cost approach.
- Ample graphics (such as current photos and site plans) should be included to aid the reader's understanding of the property.

Real Property Taxes and Assessments

- A description of the local tax assessment and billing process should be provided.
- The discussion should include the impact of underassessment or overassessment on the subject property.
- The following items should be considered:
  - Whether a change in assessment may be warranted based on the value conclusion relative to the assessment
  - Whether adjustment to real estate taxes used in the appraisal should result
- Partial assessment and delinquent taxes should be addressed.
- In cases when the market value conclusion suggests that the property is overassessed, a conclusion as to whether a reassessment is likely to be considered by a prospective purchaser given the costs and uncertainties associated with the process in the subject property's taxing jurisdiction should be made.

Zoning

- Permitted uses and zoning requirements, especially bulk/density levels, should be identified.
- The subject's conformity with zoning and any impact on marketability or value resulting from nonconformance should be determined.

Highest and Best Use

- Highest and best use conclusions must be logical given the facts identified in the market analysis, zoning write-ups, property descriptions, and other sections of the report.
- Financial feasibility must be supported by the opinion of market value and other conclusions in the report.
- In cases when the highest and best use conclusion is to hold for future development, support must be provided for this

conclusion. Reference should be made to softness in the market, changes in the investment climate, or any other issues substantiating the conclusion.

- When the highest and best use as improved is a continued use and it is concluded that the improvements add value, a discussion of the "as is" value relative to the value of the site as if vacant should be included. The following language provides an example:

> In the reconciliation section of this report, we conclude to a market value of the subject property, as improved, of $____. By comparison, the subject land value is considered to be substantially less than the value as improved. In our opinion, the improvements contribute significantly to the value of the site, dictating its continued use as currently improved.

Valuation Approaches Discussion

- Appropriate approaches must be used, based on the scope of work.
- A proper explanation must be included for any approaches that have been excluded.

Land Valuation

- Proper unit(s) of comparison (per square foot, per unit, etc.) must be applied.
- Comparable sales summaries should be free of misspellings as well as formatting and other types of errors.
- Appropriate adjustments must be applied in the adjustment grid.
- The narrative must match the adjustment grid.
- A well-written paragraph on how the per-unit conclusion was derived should be included (e.g., the best sales have the fewest adjustments) to lead the reader to the conclusion. Simply stating that the range is "x" to "y" and "z" was chosen is inadequate.
- The overall adjustments must not be excessive and should suggest true comparability to the subject.
- Comparable sales data should be supplemented with conversations with local brokers, owners, and investors. Market participant interviews and listings should be included.

Cost Approach

- Entrepreneurial profit and depreciation must be properly developed relative to the property description and market analysis data.

- External obsolescence must be properly considered. Overlooking this may result in a wide spread compared to the conclusions from the other approaches. Sample language that may be used in this section of the report follows:

> External obsolescence is caused by conditions extraneous to the subject, which impairs or diminishes desirability. Included in this category are items such as legislative enactments that restrict or impair property rights, neighborhood deterioration, and economic conditions. As noted earlier in the report, the current outlook for the ____ market in _____ County is declining. The global credit crisis (and current economic climate) has affected real estate values throughout the region.
>
> Based on the foregoing, it is clear that demand for _____ properties (the real estate) has diminished significantly. There is no demand to develop new buildings of the subject's size, and financing options for such a development are limited. As such, external obsolescence appears to exist for the subject, and it must be accounted for.

  This discussion must be concluded by estimating external depreciation using one of the following:

  - Allocation of market-extracted depreciation
  - Analysis of market data
  - Capitalization of an income loss

- If the property is proposed or new, a discussion of the developer's costs must be included and the developer's costs must be compared with the appraiser's conclusions.

Sales Comparison Approach

- Proper unit(s) of comparison (per square foot, per unit, etc.) must be applied.
- Comparable sales tables should be free of misspellings and formatting or other types of errors.
- In the adjustment grid, appropriate adjustments must be applied and the supporting narrative must adequately lead the reader to the conclusion.
- The narrative must match the adjustment grid.
- A well-written paragraph on how the per-unit conclusion was derived should be included (e.g., the best sales have the fewest adjustments) to lead the reader to the conclusion. Simply stating that the range is "x" to "y" and "z" was chosen is inadequate.
- The overall adjustments must not be excessive and should suggest true comparability to the subject.

- Comparable sales data should be supplemented with local broker, owner, and investor conversations. Market participant interviews and listings should be included.

Income Capitalization Approach

- The subject lease(s) must be properly analyzed (tenant profile, term, space type, etc.).
- Current subject asking and actual rents, the status of any negotiations on vacant space, and adequate rent comparables must be combined with an analysis that leads the reader to the market rent conclusion.
- Comparable rent summaries must be free of misspellings and formatting or other types of errors.
- Confidentiality must be considered when identifying comparable rentals. Some of the data is likely from prior appraisals, so the tenant should not be identified. It may also be necessary to disguise the property location, particularly for very large leases, to protect confidentiality.
- Absorption of any vacant space must be substantiated in reports. Including absorption comparables and/or a demand capture analysis usually supports the assumption well.
- Subject expenses must be adequately examined and any variations from historicals in the forecast must be explained, possibly with footnotes to the analysis table when needed.
- Expense conclusions should be supported by comparables as well.
- The initial overall capitalization rate (*OAR*) and internal rate of return (*IRR*) selections must be logical given the comparable sales and survey data, and the narrative must lead the reader to the conclusion.
- Investor survey data must be used with caution. The rates identified are often applicable to investment-grade properties, while the overwhelming majority of assignments involve non-investment-grade projects. These nuances must be recognized and/or the survey data must be directly applicable to these properties.
- For properties at stabilized occupancy and operations, the residual *OAR* must relate properly to the implied going-in *OAR, not the selected OAR in the direct capitalization method.*
- In cases when band-of-investment is used, equity dividend rates and equity yield rates should not be confused when estimating the equity portion of the process.

Reconciliation and Final Value Opinion

- The strengths and weaknesses of the approaches used must be explained.
- The conclusion must be related to any recent sales or listings of the subject property.
- The spread among the approaches used must be reasonable.

Addenda

- The actual contents should match up with what appears on the contents page.
- Addenda items must be legible and attractively presented and should add value to the analysis.

General Issues

- The report narrative and supporting data should lead the reader to the value conclusion.
- Ample maps, photographs, and so forth should be provided to aid the reader's understanding. Comparables must be properly placed on maps, and photos should be properly labeled.
- Copyright, sourcing, and use permission should be properly identified.
- Attention to detail (such as limiting typos, math errors, and so forth) must adhere to the highest standards.
- The depth of analysis must be appropriate for the report type.
- Grammar and style in the report must be professional and aligned with Appraisal Institute and other standards.
- For appraisers in multistate areas, proper licensing must be ensured. The appraiser and all signatories must be certified within the subject state.
- Page headers and footers should be consistent and correct.
- There should not be any unnecessary blank pages.
- Tables should be sized properly for the sake of legibility and attractive appearance.
- The report must match what is requested in the engagement letter.

Among the items in this list, certain sections of the report have an elevated propensity to include errors. Many of these errors, in turn, have a high probability of being detected by clients. For example, appraisers and QC reviewers should pay special attention to any sections that contain original writing or that are not part of standard boilerplate or templates. The opportunity for error in these sections as well as the odds that the client will read such sections are high, increasing the likelihood of error detection.

This list can be used as a basis for QC reviews and can be tailored to fit the practice's customer base. By considering the items in this list and employing the client listening tools discussed earlier in this book, the "vital few" issues to focus on can be selected as appropriate for each firm.

Time Allocation

The fee for an appraisal assignment is sometimes used as a general guideline for the amount of time that should be expended on the quality control review. While this is often a reasonable indicator of the complexity of the property and the appraisal problem, it is not necessarily the best gauge for the amount of time to be spent on the QC review. Instead, a number of factors should be considered, including:

- The complexity of the property and the appraisal problem
- The type of appraisal
- The experience level of the appraiser
- Whether previously approved templates or reports are used
- Whether the property was appraised and reviewed previously

Even taking into account these factors, each reviewer still operates at his or her own pace. As a result, it is difficult to identify an ideal amount of time to spend on each appraisal review. In an attempt to offer general guidelines, however, a study was conducted to identify broad parameters that reviewers can follow. This research included a nationwide sampling of QC reviews and encompassed

Exhibit 5.2 Quality Control Reviewer Time Study Summary

Category	Avg. Number of Minutes per Review	Category	Avg. Number of Minutes per Review
By report type		By apppraiser experience	
Self-contained	72	High	69
Summary	44	Medium	50
Restricted	29	Low	54
Updates only		By property complexity	
Self-contained	62	Raw land	39
Summary	30	Subdivisions	38
Restricted	–	Apartments	49
		1-2 tenants	47
		3-15 tenants	71
		> 15 tenants	79

over 270 commercial appraisal assignments. The results are summarized in Exhibit 5.2.

The data presented in Exhibit 5.2 was examined for four separate categories to see what patterns could be identified. The range of minutes recorded for each category was wide, reflecting the nuances associated with each assignment and the differences in reviewer speed. Despite this variation, the averages are logical. This research has uncovered the following notable items:

- As might be expected, self-contained reports require the longest reviews. In fact, an additional 28 minutes (on average) is spent reviewing self-contained reports compared to summary reports. The average review time for restricted reports is 14 minutes less than the average review time for summary reports (also less than half the average review time for self-contained reports).
- Efficiency gains are sizable for updates, with reviews on previously appraised properties taking from 15% to over 33% less time than the overall average for each type of report.
- Appraisals submitted by staff with "high" experience levels actually consume more reviewer time than those produced by less experienced professionals. This appears to result, however, from the senior staff being assigned jobs that are more complex. These assignments naturally require greater scrutiny.
- The amount of time expended on reviews is heavily dependent on the type of property appraised and the number of tenants (if applicable). Raw land demands the lowest time commitment on average, while properties with over 15 tenants require the greatest commitment.

The wide range of variables associated with each appraisal makes it difficult to identify exact time expenditures, so the averages shown are not intended to be prescriptive. Rather, they are general guidelines to allow comparisons and consider opportunities for alterations to review methodology.

In addition to the previously noted variables, the amount of time required for reviews is also dependent upon the extent to which the appraisal development process is standardized at a given firm. The effectiveness of templates employed and the automation, quality, and sophistication of databases used can markedly reduce the amount of review time required across all categories of assignments. As noted previously, such tools should be used whenever possible.

6

Appraiser/Quality Control Reviewer Responsibilities and Communicating During the Review

Proofreading Prior to Submission for Review: The Appraiser's Responsibility

Reviewing any document can be tedious and difficult, and the human element guarantees that some problems will be missed. While it is difficult for a quality control reviewer to identify all of the mistakes in a document, this challenge is even more daunting when proofing one's own work.

Consider the number of times that you have gone back to look at something you previously wrote (an e-mail, letter, or any other written communication) and found mistakes that were not noticed, despite having looked at it several times prior to releasing it. Spelling, word usage, punctuation, and other undetected errors can cause embarrassment (or worse) for the writer. Despite this difficulty, it is critical that the author of the appraisal report proofread it carefully prior to submission for QC review to act as one more filter in the process. Proofreading is also a final opportunity to polish the work prior to review; it must be performed with the necessary amount of focus and enthusiasm to optimize results.

Familiarity may (or may not) breed contempt, but it surely results in a tendency to gloss over certain sections when reading your own text and increases the likelihood of missing problems when proofreading documents. National QC reviewers and other sources provided the following best practices for reviewing one's own writing:

1. **Don't begin the review immediately after finishing the report.**
   A writer is less likely to read a recently completed document that is still fresh in his or her mind *carefully,* increasing the

risk of missing mistakes. While deadlines can pose an obstacle, it is best to switch to an unrelated task for an hour or so or to wait until the following day to review your own report if time permits.

2. **Print out the sections that contain the most original writing.**
   Research shows (and logic suggests) that portions of the document with the most original writing tend to contain the most errors. It is most effective to print these sections out and review the hard copy rather than work strictly on screen.
3. **Eliminate distractions while proofreading.**
   Thorough reviewing requires full and focused attention. Any diversions from the document (conversations, radio, television, etc.) impair the ability to focus and increase the probability of missing errors.
4. **Read slowly.**
   People tend to speed through when reading their own work, often skipping over words or sentences. One suggestion for forcing a slower review is to read the narrative aloud. People speak text more slowly than they read it, and speaking also allows the writer to hear the text as the intended reader will.
5. **Use spell-check.**
   Submitting a document that contains spelling errors is embarrassing and reflects badly on the writer. The spell-check feature available in word processing software helps prevent obvious spelling errors. However, spell-check is not completely foolproof. It does not identify valid words that are improperly substituted for homophones, such as *to* versus *too* or *their* versus *there.*
6. **Use grammar-check.**
   Similar to spell-check, the grammar-check feature in word processing software can help eliminate grammar mistakes. This tool, however, is even more prone to misidentifying errors, so review the sentence carefully to make sure that the change suggested by grammar-check is proper.

While these tips may be helpful, their application requires commitment on the part of the author of the report. Proofreading should be more than a simple scan of the document to catch the most obvious mistakes. Given the propensity for errors in manual processes like writing appraisals, paying attention to proofing is critical to helping prevent defects from reaching the client.

In reality, however, even the most diligent proofreading will fail to catch all of the errors in a document. Professional editors read documents as many as 10 times, and publishers typically hire teams of readers. However, mistakes have still been found in documents that have undergone rigorous review processes.[1] Given the human propensity for missing errors, more eyes examining a document means that more mistakes will be identified. The first set of eyes (the first line of defense) needs to be those of the writer.

Quality Control Reviewer Responsibilities

As experienced members of an appraisal firm's staff, quality control reviewers play a key role in improving the skill levels of the firm's appraisers by imparting their expertise and vision during the review process. Reviewers convey these skills through written comments within a review and via any supplemental conversations relating to each appraisal. The reviewer must maximize the learning opportunity for less-experienced appraisers in particular through an appropriate response style.

The QC reviewer also has the responsibility to be consistent in what items he or she identifies as needing attention and the manner in which comments are delivered. The reviewer cannot give the impression that quality is a moving target and must convey a sense of fairness to the appraiser. Given the variability of human nature, consistency is a challenge; this is a primary reason why report and quality control standards must be carefully developed and properly communicated.

Reviewers must conduct reviews and communicate their responses in a professional and tactful manner. It is also important to keep in mind that the appraiser invested significant time in developing the report, and criticism (constructive or otherwise) may be poorly accepted. As a result, empathy should be employed when delivering feedback.

Care should be taken, however, to make sure that proper balance is included in the response. A critique that is too delicate or avoids directly addressing problems risks failing to meet the objective of improving appraiser performance. Conversely, an overly harsh tone can result in unnecessary confrontation and be demoralizing to the appraiser. If the reviewer's critique is delivered poorly, the appraiser may "shut down" and disengage from committing to producing a quality product.

1. The Writing Center, University of North Carolina at Chapel Hill, "Editing and Proofreading," 2009, http://www.unc.edu/depts/wcweb/handouts/proofread.html/.

Maintaining professionalism can be challenging when frequently cited problems recur in an appraiser's work. Repeat problems suggest that the critiques are ignored or misunderstood; this can be a major source of frustration for the QC professional. In such instances, there is often the temptation to respond in a harsh, sarcastic, or derogatory manner. Obviously, this type of reaction should be avoided. Instead, a respectful tone should be maintained while noting that the issue in question was identified previously and that steps must be taken to prevent further recurrences. A stern tone can be effectively deployed when appropriate to modify behavior and emphasize the need for improvement and preventing repeat errors.

It is sometimes necessary for the reviewer to discuss the issue with the appraiser rather than simply leave a written comment. The request for a conversation forces the author of the report to delve into the quality issue or issues identified in detail and eliminates any hesitation (or embarrassment) he or she may have in asking for help on complex or abstract concepts. It can also help establish a high level of trust with the review professional.

Drawing from best practices and conversations with QC review professionals nationwide, the following general guidelines should be followed in developing and delivering the results of a review:

1. **Balance the response.**
   Address any problems head-on, but avoid being overly critical or harsh in tone.
2. **Provide reasoning when needed.**
   While corrections to obvious errors do not require a rationale, it may be necessary to include explanations when advanced or abstract concepts are identified. This is particularly true when inexperienced appraisers are involved.
3. **Offer alternatives when possible.**
   It is helpful to provide alternatives when the QC reviewer disagrees with the approach taken to the assignment, the wording of a section of the report, or other issues. This improves the appraiser's understanding of the point and presents a valuable learning opportunity.
4. **Accentuate the positives.**
   Positive feedback reinforces the firm's (and the reviewer's) desire to produce quality work, and it can balance any criticism included in the review. Authors also appreciate praise delivered genuinely and in the proper measure.

5. **Apply the "golden rule."**
   Every appraiser has been critiqued sometime during his or her career, and chances are that you have made many of the errors that you are now pointing out to the appraiser. Always deliver a review in the form and substance that you would like if you were the receiver of the evaluation.
6. **Be clear in the delivery.**
   To avoid confusion and unnecessary follow-up, the critique should be organized, clear, and coherent. Any handwritten remarks must be neat and legible.

The review must clearly indicate the issues identified with explanatory notes to assist the appraiser in understanding the reasoning behind the critique. Support should be included for any items noted in the review that are not obvious, and an offer should be made to answer any questions that the appraiser may have. The experience levels of appraisers should also be considered in crafting explanatory comments.

Exhibits 6.1 through 6.6 show examples of appropriate review comments applied in various situations. Note that in these examples the reviewer took the time to explain his rationale rather than simply identifying problems without providing backup. In addition, the offer to discuss the items opens the door for the appraiser to approach the reviewer for more information if desired or needed.

A major challenge for a QC review professional can be accepting the diverse writing and communicating styles of various appraisers.

Exhibit 6.1 Offering an Alternative for Consideration

Sticky Note 5/9/2010 1:10:37 PM
sschafer Options

We state in the market analysis that vacancy is over 20 percent and that negative absorption was realized the last several quarters. In the area analysis, employment is forecast to decrease the next two years. Given these negative trends, is it likely that the tract would be developed in the near term? It seems that the property would be held for future development when market conditions improve.

Conclusion – Highest and Best Use As Vacant

We considered the issues related to zoning and legal restrictions and analyzed the physical characteristics of the site to determine what legal uses would be possible. We also analyzed the financial feasibility of these uses to determine the use that is maximally productive. Given the subject site's physical characteristics and location, as well as the state of the local market, we conclude that the highest and best use of the subject site as if vacant is an office building developed to the highest density possible.

Exhibit 6.2 Requesting a Discussion

> Sticky Note — sschafer — 5/9/2010 1:21:11 PM
>
> The property photos show graffiti, stained ceiling tiles, peeling paint, and other examples of deferred maintenance. A purchaser would likely address these items to assist with marketing the vacant space. Let's discuss how we should address this in the valuation approaches.

DEFERRED MAINTENANCE

Cost to Cure: Curable physical deterioration refers to those items that are economically feasible to cure as of the effective date of the appraisal. This element of depreciation is commonly referred to as *deferred maintenance* and is measured as the cost of repairing or restoring the item to new or reasonably new condition. We did not receive a capital expenditure plan or an engineering report that would identify specific costs required to repair deficiencies at the subject property.

During our inspection, we did not notice any apparent deferred maintenance that would require immediate repair.

Exhibit 6.3 Offering an Example for a Complex Concept

> Sticky Note — sschafer — 5/9/2010 1:55:28 PM
>
> These taxes reflect a PILOT agreement that has several years remaining. It is not appropriate to capitalize the resulting net operating income into perpetuity. We need to use stabilized (market) taxes and add the present value of the PILOT benefit to the value conclusion. An example of this methodology is included in job #10-115.

Real Estate Taxes

Real estate taxes are estimated at $[illegible]00, or roughly $0.33 per square foot of rentable area. Our estimate is at the extreme low end of the comparable range but is in line with historical subject figures. Our conclusion is supported by the subject history and the comparable properties.

Exhibit 6.4 Leveraging the Reviewer's Market Knowledge

> Sticky Note — sschafer — 5/9/2010 1:54:54 PM
>
> This is an awfully large number for a leasehold in that location. It's based on a fee simple value determined using sales of much smaller properties of limited comparability. Please expand your search for larger/more comparable property sales and listings within the county.

RECONCILIATION AND FINAL VALUE OPINION

Based on the scope of work agreed to with the client, and as outlined in the accompanying report, we developed the following opinion of market value:

Appraisal Premise	Real Property Interest	Date of Value	Value Conclusion
As Is Market Value	Leasehold	May 7, 2010	$ 15,600,00[illegible]

Exhibit 6.5 Offering Positive Reinforcement

> **Sticky Note** sschafer 5/9/2010 1:47:16 PM
>
> Nice description Ellen; it really helps the reader understand that property better. The information is also worked well into the depreciation section and appropriately reflected in the cost approach. Good work!

Building Description

Property Type:	Office building
Year Built:	1975
Renovations/Additions:	The property was renovated in 2005, including new windows, flooring, ceiling tiles, landscaping, and other upgrades at a cost of roughly $5,600,000. In addition, the building engineer indicated during our inspection that the building received regular maintenance and upgrades since renovation, including a new fire safety system and new chillers.

Exhibit 6.6 Dealing with a Repeat Occurrence

> **Sticky Note** sschafer 5/9/2010 1:43:27 PM
>
> Why is this reasonable? There are a few instances when the residual rate should be lower than the initial rate, but those factors are not apparent in this case. Similar problems were noted in two jobs last month. There are apparently some concepts that we need to review. Please see me this afternoon.

Terminal Capitalization Rate Selection

As a result, we applied a terminal rate of 9.0 percent to calculate the building residual value in the cash flow forecast. This rate is 25 basis points below the implied overall rate in the initial year of the forecast. Though unusual, the lower residual rate is considered reasonable.

A key to success in the review process is recognizing that ideas can be communicated in different ways. A message is generally acceptable as long as it is delivered in a professional manner, even if it does not exactly align with the QC reviewer's preferred technique. Constantly forcing text to be rewritten simply to comply with the QC professional's style can frustrate the writer and lead to undue animosity.

Other Communication Issues

The appraiser also has a responsibility to inform the quality control reviewer about any nuances associated with the assignment or the property. Imparting knowledge about the property and the appraisal problem to the reviewer when the report is submitted for review lowers the probability of follow-up questions that can reduce the efficiency of the process.

The appraiser is often privy to information at the outset of an assignment or uncovers information during the appraisal process that is not necessarily included in the report. Such information should be conveyed to the reviewer at the beginning of the review process. Facts that are useful to the QC reviewer include:

- A summary of any work previously performed on the property, including appraisals, reviews, and so forth
- Unique features of the property or special circumstances surrounding it
- Any particular client concerns or special instructions
- Conversations conducted about the property that may not be appropriate to include in the report but influenced the appraiser's judgment

Communication (written and verbal) is obviously critical to a smooth QC process. Communication can, however, be compromised if the appraiser-reviewer relationship is weak or if the parties are not located in the same office. The latter case is becoming more prevalent today due to the growth in telecommuting and the rise of the virtual office and presents its own unique communications challenges.

Distance can inhibit communication, since the review professional cannot hold impromptu conversations with the appraiser or simply pop into the appraiser's office. In this situation, the required extra effort of making a call or sending an e-mail can act as a barrier to communication. As the senior staff member, the QC reviewer is responsible for ensuring that lines of communication remain open and clear despite such challenges.

A sizable portion of business communication occurs via e-mail. Sole or primary reliance on e-mail, though efficient, can stifle QC communication, particularly if the parties are not familiar with each other. Scheduling regular calls to discuss issues can foster an improved relationship and help ensure a smooth review process. During such calls, it is also helpful to solicit feedback from the appraiser on how the QC review procedure can be improved, thus empowering the appraiser to influence the process.

A positive rapport and high level of trust in the appraiser/reviewer relationship helps guarantee that any issues will be properly examined. This, in turn, maximizes the learning opportunity for the appraiser and ensures a clear path to the continuous improvement of the final product.

Review Delivery Methods

Research indicates that a wide variety of methods are employed in delivering the review results to the appraiser, including:

- Electronic "post it" notes in the PDF file
- Scanned and e-mailed handwritten notes
- Face-to-face discussions
- Phone calls
- Faxes
- Electronic notes added to the Word document

Note that the first two items are preferred, as will be discussed later in this section.

Each approach has its strengths and weaknesses. Comments delivered in written form provide a clear record of what was conveyed and can be referenced in the future for audit or instructional purposes. Conversely, the lack of face-to-face contact can inhibit interaction and questions from the appraiser and impair a full understanding of underlying concepts. Written reviews can also take longer to formulate and type and may be less desirable in rush situations.

In-person communication (either face-to-face or by phone) allows for greater interplay between the parties and facilitates deeper discussion of a topic and, therefore, improved understanding. The lack of a written audit trail and the potential for missing some or many of the QC professional's points are negative aspects of verbally delivered critiques.

The method of review delivery is largely a matter of personal preference that is usually left up to the QC reviewer in conjunction with the appraiser, and a combination of approaches is feasible. Whatever method the parties select, however, should maximize efficiency and be as timely and simple as possible. Some reviewers, for instance, prefer to read noncomplex reports entirely on screen and affix notes in the electronic document. This eliminates the need for printing and facilitates an easy, legible electronic response to the appraiser.

To effectively enable a QC audit process (as will be discussed in a later chapter), however, a written trail of communication between the two parties is needed. As a result, the first two options–PDF "post its" and scanned comments–should be applied. These methods should, however, be combined with in-person discussions frequently to maintain a rapport between the reviewer and the appraiser.

Handling Disputes

While many issues identified in QC are clear cut (such as obvious errors, typos, and format issues), some ideas and methodologies are abstract and/or opinion based. Appraisal, after all, is more art than science, and disagreements can occur among professionals. The QC review process is particularly prone to disputes.

Such disagreements are less of an issue in small firms where the owner or principal is responsible for the company's QC reviews and that individual has final say by virtue of his or her position. Being an owner, however, does not relieve the individual from the responsibility of listening to and considering alternative viewpoints. In addition, the appraiser cannot be forced to sign a report that includes opinions and conclusions with which he or she cannot agree.

The QC review group within a practice typically consists of appraisers with extensive and wide-ranging appraisal and appraisal review experience. Each individual's selection as a reviewer is an acknowledgement that his or her views are highly valued. As a result, opinions, suggested changes, and other issues identified in the review should be binding and must be addressed prior to delivery to the client.

The QC reviewer's comments are expected to be heeded by the appraiser, unless there is confusion about the edits or a significant disagreement. In those instances, a dialogue should occur among the various parties involved to help guarantee that proper understanding is maintained by all and to surface any disagreements. This is a valuable learning opportunity, and adequate time should be spent to discuss all relevant issues.

Misinterpretations, disagreements, and other issues may arise that are not easily resolved among the parties involved. As a result, a dispute resolution process should be established through which an appraiser or manager can appeal a reviewer's decision if the parties are unable to resolve the dispute among themselves.

At small firms, the dispute resolution path is clear: the owner or principal has final say. For larger companies, the appeal process can involve forwarding the review comment(s) in dispute along with a brief summary of the issues from each party's perspective to the appropriate manager. The manager reviews the information, initiates a discussion with each of the individuals involved in the dispute, and renders a decision on the case once all of the facts are understood.

Occasionally, there will be conflicts between an appraiser and QC reviewer that are difficult to resolve and may result in confrontation. Frequent disputes can be counterproductive and result in unhealthy animosity. Should such a situation occur, a reassignment of QC reviewers may be warranted.

7

Evaluating Report Quality and Taking Corrective Action

Conducting the Quality Control Review

The importance of the quality control review as the last line of defense to prevent external failure is sizable. Unfortunately, with appraisals, this inspection is subject to the QC reviewer's itnterpretation of quality standards and the ever-present potential for human error, thus introducing another layer of variation into an already nonstandardized process. Even with requisite reviewer training and well-defined review standards, inspection error rates can range from 10%-50%.[1]

In fact, even a group of experienced QC reviewers can miss obvious problems when given the same report to review. As an experiment to gauge the amount of variation in problem identification, three reviewers with over 20 years of experience each reviewed the same appraisal report. Comments on each report were compiled and the results were analyzed to identify patterns.

Although there were similarities in some of the issues noted, the test vividly demonstrated the amount of variation in the review process, with each individual identifying different issues. For example, the three reviewers collectively identified six errors on one page, but none identified more than three items on his own. This page from the appraisal report appears in Exhibit 7.1.

Incidentally, one grammar error and two wording problems on this page remained unnoticed by all three reviewers. The use of the word *either* in the first full sentence on the page is incorrect. Three elements are being listed in the sentence (turnover, non-payment, and slow payment), and *either* would only be appropriate for two elements. As a result, the word should be deleted from the sentence.

1. James R. Evans and William M. Lindsay, *The Management and Control of Quality* (Cincinnati: South-Western College Publishing, 1999), 571.

Exhibit 7.1 Reviewer Variability Example

were actually paying their rent in full and on time. It is normally prudent to expect some income loss either in the form of turnover, non-payment, or slow payment of rent. Since we are valuing the leased fee estate with a national tenant occupying the space for a minimum of 20 years (and the potential for 45 years), we forecasted a no vacancy and collection loss factor. While we believe the ground lease is written at market levels, the risk associated with this lease is increased given the decline in the tenant's credit standing. Any risk will be accounted for in our capitalization rate selection as discussed later in this report. — Delete

OPERATING EXPENSES

Management Fee

This fee includes rent collection, property supervision, budgeting, and miscellaneous oversight of the property. We discussed typical management fee agreements with various property managers within the market. The typical management fee for net leased properties is fairly small due to the limited responsibilities of the lessor. The actual fee is expected to fall in the range of 1.0 to 3.0 percent of the contract rental rate. Given the minimal management involved with a ground lease, we projected a management fee at the low end of the range of 1.0 percent.

Real Estate Taxes

According to the lease agreement, all real estate taxes are the obligation of the landlord. As such, we will not factor any taxes into our rather simple discounted cash flow analysis. — Tenant pays, see p. 21

Reserves for Replacement

As a ground lease there is no reason to establish a reserve for replacement account, therefore no deductions are necessary.

DISCOUNTED CASH FLOW ANALYSIS

A spreadsheet program was used to model future income and expenses. Our discounted cash flow analysis is presented on a subsequent page. In formulating this model, the following assumptions were used:

1. The pro forma is based on a sixteen-year holding period. The correlates to the remaining term of the base lease. A sale is projected at the end of this term. — This
2. All revenue and expense items have been entered based on actual lease terms and our current estimates.
3. The reversion estimate was based on a resale at the end of the twentieth year of the analysis period. It was formulated by applying a 8.75 percent overall rate to the first option year of the lease and subtracting a 2.5 percent selling cost. — 16 years in cash flow; an
4. The net cash flow and net reversion were discounted to net present value using a discount rate of 8.0 ~~percent as derived~~ below. — Different rate in cash flow

Identified by one reviewer (not necessarily the same individual for each item)

Identified by two reviewers

Identified by all three reviewers

Secondly, while one reviewer was correct in indicating that *a* should be deleted from the second full sentence on the page, the wording of that sentence (particularly the word *factor*) still sounds awkward even after *a* is deleted. Deleting the word *factor* results in a better-sounding sentence: "Since we are valuing the leased fee estate with a national tenant occupying the space for a minimum of 20 years (and the potential for 45 years), we forecasted no vacancy and collection loss."

Finally, the sentence under the "Reserves for Replacement" heading also sounds awkward. One way to rewrite this sentence to sound more clear and concise is "Because there is a ground lease, it is not necessary to establish a reserve for replacement account and no deductions are necessary."

This experiment suggests that the more sets of eyes that view a report, the higher the probability that all problems will be identified. Unfortunately, such an approach is very costly, and few firms have the luxury of applying multiple reviews. It is therefore critical that the appraiser proofreads the report carefully prior to submission for QC review.

Visual inspections such as QC reviews can be affected by several factors:

- **Complexity of the product**
  The number of "parts" in a product and the order or structure surrounding those parts affects an inspector's ability to identify defects. Complex products that are randomly structured inhibit the detection of problems. As a result, the need to simplify and standardize appraisal report contents and sections is clear.
- **Number of defects**
  In a seeming paradox, inspectors miss more defects when problem rates are low than when the rates are high. In an appraisal QC review, the reviewer can become complacent when the property type, location, and appraiser are familiar and trusted. As problems become apparent, however, complacency is often abandoned in favor of a more thorough inspection.
- **Duplicate inspections**
  Individuals tend to focus on and detect different issues within the same product, so the greater the number of inspections, the larger the number of problems that will be identified. However, the drawback to multiple inspections is the associated cost and required time.
- **Inspection volume**
  An inspector's ability to detect errors decreases markedly as the number of inspections increases. Combined with tight turn-

around requirements, performance can be considerably degraded when volume is high, limiting the effectiveness of the review.[2]

With these factors in mind, it is important to ensure that reports arrive at a QC reviewer's desk as error-free as possible, and the appraisal must be the result of a well-designed process aimed at maximizing standardization. Submitting the report with ample lead time prior to the due date also helps enhance reviewer effectiveness.

Research indicates, however, that reports vary widely and some reports may be submitted for QC review that are of low quality and contain numerous problems. These reports require an inordinate amount of review time, and the relatively large number of problems increases the probability that not all of the issues will be caught or corrected prior to submission to the client.

Analysis of the appraisal process and discussions with QC reviewers across the country indicate that a root cause of the problem is a lack of focus on "getting it right the first time" on the part of the appraisers. Appraisers may assure themselves that any errors in their report will be identified in the QC process, and this may lessen the sense of urgency for diligent proofreading and producing an acceptable report prior to submission for review.

Any report submitted for review should represent the appraiser's best effort and should be prepared as if it were to be submitted directly to the client without any QC review. Despite the difficulty in reviewing one's own work and identifying all its problems, the report should include minimal defects and be free of such potentially embarrassing errors as:

- Typographical errors
- Boilerplate from prior assignments
- Errors in judgment
- Omitted charts, tables, or sections
- Poor grammar
- Conflicting statements or information
- Spelling errors
- Lack of property-specific analysis

Given the significant role that proofreading and final QC review play in identifying and eliminating report defects, diligence must be high for both the reviewer and the appraiser. To provide additional incentive for appraisers to produce high-quality reports, a penalty structure for significant and/or frequent offenders is an effective

2. Ibid., 572.

means of improving compliance. The benefits of a penalty structure are further detailed in the following section of this chapter.

Taking Corrective Action

Criteria for Requiring Resubmission

While many reports submitted for review contain a relatively small number of problems, others are fraught with issues. These substandard reports can be so poorly constructed and include so many problems that they require another review after the initial corrections have been completed by the appraiser.

Research indicates that exceptionally poor reports often include problems even after the first set of corrections have been completed. This necessitates a second look. Despite the additional time that must be invested by the reviewer, a second review is sometimes necessary to decrease the probability of external defects.

The decision to require resubmission is subjective and depends on the reviewer, but the following guidelines are general criteria that can be applied:

- Large number of problems and questions identified
- Significance of the issues identified and their impact on value
- Complexity of the property and appraisal problem
- Value change indicated
- Inadequate analysis to lead reader to the conclusion(s) presented
- Overall sloppiness or lack of attention to detail

The decision to require a second review is based on any one or a combination of these criteria, depending on the severity and frequency of the issues identified. The second review may entail simply checking that the specific issues identified have been addressed or reading the entire report again to make sure that it is adequate. A full second reading of the report should be rare, but it may be necessary if the number and significance of changes warrant it. While a second review is often adequate, this may not always be the case.

Above all, the reviewer must be comfortable that the report adheres to the firm's standards before it is delivered to the client, regardless of the number of reviews required for it to meet quality standards.

Imposing Penalties for Substandard Reports

The quality control review process is intended to correct errors and educate appraisers. While the review is highly effective in elevating overall report quality, care should be taken to address the need for appraisers to take ownership of the quality of their reports. To provide a disincentive for sloppy report production (and an incentive for good quality work), there is widespread agreement among QC reviewers that monetary penalties are a reliable means of effecting appraiser improvement.

A penalty achieves two objectives:

- It provides a financial incentive for appraisers to be diligent in completing reports before they are submitted for QC review.
- It can compensate reviewers for the additional amount of time required to elevate poor quality reports to an acceptable standard. The additional compensation also helps ensure that the required effort will be expended by the QC reviewer to assist the appraiser in correcting the problems in the report.

Based on feedback received from clients and QC professionals across the nation, additional review charges should be applied to reports that are substandard and require an excessive amount of time for review. The fee may be a flat charge based on the number of incremental review hours expended, based on a percentage of the appraisal fee, or determined by some other methodology.

The levying of a poor-quality fine is often avoided by reviewers due to the prospect of confrontation with the appraiser or the financial hardship that it may cause the appraiser. Despite the awkwardness or outright conflict that may result, the use of penalties to help foster improvement in reports is a major factor in ensuring the success of the review process.

Most appraisers are compensated based on their production, and any drops in revenue resulting from penalties will clearly get their attention. Evidence indicates that improved performance is typically realized quickly with minimal need for repeat penalties. Given this effectiveness and the overriding importance of defect-free reports, penalties should be levied as needed.

Handling Repeat Occurrences

While consumers should expect a base level of errors in any appraisal report, the incidence of problems should ideally be kept to a minimum. Less experienced appraisers theoretically have a higher propensity for mistakes than those with several years in the business, and greater latitude is typically afforded to those individuals relative to the quality of the reports. Nevertheless, errors are to be expected regardless of the appraiser's level of experience, and any QC process is implemented to help minimize those errors.

In addition to error trapping, the QC review provides a learning opportunity. As such, it is expected that appraisers will heed any suggestions identified and learn from them, so that repetition of the same mistakes is prevented. Continual repeat errors and lack of overall improvement can be indications that the individual is not committed to producing high-quality reports or lacks the mental acuity or desire to improve.

Repeat errors are not aligned with a client-focused firm's commitment to delivering top-quality appraisal services. The QC reviewer is a front-line resource to help identify appraisers who consistently lag in terms of quality, and it is the reviewer's responsibility to assist in improving the appraiser's performance. The first step is to ensure that the comments included in the review are clear and that any needed explanation is included in the review or in subsequent discussions with the appraiser.

If repeated comments and discussions show limited or no progress even after penalties are applied, the QC reviewer must elevate the concerns to the appropriate level or levels of management. These issues are best delivered in writing and should include specific examples and approximate dates as well as the number of times that discussions were held with the individual.

After the document is forwarded to the appropriate manager, a meeting should be planned with the manager and any other appropriate individuals to discuss the case. The meeting should review the history of problems identified and corrective actions taken to agree upon the next course of action.

If it is concluded that a problem exists, potential corrective actions include:

- Personal counseling by senior staff and/or firm management personnel
- Additional training offered by the Appraisal Institute or other recognized appraisal authorities
- Adjustment of the appraiser's fee split, with the differential allocated to the QC reviewer to compensate for the additional amount of time spent on review and counseling
- Appraiser dismissal (following requisite written warning)

Any of these actions or a combination of them may be appropriate, depending on the situation. However, the primary objective is to assist the appraiser in obtaining the level of skill needed to perform his or her job effectively. If it is concluded that no corrective actions are necessary, then there may be a disconnect on the reviewer's part. Analysis of the reviewer's actions or a QC audit of that reviewer may be appropriate in such instances.

8 Putting It All Together

Writing Style and Professionalism

Writing is the basis for any appraisal practice, since appraisal reports are the appraisal professional's primary products. These documents do not simply provide value conclusions, they serve as critical marketing tools as well. Clear, accurate, and professional writing is vital to delivering a top-quality product and maximizing the effectiveness of the report as a sales tool.

Producing a professionally written appraisal is also critical to building a best-in-class reputation. Every appraisal report presents an opportunity to impress a client by communicating in a manner that sets the individual or practice apart from the competition.

An appraiser spends a significant amount of time and effort researching information and analyzing data to arrive at a well-supported conclusion. Conveying all of that hard work in a sloppy, poorly formatted report is akin to buying an expensive gift and handing it to the recipient in a grease-stained paper bag.

Presentation clearly impacts readers' overall impressions of the appraisal report. Clients consistently indicate that an appraisal's credibility is compromised, despite solid research and analysis, if the report contains typos, stale boilerplate, grammatical errors, and a format that is unfriendly to the reader. A pleasing appearance and high level of readability are also criteria against which vendors are judged in some clients' rating systems.

Consistent professionalism in writing style, a user-friendly design, and use of proper grammar are all methods of improving report quality and client satisfaction that are nearly *cost free.* Proper grammar and style can be used for a lifetime at no additional cost to the appraiser (after the initial investment in learning).

A client-friendly format can be developed by using customer input and applying best practices from within and outside the industry. Some firms also engage professional writers to review and critique their formats to help ensure a top-notch appearance.

In addition to enhancing one's reputation, well-written appraisals have economic benefits. By communicating ideas clearly and convincingly, the number of follow-up calls and amount of required revisions to reports is diminished. The perception that a firm's reports are clearer and more visually appealing than those of competitors also results in additional bidding opportunities and increased revenue.

While the amount of original writing required in reports is (or should be) minimized through the use of boilerplate, a considerable opportunity for fresh content exists in every assignment. This original writing is critical, since it typically involves the analysis that is the foundation for any value estimate. Special attention and care should be given to writing these report sections. Despite this obvious need for attention, analysis of appraisals submitted for QC review and discussions with clients indicate that those report sections that contain original writing are of inconsistent quality.

Based on an analysis of the problems identified in a broad sample of appraisal reports, substandard text is typically rooted in one or more of the following issues:

- Appraisers' lack of familiarity with, and attention to, writing fundamentals
- Limited opportunities to develop and improve writing skills
- Lack of focus on grammatical and style issues during the QC review process
- Turnaround time demands limiting the amount of time spent writing and proofing drafts for readability and professionalism

Lack of attention to detail, which is the root cause of the last two bullet points, is easily addressed through improved focus and commitment. The remaining issues, however, result from a lack of knowledge of the fundamentals of grammar and writing. Fortunately, numerous sources are available to assist writers in improving their skills. The Appraisal Institute and a variety of educational groups in local markets offer writing classes and seminars that can greatly enhance writing styles.

The list of available textbooks and other reference materials on writing style is extensive as well. The exceptionally popular book *The Elements of Style* has been in print for five decades and remains a standard for all types of writing. *Garner's Modern American Usage* is another handy reference guide to grammar, usage, and style. Several common writing pitfalls are also highlighted in the classic *Appraisal Journal* article "Some Thoughts on Lexicon and Syntax" by John White, a copy of which is included in Appendix D in the back of this book. Its tips are timeless and serve as useful references.

While beauty may be in the eye of the beholder, certain features appeal to (or offend) readers universally. The following sections address active versus passive voice, readability, and other elements of style to help remedy those problems that have been commonly identified in appraisal reports, drawn from examples identified by clients and QC reviewers nationwide.

Active and Passive Voice

The three basic elements of a sentence are the *subject,* the *verb,* and the *object. Active* and *passive* voices relate to the relationship between the subject and the verb. In an *active* sentence, the subject (the "doer") performs the action and the object receives the action. Active sentences are structured in the following order:

1. Subject
2. Verb
3. Object

In a *passive* sentence, the subject is acted upon and the object becomes the "doer." In such a sentence, the order is changed to:

1. Object
2. Verb
3. Subject

The following are some examples of active and passive voice for pairs of sentences that have the same intended meaning:

Active: The developer estimates infrastructure costs at $2,000,000.
Passive: Infrastructure costs are estimated at $2,000,000.

Active: We compared the subject to the comparable sales.
Passive: The comparable sales were compared to the subject.

Active: The hurricane heavily damaged the building.
Passive: The building was heavily damaged by the hurricane.

In general, readers consider the passive voice to be dull and wordy, whereas the active voice is perceived as livelier and more vivid. As a result, writers are encouraged to avoid the passive voice in technical and business writing to enhance reader engagement and satisfaction.

Although active sentence structuring is usually preferred, use of the passive voice is desirable in some cases. Proper uses for the passive voice include:

- Focusing attention on the action rather than who (or what) did the action
  Example: The property was outfitted with a backup generator after the storm.
- Maintaining tact or confidentiality by not naming the entity involved
  Example: The complex had not been managed well. (This avoids implicating the property owner or manager.)
- Describing a condition in which the specific actor or actors are unknown or unimportant
  Examples: The diamond necklace was stolen from the display case. (In this case, the actor is unknown.)
  The town is visited by tens of thousands of people who ski at the local resorts every year. (In this case, the actors (the visitors) are not as important as the object (the town).)
- To create an authoritative tone.
  Example: Children are prohibited from trespassing beyond this point.
- To focus attention on the process, as in scientific or technical writing.
  Example: In the next step, the solution is distilled.

While the passive voice is useful in these examples, the active voice should be used in most cases.

Readability

To ensure reader satisfaction, it is critical that written communication be presented in a manner that is clear, concise, and visually appealing. A term commonly used to test a writer's success at achieving those goals is *readability*. Essentially, readability is the intended audience's ease in reading and comprehending text. A writing style that is easily read improves comprehension, retention, and reading speed for the reader.

Reading ease within text is dependent upon the content, style, and design of the document. Readability is impacted by factors such as:

- Word choice
- Sentence structure
- Line and paragraph spacing

- Font size and type

The use of illustrations, charts, and other graphics can also enhance the reader's understanding and enjoyment.[1]

Tests measuring readability were first developed in the United States in the 1920s. They were used to help teachers, librarians, and others determine the suitability of a book for an intended audience. The results gauge the approximate grade level required to comprehend a given text.

Readability tests are mathematical formulas that typically analyze the number of syllables, words, and sentences within the text. In general, the greater the number of multisyllable words, total words in a sentence, and sentences in a paragraph, the higher the grade level required to comprehend the text. A higher score translates into a lower level of readability.

Readability tests have limitations, given that they are solely based on mathematics. It is possible, for instance, to achieve a good readability score for a dull, poorly written document as long as it contains short sentences and is composed of one-syllable words. In addition, readability indexes cannot gauge the user friendliness of the layout and design, overall visual appeal, and comprehensibility of a document.

Popular readability tests include:

- Automated Readability Index
- Coleman-Liau
- Flesch Reading Ease
- Flesch Kincaid Grade Level
- FOG (or Gunning FOG)
- SMOG

Despite their limitations, these readability tests can be very useful for writers who want to match their style to their intended audience. For instance, a national literacy survey indicated that the average American adult reads at an eighth-grade level. As a result, authors, screenwriters, government entities, and others who communicate with the general public typically attempt to match their writing styles to this level.

By contrast, the Apple and Microsoft websites are geared to a tenth-grade level, as are the popular "Dummies" and "Idiots" book series. At a tenth-grade level, these texts are theoretically too difficult for 80% of the adult population to comprehend.[2] Presumably, the

---

1. W. S. Gray and B. E. Leary, *What Makes a Book Readable?* (Chicago: University of Chicago Press, 1935): 261-292.
2. National Center for Education Statistics, US Dept. of Education, "Adult Literacy in America," Washington, DC, 1993, http://www.nald.ca/fulltext/Report2/rep15-01.htm/; William H. Dubay, *The Principles of Readability* (Costa Mesa, CA: Impact Information, 2004), 9.

authors of these works understood this, and their styles are properly matched to their target audiences. For reference, this book is rated at roughly a twelfth- to thirteenth-grade level, according to the Flesch Kincaid scale.

For any type of writing, the style must be selected based on the characteristics of the target audiences. In business writing, for example, the use of jargon and technical terminology characteristic of the specific business or industry can and should be used for clear and effective communication.

Although using these terms lowers readability according to the tests, their inclusion is often critical to properly conveying the desired message. The extent of jargon used, however, should be based on the author's familiarity with the target audience (and the audience's familiarity with the jargon). Above all, the document must be suitable for the reader's needs and written to effectively convey the intended message while maintaining the reader's interest.

The following general rules should be followed to develop effective and appealing appraisal reports:

- Keep sentences and paragraphs short.
- Use simple, direct terms that are familiar to the intended reader.
- Do not include needless words. For example, use *to* instead of *in order to*.
- Use appealing document layout and design, including indentations, numbering, and other features that can help break up long blocks of narrative.
- Include tables, charts, and other graphics whenever possible to enhance visual appeal.
- Structure ideas and sentences in a logical flow. For example, discuss income and expense figures in the order in which they are shown in an income statement.
- Use bullets to highlight a list of items rather than include them in the body of the text.[3]

Many other techniques are available for improving the readability of a document and enhancing the reader's interest and enjoyment, as will be discussed here. More writing tips are included in Appendix E in the back of this book, and additional examples of common grammar and style pitfalls taken from actual appraisal reports–along with suggested solutions–are included in Appendix F.

3. Dubay, *The Principles of Readability,* 2.

More Style Tips

Rely on Simple Words

Simple, common words are more useful than long, complicated ones because common words are more likely to be understood, take less time to read, and call less attention to writing style. The question to ask when choosing the right word is, "Will the reader understand the meaning?" Technical jargon used in various professions can be particularly confusing to outsiders, so unusual terms should be defined or more easily understood terms should be used as alternatives in reports prepared for nonprofessionals.

Avoid Insincere or Emotionally Charged Words

Because the appraisal represents the most objective treatment the appraiser can apply to the estimation of value, the report should be written in objective language and exclude words that are emotionally charged or that could be perceived as insincere, such as the following:

- Good
- Bad
- Beautiful
- Superior
- Wonderful
- Marvelous
- Tremendous
- Amazing
- Perfect
- Absolutely

Avoid Worn-Out Expressions

Expressions that are used over and over again in business lose their impact and risk causing a negative reaction. The following table lists some worn-out words and phrases with more modern and effective alternatives.

Worn Out	Modern
pursuant to your request	*as you requested*
at this time	*now*
attached please find	*attached is*
according to our records	Simply omit the phrase and continue.
please do not hesitate	*please*
the undersigned	*me* or *I*
hereto, herewith, hereby, above-mentioned, same, hereinafter	All are legal terms. Omit or state in layman's language.
under separate cover	State how you are sending the material.

Use Words Economically

Writing can be made even more concise by avoiding redundancies, or situations in which a word or phrase unnecessarily repeats the idea expressed in another word or phrase. The following table lists some examples of redundant phrases with more desirable alternatives.

Redundancy	More Desirable Alternative
whether or not	*whether*
exact same	*same*
personal opinion	*opinion*
each and every	*each* or *every*
consensus of opinion	*consensus* or *opinion*
period of time	*period* or *time*

Use Specific Words
Because words are subject to a variety of interpretations, clearer understanding can be achieved by using specifics rather than generalities. Consider the following examples:

1. **General:** The area has a moderate average temperature.
   Specific: The area has an average temperature of 64 degrees.
2. **General:** Income on investment is good.
   Specific: Income on investment averages 12%.
3. **General:** The lease expires soon.
   Specific: The lease expires on December 31.

Consider Sentence Length
A good rule to follow in writing is to limit a sentence to one idea. Short sentences, like short words, are easy to read. However, because a sentence is a group of words expressing an idea, it must be long enough to effectively do the job. Most business writing authorities recommend an average length of 16 to 25 words per sentence.

Varying the Sentence Structure
Limiting sentences to one idea and at the same time keeping them short can lead to a monotonous and choppy report. Good writers vary sentence structure to avoid such shortcomings, sometimes through the use of *compound* sentences, which are composed of two or more independent clauses. Some words and phrases, such as those in the following list, can also be used at the beginning of sentences to add variety and to show the relationship of the idea to the one preceding it:

- However
- Therefore
- Nevertheless
- In addition
- Additionally
- Also
- Furthermore
- Consequently

Avoid Long Paragraphs
The typical reader prefers short paragraphs, and short paragraphs can assist the reader in understanding the report. As a general rule, paragraphs longer than six lines increase reading difficulty and should be avoided.

Use Tabulations
The tabulation technique enables the report writer to enumerate items which might otherwise contribute to long sentences and focuses the reader's attention on each item. Listing related items using indented numbers or bullet points aids the reader's understanding.[4]

Employee Motivation and Client Satisfaction

The Employee-Client Link

Clearly, appraisal firms should not only focus on generating error-free reports. Making sure that all staff members are motivated and empowered to meet their clients' needs is equally important. Recall

4. William C. Himstreet, *Writing Appraisal Reports* (Chicago: American Institute of Real Estate Appraisers, 1974), 6-13.

the inverted pyramid organizational structure referred to in Chapter 1 of this book, in which the "lowest" level of employees have the greatest amount of customer contact. These employees–rather than the firm's CEO or senior executives–are usually the "face" of the company to most clients, and their interactions with clients heavily influence the overall client experience.

Unfortunately for many companies, the employees who have the most contact with customers are the lowest paid, least trained, and least empowered to make independent decisions. These characteristics are not aligned with properly motivating employees. A lack of staff enthusiasm can result in high turnover, unenthusiastic attitudes, and other issues that negatively influence the customer experience.

Front-line worker loss is often harmful to maintaining long-term client relationships and compromises profitability. In fact, evidence clearly indicates that client relations reflect employees' relationships within the company.[5] To put it simply, happy and motivated employees result in happy and satisfied clients. Regrettably, the converse is also true. As a result, keeping employees motivated and engaged in satisfying client needs is one of the key facets of most quality-management philosophies. Consider the accompanying example involving bank tellers.

Front-line employee satisfaction is enhanced when these employees believe that they have the power to deliver what clients want.

Bank Tellers: Employees on the "Front Lines" of Customer Contact

Customer service representatives (tellers) in a bank branch represent the "face" of the bank to most customers, often handling transactions for hundreds of customers in a given day. These workers, however, are typically near the low end of the pay scale in comparison to other types of bank employees and must obtain supervisor approval for many seemingly trivial customer-related service issues. They also have the pressure of balancing sizable cash transactions every day and complying with seemingly endless regulations and policies.

Due to the challenges involved on the job, the turnover rate for customer service representatives (and other branch positions) is quite high at most banks. Not surprisingly, these institutions often lag behind other service businesses in client satisfaction survey rankings. Fortunately, airlines and cable TV providers are around to make banks and other service providers look good by comparison.[6]

---

5. Timothy L. Keiningham and Terry Vavra, *The Customer Delight Principle: Exceeding Customers' Expectations for Bottom-Line Success* (New York: McGraw-Hill, 2001), Preface.
6. The American Customer Satisfaction Index, Scores by Industry, 2010, http://www.theacsi.org/index.php?option=com_content&task=view&id=18&Itemid=33/.

This can be accomplished by providing employees with the proper resources (technology, information, and so forth), training, and decision-making latitude to correct problems when they arise. Management's commitment to improving procedures and processes to avoid repeat occurrences is also highly valued by staff members.[7]

Given the link between employees, clients, and (ultimately) the success of the company, the time-honored idea that "the company is its employees" rings very true. In fact, Six Sigma and other quality programs typically include employee satisfaction as a main ingredient for successful companies.

While the elements vary depending on the source, certain general key factors influencing employee satisfaction and engagement are displayed in Exhibit 8.1. Each factor is then discussed in the next section of this chapter. However, this discussion merely scratches the surface of these critical topics. Detailed information on each is available from a variety of sources, and these concepts should be researched in detail before implementing any quality-management program.

Education and Training

Educating employees is limited at many companies and often only includes some form of technical training or education. While it is important to enhance technical skills to improve effectiveness and better serve customers, technical competence is only one of several features of a well-balanced training program.

A proper training program should also feature instructions on such varied topics as communication skills, problem solving/lateral thinking, and quality management principles (including process analysis and simplification, identifying and meeting customer requirements, waste elimination, and cycle time reduction).

To be effective, any training program also needs some customization to each job function and to the experience level of the employee.

Exhibit 8.1 Engaging Employees

7. Stefan Michel, David Bowen, and Robert Johnston, "Making the Most of Customer Complaints," *The Wall Street Journal* (September 22, 2008), http://online.wsj.com/article/SB122160026028144779.html?mod= todays_us_the_journal_r/.

For instance, individuals with heavy client contact should be trained more extensively in interpersonal skills than engineers or other employees who have more limited contact with clients. Likewise, a relatively new staff member may require greater technical training than a 15-year veteran.

Depending on the size and nature of the company, training and education can be delivered through in-house resources, external institutions or consultants, or (more likely) a combination of both. Many large companies maintain in-house trainers who often deliver instruction on concepts that are specific to the firm or industry, in addition to more generic topics.

Even in large companies with dedicated training departments, however, senior staff and executives cannot neglect their responsibility to train subordinates. Mentoring and coaching provided by experienced staff members is a critical tool to help individuals develop the skills necessary for improving performance. Managers who act as mentors are also integral to enhancing employees' satisfaction as well as their engagement in customer satisfaction.

Regardless of the delivery source, it is vital that the company commits to continuous training. The best customer-focused firms in any industry maintain regular training requirements for their staff, up to and including executive management, to make sure that skills are reinforced and new developments within the industry are delivered.[8]

Empowerment and Involvement

Involving employees in the process design and decision-making for various facets of the company's operations is a key to assuring higher quality, lower defect rates, and improved productivity. After all, involving those actually doing the work in the analysis of it ensures inclusion of critical intelligence "from the trenches." Employees involved in the process are also better equipped to spot future improvement opportunities, are more likely to offer suggestions, and typically have higher morale.

Giving license to employees to take greater control of their work and assume increased responsibility for the results is the essence of empowerment. This concept is not new, but it is resisted in some organizations. Managers may fear changes that can result from giving up some amount of control, or they may cling to the archaic concept that effective management entails possession of power.[9]

8. James R. Evans and William M. Lindsay, *The Management and Control of Quality* (Cincinnati: South-Western College Publishing, 1999), 54; Peter Murley, *Handbook of Customer Service* (Cheltenham, UK: Gower Publishing Limited, 1997), 448.
9. Dale H. Besterfield, *Quality Control* (Upper Saddle River, NJ: Prentice Hall, 2001), 40; Murley, *Handbook of Customer Service*, 491.

Simply dictating procedures and processes from above relegates workers to "robot" status and depletes interest from any job activity. Employees work unenthusiastically under such conditions, and this lack of motivation results in lower production and quality. Improvement is enabled, however, when individuals are encouraged to think about how their jobs are accomplished and are involved in process development. Greater employee "buy-in" to change is also realized, since the employees themselves had a hand in its development.

For firms that cultivate employee involvement, the number of improvement suggestions generated increases markedly and the quality of those ideas improves. For example, companies implementing quality-management programs can receive over four times the amount of employee suggestions as compared to companies that do not use quality-management programs, and 60%-70% of those ideas are usually deemed worthy of implementation.[10] These suggestions are a key ingredient in the continuous improvement aspect of quality programs.

While empowering staff is a significant element of employee motivation and achieving higher quality and customer satisfaction, this delegation of responsibility cannot be passed along until proper training programs are in place. As a result, these two initiatives must be rolled out in concert to minimize the risk of failure.

There are numerous methods of fostering employee involvement and empowerment, ranging from establishing suggestion programs that encourage individuals to submit ideas (and receive rewards) to formal quality teams that meet regularly to tackle specific issues. As with other quality initiatives, the Japanese utilize suggestion programs with great success. These efforts, however, typically focus on many small but continuous improvements, rather than a handful of major proposals. The cumulative effect of these gradual enhancements can be significant when continuously applied, and the downside risk relative to major "silver bullet" initiatives is minimized.

Whatever form of implementation (or combination of options) is selected, it is important that managers continuously and enthusiastically promote and encourage suggestions at every level. Inclusion of incentives (cash, peer recognition, and other forms) for successful ideas is also useful in encouraging suggestion development.

Teamwork and Cooperation

The Japanese success with quality management practices is rooted, in no small measure, to their establishing quality control circles and other teams focused on identifying interdepartmental and cross-func-

10. Kaoru Ishikawa, *Introduction to Quality Control* (Tokyo: 3A Corporation, 1989), 67.

tional solutions to problems. These are essentially groups of workers who are assembled to solve specific problems, identify improvement opportunities, monitor progress on selected solutions, and so forth.

Using the concept of the team leverages the collective knowledge of staff from different disciplines and varied levels in the hierarchy within an organization. It facilitates idea generation and problem solving that could not be accomplished by individuals working independently. The team approach is also an effective means of increasing peoples' sense of empowerment within the organization.

Teamwork and cooperation also promote an aligned sense of purpose with the firm and can eliminate the unproductive rivalry that may result from focusing on individuals. Companies whose workers collaborate in harmony with this purpose typically attract the most discerning and loyal customers.[11]

In quality-management programs, teams generally take one of the following forms:

- **Quality circles**
  Quality circles consist of a small collection of workers from a single department or related departments who are assembled to address a specific issue. Quality circles may be standing or formed with a specific goal in mind and are typically headed by the supervisor of the particular department that is contemplating the change or improvement.
- **Multifunctional project teams**
  Multifunctional project teams are broader in scope than quality circles and are typically larger groups. Multifunctional groups are most often deployed to develop new processes and/or improve existing ones and are usually chaired by the manager of the area that is most affected by the problem. Like quality circles, these teams may be standing or created for a specific purpose, but it is important to include all appropriate personnel from the required disciplines early in the meeting process.[12]

The frequency of meetings may vary based on the scope and nature of the problem being addressed. Consideration should be given, however, to gathering with enough regularity that critical points and related data are not forgotten between meetings. Background information on the topic and the group's main objective should also be highlighted, and the team members should be properly educated on, or familiar with, the operations involved.

11. Rich Karlgaard, "Recovery's Seven Secrets," *Forbes* (June 7, 2010), 17.
12. Besterfield, *Quality Control,* 38.

Compensation and Recognition

Significant components of motivating employees include a company's compensation package as well as the social/emotional issue of recognition for employees' efforts and accomplishments. In addition to base pay, compensation includes bonuses, promotions, titles, and other forms of recognition (both monetary and nonmonetary).

While money is a factor in employees' happiness and motivation levels, its significance can be heightened if the individual feels that his or her pay is not at the same level as those of others in similar positions at the firm or competing organizations. To avoid this pitfall, many large corporations base compensation on "the market," made up of similar and competing firms, and they attempt to maintain employee compensation within these market ranges. This helps minimize employees' perceptions of being underpaid and the often-powerful negative emotions associated with this view.

Company compensation plans may also include some form of sharing in the company's success and achievements realized by the employee's group or team. These programs help keep the focus on the organization (or its subparts) as a whole rather than on individuals and encourage teamwork.

Recognition is used as a complement to direct compensation, as was discussed in the "Celebrate Successes" section in Chapter 3. This technique acknowledges employee achievements through cash, gifts, praise, or other means, and is highly effective at encouraging desirable performance. To maximize the impact of such a program, however, it is important to publicize the award to the appropriate audience within or outside the organization.

> "If change is happening on the outside faster than on the inside, the end is in sight."
> - Jack Welch, retired CEO of General Electric

Beating Resistance to Change

Constant technological and competitive innovations force companies and individuals to change or face a challenge to their long-term survival. When combined with the pace of social and political change that can quickly influence customers, the imperative for nimbly adapting is clear.

While there are those who enjoy and embrace transformation, humans tend to resist any disruption of tried-and-true methodologies. In addition to their natural bias against change, employees can view new programs as the "flavor of the month" or harbor suspicions that management's true motivation is to force additional work on employees or make staff cuts.

Employees' reactions to change can range from actively rebelling against the new process or system to paying it lip service and following up with only half-hearted effort. A common employee reaction to change is something along the lines of "My job (or business) is different, so this won't work here." The widespread restructurings and downsizings pervasive in American industry over the last several years have contributed to worker distrust of management and have left many employees wary of change.[13]

The root cause of some employees' trepidation is a lack of trust or confidence in management. This issue can be overcome by involving employees in the change management process, ensuring ongoing open and honest dialogue among all parties, fostering mutual trust, and providing proper training and rewards. Actions that managers can take to accomplish these objectives include:

- Ensuring proper management involvement and engagement in all changes.
- Instilling a high sense of urgency about the need for change and continuous improvement, including the identification and highlighting of pressure from competing organizations.
- Providing ample rationale for the change to ensure buy-in and increase comfort levels with the transformation.
- Leading by example and being consistent.
- Dealing quickly and decisively with those who deliberately and regularly resist change.[14]

The implementation of Six Sigma and other quality-management philosophies involves challenging every individual in a company to identify new and improved ways of working to continually improve customer satisfaction. This continuous improvement will not occur, however, unless workers buy into the concept and are willing to step outside their comfort zones.

Given the influence of competition and the imperative for continuous improvement, the need for managers to calm individual

Source: Adapted from an HSBC Bank USA internal quality training program.

13. Michael Lee Marks, "In With the New," *The Wall Street Journal* (May 24, 2010), R4.
14. Evans and Lindsay, *Management and Control of Quality,* 303.

employees' fear of change is significant. Stressing competitors' actions or innovations that could threaten the company and identifying where the firm is lagging behind the rest of the industry can help employees recognize the case for change. Highlighting successes from previous process-improvement efforts (including the impact on the employees involved) can also help prove that change is beneficial.

Reducing or (preferably) eliminating employees' fear of change helps them adapt readily to quality improvement efforts and can reduce employee stress levels. Management's success with enticing its workers to actually embrace change can propel the firm to quicker and more meaningful improvement over time, helping it to become a more nimble competitor in the market.

Implications for Appraisal Practices

Appraisal firms are no different from other companies, with individual appraisers often having the greatest amount of customer contact. Keeping appraisers properly motivated and aligned with the practice's client focus will ensure long-term success.

Front-line appraisal employees can gain training (especially technical training) from the Appraisal Institute and other industry sources. However, it is important that managers, quality control reviewers, and others supplement this technical training with real-world examples. Managers must also make sure that appraisers are part of the team and are empowered to make customer-impacting decisions and process-change suggestions.

A valuable tool in training, empowerment, change management, and motivation is an effective QC process. As previously discussed, QC procedures must be designed to impart not only how to properly develop a value estimate but also how to make best use of proper writing styles, attractive formatting, and positive communication techniques with clients.

The responsibility to provide training and guidance to less-experienced appraisers and those requiring assistance in meeting quality standards is shared by those individuals' managers as well as the QC staff and executives within the organization. The professional improvement of these individuals, and all staff, is vital to the continued growth and success of any appraisal organization.

When properly applied, mentoring through the QC process is a primary means of achieving appraiser satisfaction and motivation that can yield the following desirable results:

- Faster acclimation of staff members to the company's report standards

- Productivity gains for the appraiser, QC reviewer, and others involved in report production
- Greater professional satisfaction
- Improved staff retention
- Overall enhanced customer satisfaction

The QC review process is a primary underpinning of the professional development effort, and it is important that reviewers (some of the most talented and experienced professionals in the practice) provide guidance and mentoring. While the success of the program lies largely with the appraiser's commitment to improve, the QC reviewer can enhance the experience by:

- Taking the necessary time to explain comments and concepts with the appraiser
- Maintaining a positive and supportive attitude
- Demonstrating an enthusiastic attitude toward delivering a quality product
- Offering assistance as a "sounding board" for questions and concerns
- Leading by example
- Soliciting feedback from the appraiser on opportunities for improvement in reports, the QC process, and other facets of the operation

While QC reviewer fees often do not compensate for the amount of time spent in mentoring, dividends will be realized over the long term. Greater appraiser and reviewer efficiency, improved engagement in the process by the appraisers, and enhanced client satisfaction will result in improved individual and group profitability over the long term.

Establishing an Effective Quality Control Audit Process

As previously noted, the effectiveness of any QC review program is rooted in the proper definition of product standards (as identified in minimum report standards documents) and establishing specific written criteria for QC review. These set the standards by which products are judged.

Even the best-conceived standards, however, can be rendered ineffective if the appraisers and QC reviewers do not consistently adhere to the prescribed parameters. Research indicates that report content, analysis, formatting, and other facets can vary from appraiser to appraiser within a firm despite the existence of standards. This problem can be compounded for larger companies with multiple offices and a broader diversity of appraisers and products. The result is variation in report content and quality, and this is a primary source of frustration for customers.

Reasons for this inconsistency in quality levels include inadequate commitment to quality and lack of understanding or misinterpretation of the standards. An effective means of eliminating these root causes of noncompliance with standards is conducting periodic inspections (audits) to ensure that defects are consistently identified and corrected by QC reviewers.

The QC audit process directly addresses any problems through examining finished products and identifying and correcting any weaknesses in the QC review process.[15] In addition, appraiser and QC reviewer awareness that an audit process exists (and that any findings will be reported to management) is also very useful in motivating individuals to comply. The audit, therefore, is an integral part of an effective QC process.

Essentially, auditing is an exercise in examining the quality control process itself, or "checking the checkers." Its objectives are to ensure that QC reviewers are interpreting the defined product and QC standards consistently and to determine if reviewers are effective in upholding those standards during the QC process.

Benefits of a properly designed QC audit process include:

- Verification of compliance (and non-compliance) with standards
- Identification of problems and areas in need of improvement
- Improved staff training and understanding of standards
- Continuous process/product improvement through best-practice identification and implementation

The scope and level of formality of the audit program depends largely on the size of the firm and the type of practice involved. Large firms with multiple offices that produce appraisals on a wide array of property types are prone to wider variations in report quality and consistency, and should consider a formal, structured program.

Small firms, however, benefit from audits too. Although the program may be less formal (as a result of a limited number of producers and resources), inconsistencies in product quality should still be identified. This often happens when a prior assignment is selected for use as a template for a current appraisal and problems are noted. Even in such a nonstructured environment, the issues found must be addressed and documented to effect appropriate and sustained change.

15. Ishikawa, *Introduction to Quality Control,* 421.

An audit is conducted by internal staff or an external vendor and may involve one individual or a team, gauged appropriately for the firm size and type. The most practical form of inspection used in professions such as appraisal, however, is usually an audit performed by internal staff. This is a reasonably cost-effective approach that ensures auditors are technically proficient and familiar with the specific standards applicable in the industry.

To help ensure consistent, standardized audits, the number of auditors within a firm must be limited (to minimize differences in opinion), and those individuals must have a common concept of the critical factors to be examined in an audit. In smaller firms, the audit team may be limited to one or two individuals, often the principal(s) of the firm or other senior staff members.

Each member of the audit staff should be carefully selected to guarantee that they possess the following qualities:

- In-depth knowledge of the appraisal process from start to finish
- Ample experience in the field
- In-depth familiarity with product and QC standards
- A sincere interest in producing products that meet or exceed customer expectations
- Diplomacy
- Objectivity
- Empathy[16]

As in the QC review process, the auditor should be open-minded and focus on correcting the problems rather than demeaning the report producer. Individuals conducting such examinations must also be aware of the confidential nature of the process and exercise decorum.

The QC audit program is designed for periodic examination of the final work product on a post-delivery basis. Both the appraisal and the original QC review comments are examined against defined appraisal report and QC review criteria. As a result, it is imperative that the auditors are well versed in both the firm's minimum report and QC review standards. The general QC audit process is summarized in Exhibit 8.2.

Quality Control Audit Preparation

As part of the preparation process, checklists and/or score sheets must be developed for use in conducting the audit and reporting findings from the examination. Checklists serve as the audit guidelines and help ensure that auditors follow a standardized approach. Items

16. L. Marvin Johnson, *Quality Assurance Program Evaluation* (West Covina, CA: L. Marvin Johnson, 1990), 43-47.

Exhibit 8.2 The Quality Control Audit Process

Audit Preparation →	Field Work →	Report Preparation and Distribution →	Follow Up
· Determine the focus · Develop checklist(s) · Identify auditee(s) · Identify samples · Establish schedule · Inform auditee(s) of dates	· Read appraisal · Read QC comments · Complete checklist · Copy examples for file · Determine overall rating · Note corrective actions · Identify best practices	· Prepare findings report · Distribute to auditee(s) · Review with auditee(s) · Determine overall rating · Identify corrective actions · Note process upgrades · Meet with auditee(s)	· Set completion dates · Follow-up audit · Note compliance · Any additional actions · Apply process upgrades · Note final outcome in file

in the list should be standard, but the form must allow for additional non-standard issues uncovered during the fieldwork. Providing ample space for comments accomplishes this objective.

In developing questions and topics for the checklist, a team should be convened that includes those likely to conduct the examinations. The group should brainstorm ideas for topics, keeping in mind the objectives of the audit (adherence to minimum report and QC standards in this case).

As with any activity conducted by a customer-driven organization, the checklist items should follow customer CTQs. For example, the customer-defined features identified in the section on "Significant Issues Found in Appraisal Reports" in Chapter 5 can serve as an outline for such a checklist. Including these items in the checklist highlights their importance to the individuals being audited (the auditees) and, over time, ensures that they receive attention from both appraisers and QC reviewers.

The sample quality control audit checklist found in Appendix G in the back of this book is derived from these items discussed in Chapter 5. The general structure of this list is shown in Exhibit 8.3.

The QC audit checklist can be structured in a number of different ways, ranging from open-ended survey questions (intended to evoke qualitative responses) to checklists like the one shown in Exhibit 8.3 that allow for graded numerical ratings for the various facets of the examination. The graded checklist enables auditors to identify and amplify any of the significant items that may be encountered during the audit.[17]

17. B. Scott Parsowith, *Fundamentals of Quality Auditing* (Milwaukee: ASQC Quality Press, 1995), 19.

Exhibit 8.3 Quality Control Audit Checklist

Auditor Name: ____________________

Audit Date(s): ____________________

File No.: ____________________

Property Name: ____________________

Property Address: ____________________

Appraisal Office: ____________________

Primary Appraiser Name: ____________________

Other Report Signer(s): ____________________

QC Reviewer: ____________________

				Internal Use Only		
Content Items	**Rating**	**Corrective Action?**	**Comments**	**Weighting**	**Wtd. Score**	**Max. Score**
1. Letter of Transmittal						
a. Client, date(s) of value, extraordinary assumptions, hypothetical conditions identified					0	0
b. Client title field completed					0	0
c. Client file number completed					0	0
2. Extraordinary Assumptions and Hypothetical Conditions						
a. Extended lease-up properly addressed					0	0
b. Retrospective value properly addressed					0	0
c. Proposed construction properly addressed					0	0
d. Proposed lease(s) properly addressed					0	0
e. Other issues properly addressed					0	0

Each item in the checklist is rated on a scale of one to three, with three indicating an above-standard effort and one representing below-standard work. An overall rating is determined based on the scores for the individual item and given the auditor's opinion of each item's importance. Ratings are used to provide quantitative feedback to help identify the relative performance of each appraiser and QC reviewer.

Audits are typically performed by examining a sampling of the products completed. In selecting the sample, the widest possible population of variables should be covered. The population should also be selected randomly in order to prevent sample bias and should be of sufficient size to achieve the audit's objective.

Sample size can fluctuate widely depending on the variability in the product and the process. Mechanized processes involving homogenous products typically require a smaller inspection percentage than manual processes supporting unique products. As a practical matter, sample size can be limited by the resources allocated to complete the examination. This is particularly true if the audit is conducted using in-house staff rather than an outside vendor.

There are various scientific methods for selecting a sample size, although many are applicable primarily to high-volume production environments. In an appraisal practice, the sample must include an ample number of reports to gauge the performance of each appraiser and QC reviewer. It is generally true that the larger the sample size, the greater the ability to detect defects (known as the *confidence level*), but there are clear diminishing returns as the sample population increases.

While it is preferable to review several reports from each appraiser, the number of appraisers relative to available auditing resources often prevents such a comprehensive program. An effective solution is to select a set number of reports for each QC reviewer, based on the theory that as long as the "checkers" are performing competently, most defects included in reports that they review will be identified and corrected.

Once the sample is identified, the schedule must be set, taking into consideration the availability of the auditors over the audit cycle (often the calendar year). Some audit programs include the "surprise" approach, wherein the auditee is not informed prior to the audit's commencement. This methodology is typically used to detect fraud or misconduct, particularly for cash businesses and those with large amounts of inventory on hand.

When the audit is conducted after the completion of the product (as with appraisals), however, the need for surprise is essentially eliminated. Informing the auditee of the audit date(s) and subject matter is a common courtesy for such an examination.

Fieldwork

Fieldwork involves accumulating and grading information to express an opinion and providing recommendations for improvement and identification of best practices to be applied to the broader production group. Although this effort can be conducted using surveys, detailed end-product testing is usually more effective for firms producing low-volume, relatively non-standardized products, such as appraisals. (Note that *fieldwork* is a generic term; the audit could actually occur without the auditor leaving the office.)

Fieldwork, as applied to appraisal, involves comparing the sample report with the criteria identified in the established audit checklist and rating each item in the sample relative to the appropriate criteria. The original appraisal is reviewed, along with any comments made by the QC reviewer, to gauge compliance with standards.

Problems, best practices, or other items can be best demonstrated using specific examples from the report. Copies of the appropriate text should be included in the audit file. These samples are useful for post-audit discussions and to facilitate the implementation of best practices.

As mentioned previously, the overall rating is determined by reviewing scores for each individual audit point in the checklist. Auditors must consider the relative significance of each point. It is important to establish weighting parameters in the audit preparation phase, taking into account that certain CTQs (such as those affecting value, scope, and so forth) are more significant to clients and should be more heavily weighted than others. Particular attention must be paid to properly weighting any client "delighter" attributes.

Even with defined parameters, scoring remains inherently subjective and challenging for an auditor. The following table provides guidelines that can be used to help arrive at audit scores.

Rating	Parameters
1	· Materially below standard and/or violates procedures
	· Key elements are omitted or wrong
	· Likely to be identified by the client as not conforming to standards
	· Corrective action needed
2	· Meets all requirements specified in the procedures manual, with minor exceptions
	· Limited amount of risk that client would identify the item as a problem
	· No corrective action needed
3	· Meets all facets of the policy/procedure and exceeds many
	· Exemplary effort
	· Serves as a model for how to complete the task

Preparing and Distributing the Report

The end product of the audit process is a written report that is distributed to the appraiser or appraisers, any manager that might be involved (possibly as a co-signer), and the QC reviewer. The report should be issued as close to the completion of the field review as possible so that the findings are fresh in the auditor's mind, minimizing misrepresentation of the facts and improving accuracy.

The report summarizes audit results and includes an opinion on the report's compliance with standards, along with significant explanations, examples, and comments identified in the checklist. The formal report should be standardized to ensure that the information is delivered consistently, and it should include the following items:

- Audit scope and objective, including standards against which the audit occurred
- Auditor's name
- Date(s) of the audit
- Identification of the appraisal(s) examined, including any file numbers, dates, etc.

- Comments, supporting evidence, findings, and corrective actions
- Identification of any noteworthy techniques or best practices that should be considered for system-wide implementation[18]

The final two bullets are critical to ensuring adherence with standards and achieving continuous improvement. The audit team should be vigilant in identifying problems that are pervasive across the company and adjusting processes and procedures to eliminate these problems. Similarly, a mechanism for implementing best practices should be designed to maximize creativity and ingenuity. A sample QC audit findings report is shown in Exhibit 8.4.

The audit report should not stray from the facts and should use specific examples as much as needed to ensure the auditee's clear understanding of any issues uncovered. Any corrective actions that are noted in the findings should also include a time frame by which the issues must be addressed.

Depending on the severity and number of corrective actions surfaced, it may be necessary to increase the frequency of audits for the appraiser(s) or require that all reports over a certain period of time be examined to make sure that the issue is corrected. Personal counseling by appropriate levels of management may also be warranted when significant problems (standards or ethics violations, for instance) are identified.

It is important to note any best practices identified in the audit and to appropriately recognize the individuals involved for exemplary conduct. The innovation should be addressed separately from the other audit issues, and a mechanism must be established for the implementation of these critical opportunities for product and process enhancement.

The final report, any source documents (such as the appropriate sections of the appraisal, QC reviewer comments, and so forth), completed checklists, and other documents used in the process should be retained so that they may be accessed in the future. Electronic media is often the best means of maintaining these records, and a minimum timetable for retention should be established. As a result, the audit file should be scanned and saved to the appropriate server in the auditor's office.

Although it is not necessarily required if no significant issues are identified in the examination, it is a good practice to meet with the auditees to review the report. Such a dialogue provides an opportunity to better explain how ratings were derived and discuss findings in greater detail. This presents an important learning opportunity for the auditees.

18. Ibid., 31.

Exhibit 8.4 Quality Control Audit Report

Auditor Name: ______________________________

Audit Date(s): ______________________________

File No.: ______________________________

Property Name: ______________________________

Property Address: ______________________________

Appraisal Office: ______________________________

Primary Appraiser Name: ______________________________

Other Report Signer(s): ______________________________

QC Reviewer: ______________________________

Scope

The audit scope included the following:

- The above-identified appraisal was read, along with any comments from the QC reviewer.
- The report and QC reviewer comments were compared to the existing minimum appraisal and QC review standards.
- The report sections were scored using a checklist, and each section was rated (see attached checklist).
- A detailed review of the appraisal file, checking of mathematical calculations, and cash flow modeling analysis (if any) were not performed.

Objectives

The auditing was performed to gauge compliance with the firm's minimum appraisal report and QC review standards to help ensure that a consistently high level of quality is produced. The audit examines the report based upon client-defined quality parameters, and the results of the audit program assist in:

- Verifying compliance (and noncompliance) with standards
- Identifying problems and areas in need of improvement
- Improving staff training and understanding of standards
- Continuous process/product improvement through best-practice identification and implementation

Summary of Findings from Appraisal Report

The overall report rating is ____, indicating that the appraisal and the QC review exceeded/met/did not meet the firm's standards. Ratings for each report section are included in the attached checklist, along with explanatory comments, where appropriate. Supporting documentation from the appraisal or the QC review is also attached to highlight any issues identified. Also, the corrective actions identified below (if any) require actions from you and will be discussed in greater detail in our meeting to review the findings.

You will be contacted shortly to set up a meeting to review the findings. Thank you for your participation in our QC audit program.

Timing

Our clients consistently identify on-time performance as a key driver of their satisfaction with our service. Keeping them informed of any events that may impact delivery of the report as agreed is very important. System information indicates this report was delivered ____ days past the agreed-upon delivery date.

Corrective Actions

1. ______________________________

____

____

Responsible Party: ______________________________

Completion Date: ______________________________

2. ______________________________

____

____

Responsible Party: ______________________________

Completion Date: ______________________________

Best Practices

____

____

____

The meeting is also a chance for the auditees to respond to the findings and possibly cast new light on one or more of the audit points. If changes are warranted as a result of this dialogue, the report must be promptly revised (including any ratings changes) and reissued. Feedback on the audit process should be solicited from the auditees during this exit interview as well.

Follow Up

Any issues identified as requiring corrective actions are subject to follow-up by the auditee(s), the appropriate levels of management, and/or the auditor. The corrective action should be clearly identified, and an attainable date for the corrective action should be included. These must be spelled out clearly in the audit report. The auditor must be notified when the action is complete, and this should be done in writing and included in the audit file.

A mechanism for follow-up must also be identified to guarantee that the learning point is resolved. This often involves informing the auditor when the action is complete, and should be made in writing and included in the file.

As was previously noted, it is critical that any best practices noted are implemented through alteration of the process and distribution to the appraisers in the firm. This task falls to the manager(s) at the firm, the auditor, the appraisers, the QC reviewers, or any combination of these that can properly effect the change.

Finally, the outcome of the actions and any related activities that occurred following report issuance should be noted in the file to establish a proper audit trail.

Conclusion

Driven by competition and the resulting need for continuous improvement, businesses evolved over time to increase the quality of the goods and services they produced, while simultaneously reducing the costs and cycle times associated with their production. The application of quality-management methodologies like Six Sigma helped accelerate this improvement.

The appraisal industry, like many service businesses, has been slow to embrace quality-management principles. Despite this lack of adoption, appraisers realized substantial efficiency and quality gains through leveraging technology over the last several years. The resulting process streamlining and product standardization are hallmarks of quality management, although the relationship in this case may be more serendipitous than intentional.

Although these gains were significant, a sizable opportunity remains to improve quality and enhance efficiency using quality-management techniques. This begins with listening to clients and tailoring reports and other products to their needs. Fashioning production processes to ensure consistently high-quality reports (as perceived by customers) enhances client satisfaction and the firm's brand image. Appraisal firms that are committed to continuous improvement and product delivery by engaged, motivated employees can consistently exceed client expectations and find themselves well along the road to client delight and the related benefits it brings.

> Whenever I go on a ride, I'm always thinking of what's wrong with the thing and how it can be improved.
> - Walt Disney

Appendix A

Active Listening

Hear What People Are Really Saying

Listening is one of the most important skills you can have. How well you listen has a major impact on your job effectiveness, and on the quality of your relationships with others.

- We listen to obtain information.
- We listen to understand.
- We listen for enjoyment.
- We listen to learn.

Given all this listening we do, you would think we'd be good at it! In fact we're not. Depending on the study being quoted, we remember a dismal 25-50% of what we hear. That means that when you talk to your boss, colleagues, customers or spouse for 10 minutes, they only really hear 2½-5 minutes of the conversation.

Turn it around and it reveals that when you are receiving directions or being presented with information, you aren't hearing the whole message either. You hope the important parts are captured in your 25-50%, but what if they're not?

Good communication skills require a high level of self-awareness. By understanding your personal style of communicating, you will go a long way towards creating good and lasting impressions with others.

Tip:
If you're finding it particularly difficult to concentrate on what someone is saying, try repeating their words mentally as they say it. This will reinforce their message and help you control mind drift.

Clearly, listening is a skill that we can all benefit from improving. By becoming a better listener, you will improve your productivity, as well as your ability to influence, persuade, negotiate. What's more, you'll avoid conflict and misunderstandings–all necessary for workplace success.

The way to become a better listener is to practice "active listening." This is where you make a conscious effort to hear not only the words that another person is saying but, more importantly, to try and understand the total message being sent.

In order to do this you must pay attention to the other person very carefully.

You cannot allow yourself to become distracted by what else may be going on around you, or by forming counter arguments that you'll make when the other person stops speaking. Nor can you allow yourself to lose focus on what the other person is saying. All of these barriers contribute to a lack of listening and understanding.

To enhance your listening skills, you need to let the other person know that you are listening to what he or she is saying. To understand the importance of this, ask yourself if you've ever been engaged in a conversation when you wondered if the other person was listening to what you were saying. You wonder if your message is getting across, or if it's even worthwhile to continue speaking. It feels like talking to a brick wall and it's something you want to avoid.

Acknowledgement can be something as simple as a nod of the head or a simple "uh huh." You aren't necessarily agreeing with the person, you are simply indicating that you are listening. Using body language and other signs to acknowledge you are listening also reminds you to pay attention and not let your mind wander.

You should also try to respond to the speaker in a way that will both encourage him or her to continue speaking, so that you can get the information you need. While nodding and "uh huhing" says you're interested, an occasional question or comment to recap what has been said communicates that you understand the message as well.

Becoming an Active Listener

There are five key elements of active listening. They all help you ensure that you hear the other person, and that the other person knows you are hearing what they are saying.

1. **Pay attention.**
   Give the speaker your undivided attention and acknowledge the message. Recognize that what is not said also speaks loudly.
   - Look at the speaker directly.
   - Put aside distracting thoughts. Don't mentally prepare a rebuttal!
   - Avoid being distracted by environmental factors.
   - "Listen" to the speaker's body language.
   - Refrain from side conversations when listening in a group setting.
2. **Show that you are listening.**
   Use your own body language and gestures to convey your attention.
   - Nod occasionally.
   - Smile and use other facial expressions.
   - Note your posture and make sure it is open and inviting.
   - Encourage the speaker to continue with small verbal comments like "yes" and "uh huh."
3. **Provide feedback.**
   Our personal filters, assumptions, judgments, and beliefs can distort what we hear. As a listener, your role is to understand what is being said. This may require you to reflect what is being said and ask questions.
   - Reflect what has been said by paraphrasing. "What I'm hearing is..." and "Sounds like you are saying..." are great ways to reflect back.
   - Ask questions to clarify certain points. "What do you mean when you say..." "Is this what you mean?"
   - Summarize the speaker's comments periodically.
4. **Defer judgment.**
   Interrupting is a waste of time. It frustrates the speaker and limits full understanding of the message.
   - Allow the speaker to finish.
   - Don't interrupt with counter-arguments.

Tip:
If you find yourself responding emotionally to what someone said, say so, and ask for more information: "I may not be understanding you correctly, and I find myself taking what you said personally. What I thought you just said is XXX; is that what you meant?"

5. **Respond appropriately.**
   Active listening is a model for respect and understanding. You are gaining information and perspective. You add nothing by attacking the speaker or otherwise putting him or her down.
   - Be candid, open, and honest in your response.
   - Assert your opinions respectfully.
   - Treat the other person as he or she would want to be treated.

Key Points

It takes a lot of concentration and determination to be an active listener. Old habits are hard to break, and if your listening habits are as bad as many people's are, then there's a lot of habit-breaking to do!

Be deliberate with your listening and remind yourself constantly that your goal is to truly hear what the other person is saying. Set aside all other thoughts and behaviors and concentrate on the message. Ask questions, reflect, and paraphrase to ensure you understand the message. If you don't, then you'll find that what someone says to you and what you hear can be amazingly different!

Start using active listening today to become a better communicator and improve your workplace productivity and relationships.

Appendix B

Common Errors and Issues in the Appraisal Report

The following 2008 white paper discusses common errors and issues in appraisal reports noted by the Appraisal Institute's Senior Manager of Experience Review and Senior Manager of Ethics and Standards. It is used as a supplement in a number of Appraisal Institute courses, including *Residential Report Writing and Case Studies, General Appraiser Report Writing and Case Studies, Report Writing and Valuation Analysis,* and *Business Practices and Ethics.*

The following are some of the errors commonly noted by the Appraisal Institute's Senior Manager of Experience Review and Senior Manager of Ethics and Standards. This information is pertinent to both general and residential appraisal practice. These items are not listed in order of occurrence or importance.

Certification Statement

The most common errors we see in appraisal reports have to do with certification statements. These errors are also the easiest to avoid. The key is to remain cognizant of current certification requirements in USPAP (Standards Rule 2-3 for real property appraisal reports, Standards Rule 3-3 for appraisal review reports, and appraisal consulting reports) as well as the requirements of the Certification Standard of the Appraisal Institute.

Designated and Associate Members of the Appraisal Institute are subject to requirements of the Appraisal Institute, which include the Certification Standard. (The Standards of Professional Appraisal

Practice of the Appraisal Institute include USPAP plus our Certification Standard.)

Certification requirements may change from time to time. It is incumbent on the appraiser to provide a certification that is contemporary with the appraisal date. To assist you with this, the Appraisal Institute provides sample certifications for appraisal, appraisal review, and appraisal consulting assignments on our Web site. These are Word documents that can be downloaded and copied directly into your own reports. They include both the statements required by USPAP and the statements required by the Appraisal Institute for its members. See www.appraisalinstitute.org; log in under Members Only; go to Resources, then Downloads, then Code of Professional Ethics and Standards, and finally Sample Certification Statements for Written Appraisal, Appraisal Review, and Appraisal Consulting Service Reports. When the Word document comes up, save it to your hard drive.

The USPAP certification does not have to be exactly the same as that in Standards Rule 2-3, but it has to be similar in content. (The Appraisal Institute's certification statements MUST be verbatim.) You must be careful not to deviate from the intent of the language if you do not use the USPAP certification language exactly. You may make additions if they are relevant to the assignment.

If you use form reports, be careful. Often the certification included in your software is out of date or doesn't comply with Appraisal Institute requirements or with your state appraisal law. With the exception of the Appraisal Institute's AI Reports® forms, the certification provided in a form report is not compliant with the Code of Professional Ethics and Standards of Professional Appraisal Practice of the Appraisal Institute–additions are required to be compliant. It doesn't matter where these additions go in the report, just as long as they're included somewhere. If they can't be added to the certification page, put them in a logical place.

If you have created your own certification template, it's helpful to put a version date on it so you can easily tell whether it is current.

The value conclusion need not be included in the certification. The certification need not be dated (except in the case of the certification retained in the workfile for an oral report).

Note that the proper nomenclature is "certification," not "certificate," "certificate of value," or "certification of value." The certification statements relate to the entire assignment and the manner in which it was completed, not just the value conclusion.

Finally, keep in mind that the certification is a very important part of an appraisal, appraisal review, or appraisal consulting report.

Only an appraiser can make such a statement. Avoid burying the certification in the back of the report or in the addenda, or putting it in tiny or unclear print. Let your reader know you are sincere about these statements and proud to be able to make them.

Identification of the Client, the Intended Use of the Appraisal, and the Intended Users

Identification of the client, intended users, and intended use is a significant and necessary step in the appraisal process. Making these identifications defines the parties to whom you are responsible, and why. When you write a report, you are writing to your client and intended users. They are the audience for your discussion and conclusions. (Note that in Standards Rule 2-1(b), USPAP says the report must contain sufficient information to enable the intended users to understand the report properly. In order to ensure that your report contains sufficient information, you must first know who the intended users are.) And you are writing to the intended users about the particular problem they wish to resolve–a question about the value of a property or about the quality of the work of another appraiser, for example.

It is a misconception that the "addressee" named in the report is necessarily the client. A very common mistake is to assume it is understood that the addressee is the client. This may or may not be the case. It is required that you specifically identify the client by name or type.

The concept of intended user is widely misunderstood. To be an intended user, THE APPRAISER MUST INTEND for that party to rely on the assignment results. An intended user is not simply anyone who "intends to rely" or "will rely" on assignment results. Further, receiving a copy of a report does not mean that a party must be identified as an intended user. See Statement 9 in USPAP for further information.

The intended use is the key driver in determining the appropriate scope of work for the assignment. Why the appraisal is needed, what the value issues are, what effective date of appraisal is required, and what interests are to be considered are among factors that make up the intended use/intended user/scope decision. Your client might not fully understand the appraisal process, the reporting requirements, or the complexities of appraisal. Your identification of these elements can help you provide your client with a valuation service that is appropriate.

Again, be careful with form reports, as they might not provide space to adequately address these key items.

Scope of Work

Scope of work is the most critical decision you will make in an assignment. In solving any problem, including an appraisal problem, there are three major steps to the process:

1. identify the problem,
2. determine the solution (or scope of work), and
3. apply the solution.

None of the three steps can be omitted, and they must be carried out in order.

The first step, identification of the problem, involves figuring out seven key assignment elements:

- Client
- Intended users in addition to the client
- Intended use
- Objective, or type of value in an appraisal
- Effective date
- Property characteristics that are relevant to the assignment (e.g., interest valued, physical and legal characteristics)
- Assignment conditions (e.g., hypothetical conditions, extraordinary assumptions, jurisdictional exceptions)

In an appraisal assignment, Standards Rule 1-2 of USPAP requires that these items be identified, or "figured out." They provide the framework for the assignment and allow the appraiser to identify the problem to be solved. Standard 2 of USPAP requires that the same items also be reported. They provide the "full story" about the value conclusion, which, by itself, is meaningless.

Once the seven assignment elements are figured out, the appraiser can move to the second step, determining the scope of work to solve the problem. Scope of work encompasses all aspects of the valuation process, including the question of which of the usual three approaches to value will be used. Also included in the scope decision are the questions of how much data is to be gathered, from what sources, from which geographic area, and over what time period; what is the extent of the data verification process; and what is the extent of the property inspection, if any, etc.

The scope of work decision is appropriate when it allows you to arrive at credible assignment results and when it's consistent with (1) the expectations (if any) of clients that are similar to yours and (2) what your peers would do if faced with the same sort of situation.

In 2006 USPAP was revised substantially with regard to scope of work. This represents a significant conceptual change in appraisal practice. It is important that all appraisers fully understand the ramifications of this change and are fully aware of its implications. You can find more information about scope of work on The Appraisal Foundation's Web site, where the Appraisal Standards Board has published a Q&A about scope of work. Also, the Appraisal Institute has published a book, *Scope of Work*, by Stephanie Coleman, MAI, SRA, which provides some practical assistance.

Extraordinary Assumptions

The proper use of extraordinary assumptions is often misunderstood. An extraordinary assumption is an underlying premise of the assignment, something that is believed to be true for the sake of the analysis, but whether or not it is in fact true is uncertain. Extraordinary assumptions differ from the general assumptions that are often made and reported in all assignments. An extraordinary assumption is specific to the assignment at hand. Further, if an extraordinary assumption is contrary to the truth, the assignment results would be affected.

It is important to understand that when an extraordinary assumption proves to be contrary to the truth, it does not mean the appraiser was "wrong." The appraiser must ascertain that the use of the extraordinary assumption is appropriate given the client's intended use of the assignment results. Then, unless agreed upon with the client at the time of the assignment, the appraiser is under no obligation to "fix" or "correct" an appraisal upon learning that the premise–the reason for the extraordinary assumption–is false. A value opinion is always developed within the context of the assignment as defined by the scope of work and other assignment parameters such as the date of value and the type of value, as well as stated hypothetical conditions and extraordinary assumptions. If an extraordinary assumption made in an appraisal subsequently turns out to be false, the appraiser could accept a new assignment that would reflect the different underlying premise.

USPAP's SR 2-2 a (x), b (x), and c (x) says the appraisal report must "clearly and conspicuously state all extraordinary assumptions; and state that their use might have affected the assignment results." This does not mean the property must be appraised twice–both with and without the extraordinary assumption. It simply means the client and intended users must be alerted to the extraordinary assumptions so that their significance, given the intended use, can be comprehended.

Many assignments involve one or more extraordinary assumptions. In reporting, extraordinary assumptions need to be handled in a specific manner. Extraordinary assumptions must be conspicuously disclosed. They cannot be inserted in fine print or buried in the addenda where they are unlikely to be read. It may be appropriate to cite extraordinary assumptions in more than one place in your report, depending on their significance to the assignment.

An example of an extraordinary assumption could involve the appraisal of an older gas station. The date of value is the current date. It is known that many gas stations of the subject's vintage have leaking underground storage tanks. If so, the cost to remediate the problem can be sizable–especially if leaking fuel has made its way into the groundwater. However, the status of the subject's tanks is uncertain. If you proceed with the assignment based on the assumption that the property does not have leaking tanks, you would be using an extraordinary assumption–it is specific to your assignment and would likely affect your value conclusion if found to be incorrect.

A second example is the very common case of a "drive-by appraisal," in which the subject improvements are visually inspected only from the curb. To proceed with such an assignment, the appraiser must establish something to be true about the size, condition, and other characteristics of the property that are relevant to the valuation problem. Sources for such information may include prior appraisals completed by another; county records; or even the verbal information from the owner or agent. The information may be true, but from the appraiser's viewpoint there is uncertainty attached to it, and the valuation will hinge on one or more extraordinary assumptions about the "gaps" in the facts.

Hypothetical Conditions

Hypothetical conditions are things that you know to be contrary to fact but you take them to be true for the purpose of the analysis. Contrast these with extraordinary assumptions, which are about uncertainties. The decision to use a hypothetical condition must be carefully considered. The hypothetical condition must be appropriate given the client's intended use of the assignment results and can't be so outlandish that it leads to non-credible results.

It may be necessary to use a hypothetical condition for legal or comparison purposes. The resulting analysis and conclusions must be credible, and the hypothetical condition must be clearly disclosed. Your client needs to know what the hypothetical condition is and how it might affect your value conclusion. In reporting, hypothetical conditions need to be handled in a specific manner. According to SR 2-2 a (x), b (x), c (x), you must "clearly and conspicuously state all hypothetical conditions; and state that their use might have affected the assignment results." The difference in reporting between a general assumption and a hypothetical condition is that the latter must be conspicuously disclosed, not buried in the back of the report or shown in tiny print. It may be appropriate to cite all hypothetical conditions in more than one place in your report, depending on their significance to the value conclusion.

One of the most common reasons for using a hypothetical condition is to develop a value opinion of a proposed property as of the current date. Almost all appraisals of residential construction projects are performed this way and therefore are based on a hypothetical condition–that is, that improvements are already complete when, in fact, the improvements don't exist.

When using a hypothetical condition, terminology is important. It is appropriate to note that the value is based on the hypothetical condition. You then explain the condition. The value itself is not hypothetical–that is, it's not a "hypothetical value." Rather, the value is based on a hypothetical condition.

Prospective Value

One key assignment element is the effective date of value, which may be a current date, a retrospective date, or a prospective date. If your assignment is for a proposed project, your client may need a value that is effective as of the date of completion and/or date of stabilization (prospective values). Or your client might need to know what the property would be worth if it were completed as of today (current value). Either is allowable. Each can provide the client with a useful conclusion. See Advisory Opinion 17, *Appraisals of Real Property with Proposed Improvements,* for further information.

There is confusion about how to qualify your reporting of a prospective value. Extraordinary assumptions help you report prospective value without being misleading; they assist you in being clear about your valuation process, opinions, and conclusions. To some it is confusing whether the value of proposed construction or of non-stabilized properties should be based on a hypothetical condition or an extraordinary assumption. If your effective value date is a current date, your appraisal will be based on the hypothetical condition that the improvements exist when, in fact, they do not. If your value date is in the future, when you anticipate completion (a prospective value), then your appraisal will be based on the extraordinary assumption that the improvements will indeed be completed as proposed as of that date.

Whenever the date of value is a prospective date (even in cases that don't involve proposed construction), there will be one "automatic" extraordinary assumption that relates to the potential changes between the current time, when you are researching and writing the report, and the effective future value date. Because you cannot see into the future, you want to point out that you assume no significant changes will take place.

Reporting prospective values must be done with care. According to Statement No. 4 in USPAP, "In prospective value opinions, use of the term 'market value' without a modifier such as 'forecasted' or 'prospective' and without future verb tenses is improper." It's correct, for example, to state your conclusion as "market value as of (future date) will be $XXX," rather than "the market value is...."

Prospective Value—Value Date

In a prospective value assignment, you may be asked for the value as of either a specific date or a specific event. The date of value to be used in an analysis is identified based on the nature of the problem to be solved.

If your client requests a value as of a specific event, such as completion of construction or stabilization of the property, you will need to figure out what future date will be associated with that event. The client, developer, or other parties to the assignment may provide you with dates reflecting their estimate of completion, lease-up, or stabilization. These may be reasonable estimates, but you cannot assume they are without some consideration. It is not appropriate for you to accept the developer's estimate of completion or stabilization at face value. You must consider the market and determine if the completion, lease-up, sellout, etc., is likely to occur by the specified date.

Analysis of the Subject Property History

It is not sufficient to simply report the subject's sales history. In fact, simply reporting it does not meet the USPAP requirements on this issue. When an opinion of market value is to be developed, you must *analyze* all sales of the subject property that occurred in the three years prior to your date of value. You must also analyze any agreements of sale (contracts), options, or listings that are current as of the date of appraisal. Listing the sales or other agreements is just a start. See Standards Rule 1-5 as well as reporting requirements covered by Standards Rule 2-2 (a) (ix), 2-2 (b) (ix), or 2-2 (c) (ix). Also see Advisory Opinion 1, *Sales History*.

USPAP has no requirement to analyze the sales history of each comparable sale. However, Fannie Mae and certain other government bodies require comparable sales histories. This regulation is applicable to lenders, and it's reflected on the URAR form.

Highest and Best Use

Highest and best use is commonly one of the weakest areas in an appraisal. It is too often viewed as a "necessary but fruitless exercise," when it is the meat of the assignment in an analysis of market value. Even though many improved properties do represent the highest and best use, there are still issues that must be considered. If you do not adequately address highest and best use, you may inappropriately analyze the property.

When your assignment objective is to develop an opinion of market value, you must address the question of the highest and best use for whatever you are valuing. That is, if you're valuing an improved property, you must address the question of the highest and best use *as currently improved.* If you're valuing a vacant site, then you must address highest and best use *as vacant.* If you're valuing a site as if vacant (as in the case of an improved property when we complete a cost approach), you must address the question of the highest and best use *as if vacant.* If you're valuing a proposed property, you must address what the highest and best use WILL be when complete. If you're valuing a proposed property as of the current date based on a hypothetical condition, you must address what the highest and best use WOULD be if the improvements were complete as proposed.

To answer the question of highest and best use of a vacant site, four tests apply: physical possibility, legal permissibility, financial feasibility, and maximum productivity. Many uses may be physically possible, but only some of those will be legally permissible. And of those, only some will be financially feasible. The question ultimately becomes, which of those uses (physically possible, legally permissible, financially feasible) brings the highest economic return to the owner of the rights to the land?

To answer the question of the highest and best use of an improved site, the same four tests apply. But they generally don't provide a sufficient framework for answering the HABU question. Rather, you need to consider three possible scenarios regarding the improvements, and which of the three makes the most sense. What would the most probable buyer of this improved site do with the improvements? Would the buyer:

1. Keep using the improvements the way they exist?
2. Make modifications to what exists?
3. Demolish the existing improvements to obtain a vacant site?

Using the framework of these three questions, you can better refine your highest and best use analysis. Many times, appraisers miss the mark because they don't recognize the opportunity to alter the existing improvements that the market sees for the property. Remember, as an appraiser you are trying to reflect the actions of the "most probable buyer" for that property. Put yourself in those shoes. If it were your property, what would you do with it to maximize its value?

An incorrect conclusion of highest and best use as improved may seriously impact your value conclusion. A common error in highest and best use analysis is failure to recognize or address property characteristics that may have been mentioned in the description sections. There are many obvious property issues that trigger additional highest and best use analysis. Excess land, a legally non-conforming use, obsolescence, the need for renovation or conversion of use, interim use, and transitional use are a few. If you do not properly address these issues, they can affect the credibility of the work. If you do not recognize them in your analysis of highest and best use, you may miss them in the valuation analysis. And, if these are issues for your property, you should expect to include some discussion in the highest and best use section.

Unfortunately, it is very common to see a statement that reads: "The subject property's highest and best use is as improved." This is a weak comment about any property, but it is particularly inappropriate for an appraisal of a proposed project or one where renovation is being analyzed. Highest and best use as improved for a proposed property should address the proposed improvements. A proposed project needs the same critical analysis as that for an existing improved property. It is crucial to recognize that a proposed project may not be the highest and best use of the property. The developer may not know the market or may be constructing something that is an over-improvement or an under-improvement to accommodate special needs of the buyer/user. It is your job to recognize the keys to highest and best use and analyze the proposed improvements AND deal with them appropriately if they are not the highest and best use of the property.

Highest and Best Use—Reporting

A common misconception is that in a Summary Appraisal Report it is acceptable to just summarize your conclusion. This is incorrect. You must summarize your analysis. If the objective is market value, there will always be some degree of analysis of highest and best use. Granted, in some cases that analysis is quick, and the highest and best use conclusion of the property as it exists doesn't take more than a flash to figure out. For example, consider the case of a single-family residence located within a subdivision of similar houses, where there is no chance that a likely buyer would demolish the house to maximize value, and where modifying the improvements would not significantly increase the value above the cost to make them. But it's still necessary to provide some reasoning or rationale for your conclusion. USPAP language reads: "summarize the support and rationale for that opinion" [SR 2-2 (b) (ix)].

It is not necessary to repeat sections of the report in the highest and best use analysis. Report sections are not intended to be stand-alone. The Market Analysis and other descriptive sections of the report can be used to support highest and best use conclusions as well as the valuation sections. Material from other report sections may be referenced in the Highest and Best Use section to support the analysis and conclusions.

Highest and Best Use—Residential Form

Another common misconception is that it is only necessary to check the box on a form report if the highest and best use is "as improved." This is incorrect. Highest and best use in a summary form report still requires some detail even when the existing improvements represent the highest and best use. (See comments above.) USPAP language relating to highest and best use in a Summary Appraisal Report reads: "summarize the support and rationale for that opinion" [SR 2-2 (b) (ix)]. You may provide a brief statement, but to meet the requirements of the Standard, you must provide more than a checked box.

Excess Land and Surplus Land

Excess land is commonly mishandled in assignments. It is often confused with surplus land. It is too often lumped in with the value of the entire property or ignored altogether. Excess land may be sold off separately from the rest of the property, so in effect, the subject property becomes two subject properties. Excess land may have a different highest and best use than the rest of the site. This must be addressed in the highest and best use analysis. Further, excess land will have to be treated separately in the valuation process. An entirely different set of comparable data may be required. The value of excess land must be reported separately. Be careful about adding the value of the excess land to the value of the rest of the property, as the sum of the parts may or may not equal the whole.

Surplus land does not have a separate value, as it cannot be sold off separately. It is "extra" land that may or may not contribute value to the overall property. It does not have an independent highest and best use. It may have the same value per unit of comparison (e.g., value per square foot, value per acre) as the rest of the site, or it may contribute less per unit of comparison.

Reporting Requirements

In 2006 the Departure Rule was eliminated from USPAP, along with all the disclosure requirements relating to departure. USPAP no longer uses the terms "complete appraisal" and "limited appraisal" to describe the development process. The change did not affect the written appraisal reporting options (Self-Contained, Summary, and Restricted Use) or the requirement to disclose which option you used.

Advisory Opinion 11 provides a good overview of the content requirements for each of the three reporting options and includes a report content comparison chart that is very helpful in determining what is required for each. It is important that you meet all of the requirements for the option that you choose. It is inappropriate and misleading to state that you are providing a Self-Contained Appraisal Report when the level of detail is no more than that required for a Summary Appraisal Report, or that you are providing a Summary Appraisal Report when its content level is that of a Restricted Use Appraisal Report.

Many clients do not fully understand the different reporting options. It's the appraiser's responsibility to explain the differences and provide the report needed. Often clients request a Self-Contained Appraisal Report but ask for a "shorter version"–it is necessary for you to explain that if you call it a Self-Contained Appraisal Report, it must be one. If the client wants one detailed approach and cursory secondary valuation approaches, you can write a Summary Appraisal Report and provide a more detailed reporting of the emphasized section. It is *not* acceptable to call this report "Self-Contained."

If you are preparing a Restricted Use Appraisal Report, you must intend that it be used by only one party. That is, it must be for client-use only. If you intend for parties other than the client to use the report, a Restricted Use Appraisal Report is not appropriate. If your client needs more than just the value conclusion (for example, data and analyses), then a Restricted Use Appraisal Report is not appropriate. It is unacceptable to provide a Restricted Use Appraisal Report just to keep costs down. Your report must include the information the client requires and address the reason why the client needs the appraisal from you.

For instance, in legal situations, often an attorney will request a Restricted Use Appraisal Report to make an initial determination about the extent of a legal issue. It may be appropriate to provide such a report if it is your intention that the attorney is the only one who will use the report. But it is not appropriate to provide a Restricted Use Appraisal Report for eminent domain purposes when it is your intention that the attorney, the client, and the court will all use it.

You may use any number of forms for reporting. Beware of forms that do not in themselves call for all of the information required under Standard 2. Some forms need to be supplemented with such items as intended use, intended user, scope of work, etc. It is incumbent on you, the appraiser, to understand whether the form or format you are using allows for compliance with the reporting requirements of Standard 2 of USPAP.

Residential Reporting Requirements

The new URAR form (March 2005) does not need addenda to meet USPAP's reporting requirements. It will need the addition of the Appraisal Institute's certification statements. This form is intended for a specific use, and you may continue to use the old URAR form for other assignments.

The old URAR form does not meet all the reporting requirements as outlined in USPAP. It is possible that with careful and concise language you could fit the majority of the additions into the body of the form; however, this is unlikely. In most instances, supplementation will be needed to address the reporting requirements not covered by the form, in addition to a current certification as required by Standards Rule 2-3.

We highly recommend the use of the Appraisal Institute's AI Reports® forms when the appraisal does not need to meet the requirements of Fannie Mae, Freddie Mac, FHA, or VA. If the assignment is with a lender who is not concerned with these entities, use of the new URAR is not required. For a non-lending client, the new URAR is not appropriate.

Reconciliation

Standards Rule 1-6 requires the appraiser to reconcile the quality and quantity of data. The corresponding reporting requirements are in Standards Rule 2-2 (a) (ix), 2-2 (b) (ix), and 2-2 (c) (ix). A reconciliation section consisting of boilerplate and stock comments does not often present useful information. A discussion of the data used, its application to the subject, how the approaches apply to the subject, and so on, is essential to a meaningful reconciliation.

Miscellaneous—Theory and Practice

The following are common errors noted in a significant number of assignments:

- Failing to complete a sufficiently thorough market analysis when analyzing highest and best use, income, vacancy, and expenses

- Including irrelevant data in the report but leaving out relevant information; for instance, including a detailed market analysis covering retail and office properties but providing only a weak analysis of the apartment market when the subject property is an apartment
- Improperly handling or ignoring excess land
- Allowing gaps in the reporting of the analysis, which require the reader to take "leaps of faith" to understand a conclusion or analysis
- Failing to recognize the market for the property–local, regional, or national
- Valuing a leased fee interest without knowing or analyzing the lease terms
- Analyzing a single-tenant, owner-occupied property using multi-tenant comparables

- Analyzing rent comparables without considering the size of the demised spaces in either the comparables or the subject
- Failing to recognize the date leases were initiated in completing rent comparable analysis
- Failing to use a DCF for leased fee analysis when it is necessary for credible results
- Not understanding what is included in Marshall Valuation Costs

- Applying percentage adjustments in an improper sequence
- Not using or citing up-to-date materials; for instance, referencing old textbooks
- Not having or reviewing current editions of the Standards–akin to filing your taxes using an old form
- Not discussing excess land or functional issues in a highest and best use analysis
- Failing to reconcile the data and analysis in the appraisal
- Careless editing of boilerplate

Resources and References

The Code of Professional Ethics and Standards of Professional Appraisal Practice of the Appraisal Institute are available on the Appraisal Institute Web site, www.appraisalinstitute.org. Copies of

USPAP can be obtained through The Appraisal Foundation, www.appraisalfoundation.org.

If you have additional questions or need more information, contact:

Stephanie Coleman, MAI, SRA
Senior Manager, Ethics and Standards
Appraisal Institute
Phone: 877-777-6939
E-mail: scoleman@appraisalinstitute.org

Janice F. Young, MAI, SRA
Senior Manager, Experience Review
Appraisal Institute
Phone: 503-235-8755
E-mail: jyoung@appraisalinstitute.org

Appendix C

Common Cash Flow Modeling Issues

The following are some tips and suggestions for modeling cash flows to help prevent common errors and problems:[1]

- Review net operating income in the reversion year to make sure that it is not an "aberrant" year (unusual lease rollover, capital expenditures, and so forth). Similarly, review occupancy to check that a normalized/stabilized occupancy is being capitalized.
- Treatment of vacancy and collection (V&C) loss must result in a normalized deduction. Specifically, V&C can be calculated in some software models using hard inputs (smoothing), lag vacancy between leases (which has varying impacts on V&C depending on lease rollover), or permanent vacancy, wherein the space is included at zero rent forever (often applied to conference rooms, leasing/management offices, maintenance rooms, and so forth). Whatever method is used, the total deduction must reflect the V&C that is identified as appropriate in the narrative. For instance, if a 6% vacancy and 1% collection loss are supported in the market, then the reversion and the average over the term should be approximately 7%.
- The discount rate and capitalization rate applied in the cash flow must match the narrative in the report.
- All market leasing assumptions must match the report narrative.

1. The author gratefully acknowledges the members of the Cushman & Wakefield QC Review Standards Subcommittee who contributed many of these points. Team members include C. Clayton Davie, MAI, Steven R. Gragg, MAI, Michael C. McNamera, MAI, Scott M. Rando, MAI, and Steven A. Zenker, MAI.

- The discounted cash flow must align with any pro forma income and expense charts included in the narrative. This is a critical element that should *always* be double-checked for income-producing assets.
- All market leasing assumptions should be named to match each classification of space for ease of auditing. For instance, category titles should be "anchor" and "in-line" for those types of spaces, rather than "MLA1," "MLA2," or some similar type of generic coding.
- Ensure that all renewal assumptions match the narrative in the report.
- Clearly identify rent growth rate assumptions in the narrative of the report (noting if any years are flat).
- The reimbursement type in the cash flow model (such as triple net) must match the text in the report.
- Check that the level of reimbursements in the cash flow is logical as a percentage of the expense and given the type of leases (such as net, gross, and so forth).
- Ensure that when rent step(s) are projected for market leases, the steps are properly modeled.
- Examine significant sections of the property-level cash flows (revenues, expenses, and net operating income) on a per-square-foot basis to make sure that they are reasonable.

Appendix D

Some Thoughts on Lexicon and Syntax

John R. White, MAI

The following article, "Some Thoughts on Lexicon and Syntax" by John R. White, MAI, was originally published in the July 1989 issue of *The Appraisal Journal.*

I have a deep personal interest in encouraging all real estate professionals to improve their writing skills to a level equal to their knowledge and ability. Under the pressure of our assignments, we sometimes forget the importance of composition or are careless in our writings. Where the English error is especially glaring, it can detract from the quality of professional findings. Reports should be phrased in a clear, concise, and crisp way. As a resolve, let's leave to nonprofessionals the trade jargon, the hackneyed words and phrases, the redundancies, and the poor syntax.

There are several basic rules that characterize an exceptional writing style. Use short sentences wherever possible. Never use an obscure, secondary meaning of a word when an understandable word is equally descriptive. Avoid two descriptive adjectives when one would suffice. Abstain from fancy and effusive language. Be careful in starting a sentence with a participle because the subject of the sentence is so frequently confused by the writer. Use of the active rather than the passive voice is more effective. Avoid language that is suggestive of a legal brief.

John R. White, MAI, is honorary chairman of Landauer Associates, Inc., New York. He has been a frequent contributor to *The Appraisal Journal* and is the author of the book, *Real Estate Valuing, Counseling, Forecasting: Selected Writings of John Robert White,* published by the American Institute of Real Estate Appraisers.

In correspondence, we may at our discretion use either the first person singular "I" or the first person plural "we." "I" is more personal. When using "I," be consistent; do not mix "I" with "we." When using "I," sign your name directly without the company name as a closing signature. Normally, the more formal the purpose of the correspondence, the more you would use "we." "We" should always be used when official or policy statements are made or company opinions offered. The company name may be substituted for "we" when findings and recommendations are presented, or as a relief from "we."

In reports, I recommend the third person: "The consultant noted that..." rather than the passive, "it was noted that...." Frequently, this traditional form can be dispensed in favor of direct language such as, "The facade lacked adequate fenestration" rather than, "The consultant noted that the facade lacked adequate fenestration." The reader knows the statement is made by the person who signs the report; thus, the third person reference frequently becomes superfluous.

It is particularly important to eliminate so-called "buzz words" from our reports. Certain words catch the fancy of the market and are used chiefly to impress. An outstanding illustration is the use of "super." I can barely tolerate references to, say, "super" design when superior or excellent design is really intended. I prefer to bring older reports current rather than to "update" them. I like to avoid stating that the profit and loss statement has been "grossed out" in favor of saying that all forms of revenue and their accompanying expenses have been presented. Another outstanding example is the use of prioritize, a blatant misuse of the meaning to put in priority. Please don't fall into the buzz word trap!

Undoubtedly the two most grating errors are, first, the constant, incorrect form of the pronoun after the linking verb "be." How many times have you heard someone say "It's me" or "That's him" rather than "It is I" or "That's he"? The second most grating error is the incorrect use of the subject form of a pronoun with a preposition, as "between you and I" rather than "between you and me."

Frequently, the rationale for mistakes is repeated misuse. To some, incorrect syntax is justified because everyone does it. But why should we impurify a language whose ground rules have evolved over centuries through scholars who have devoted their life to semantics? Our mission as professionally motivated business people is to articulate our views in the clearest possible way. As William Strunk, Jr., said, "To use the language well, do not begin by hacking it to bits; accept the whole body of it, cherish its classic form, its variety, and its richness."[1]

1. William Strunk, Jr., and E. B. White, *The Elements of Style,* 3d ed. (New York: Macmillan, 1979), 82.

With a nod to Professor Strunk and E. B. White and their book, *The Elements of Style,* I have put in columnar form phrases, expressions, and words that should probably be avoided in the professional's lexicon.[2] The ill-advised expressions have been stated and suggestions made for improvement, as well as the reason for the change. The list is not complete; it is merely illustrative of our more common mistakes. Some may react on the grounds that the examples are obvious. Please, nevertheless, accept the following table as a reminder of the importance of good English composition and word choice as an essential ingredient in our practice. I have only started the process of suggesting how to improve our composition with the enclosed examples. They are by no means all-inclusive. If you are a gifted writer, perhaps the table will be helpful to others in your employ who need help. English is not an easy language to master. It may be comforting to know that even the best writers make frequent use of reference books. Some books to turn to for English usage and style are *Line by Line,* by Claire Kehrwald Cook;[3] *The Chicago Manual of Style;*[4] *Instant English Handbook,* by Madeline Semmelmeyer;[5] and *A Dictionary of Modern English Usage,* by H. W. Fowler.[6] I earnestly hope that the examples in Table 1 and the listed reference books will serve as a reminder of our compelling need to effectively communicate.

Believe me, good English is fun! We should all take pride in the manner in which we speak and write. Make a deliberate effort to improve your verbal and writing proficiencies. Avoid slang, trite expressions, and jargon. Effective communication is essential to business success. Constantly strive to improve your vocabulary. A high proportion of appraisers write very well. Yet, as we have become more technologically minded, there is always the disposition to sacrifice lexicon and syntax for methodological proficiency. A constant reminder of the importance of good written communication is critical if the appraiser is to achieve the highest level of well-rounded performance and be regarded as a professional.

---

2. Ibid.
3. Claire Kehrwald Cook, *Line by Line* (Boston: Houghton Mifflin Company, 1985).
4. The University of Chicago Press, *The Chicago Manual of Style,* 13th ed. (Chicago: University of Chicago Press, 1982).
5. Madeline Semmelmeyer, *Instant English Handbook* (Little Falls, N.J.: Career Publishing, Inc., 1981).
6. H. W. Fowler, *A Dictionary of Modern English Usage,* 2d. ed. (Oxford: Oxford University Press, 1965).

TABLE 1 Phrases and Expressions to Avoid

Poor Usage	Preferred	Comment
Submitted, *herewith,* is our report.	We are enclosing our report. We are submitting our report. Accompanying this letter is our report.	Bury *herewith.*
With respect thereto, we offer the following opinion.	We, accordingly, offer the following opinion.	Let's also bury *thereto. With respect* is overworked.
The client can move into new space at a minor increase over *your* present rent.	*The client* can move into new space at a minor increase over *its* present rent.	*The client* is in the third person; subsequent reference in the same sentence must also be in the third person.
Racial strife *then being* experienced in the city...	Racial strife experienced in the city...	Omit needless words, especially *being.*
The lease provisions are *standard* and *normal.*	The lease provisions are standard.	Redundant adjectives
It was a splendid, breathtaking vista.	It was a breathtaking vista.	
So much for the density question. Now about the environment.	Start a new paragraph with "Setting aside the density question, the environment is described..."	Starting a new paragraph signals a new idea. Also, every sentence needs a verb.
Pursuant to your instructions ...	*In accordance with* your instructions... or *Following* your instructions...	*Pursuant to* is obsolete, awkward, and legalistic.
We are pleased to submit...	We are submitting...	*We are pleased* is obvious and thus unnecessary.
I *feel like* the terrain prevents construction.	I *feel as though* the terrain ... or The terrain prevents construction.	Ungrammatical use of like
Between *you and I,* shopping centers are a good investment.	Between *you and me,* shopping centers are a good investment.	Prepositions take the subject form of pronouns.
It was *me* who rented the space.	It was *I* who rented the space or better I rented the space.	Use of pronoun as a predicate nominitive. Test it by asking, who rented the space? I rented... not, me rented.
I dislike that *type of* shopping center.	I dislike that *kind of* shopping center.	*Type of* is not a synonym for *kind of.*
He plans *to diligently pursue* the marketing program.	He plans *to pursue diligently* the marketing program.	It's best not to split an infinitive (*to* plus a verb form) except when required for emphasis.
In regard to the renting inquiry...	*Regarding* the rental inquiry...	Stilted expression
In the final analysis, the investment will prosper.	*In conclusion...* or *Finally,* the investment will prosper.	Trite expression
I *consider* the real estate *as* fully depreciated.	I consider the real estate fully depreciated. or I *consider* the real estate *to be* fully depreciated.	Do not follow with *as* when consider means *believe to be.*
He lost the tenant *due to* his unyielding terms.	He lost the tenant *because of* his unyielding terms.	Used loosely for *through, because of,* or *owing to*
The bonus is divided *between all of us.*	The bonus is divided *among us.*	*Among* is used when more than two things or persons are involved. When more than two are involved but each is considered individually, *between* is preferred. *All of* is a needless phrase.
The analyst *did not* think the investment was wise.	The analyst thought the investment was unwise.	Put negative statements in a positive form.
Descending from the parapet wall, he observed a trailing antenna.	He observed a dangling antenna descending from the parapet wall.	A participle phrase must refer to the subject, or the sentence must be reworded.
He *affected* the transaction quickly.	He *effected* the transaction quickly.	*Effect* means *to accomplish* or *to bring about.*
This approach had the desired *affect.*	This approach had the desired *effect.*	*Effect* can also mean *result* or *to influence.*

TABLE 1 **Phrases and Expressions to Avoid *(continued)***

Poor Usage	Preferred	Comment
The report concerned the *affect* of interest...	The report concerned the *effect* of interest...	
His conclusions were *effected* by the structural problems.	His conclusions were *affected* by the structural problems.	*Affect* also means to influence.
The draperies were *flammable.*	The draperies were *inflammable.*	*Inflammable* means combustible.
No agreement has as yet been reached.	No agreement has been reached.	More succinct
First,...; secondly,...; thirdly,...	First,...; second,...; third,...	Either first or firstly is acceptable, but if you begin with first, do not continue with secondly.
The deadline requirement made her *overly* tired.	The deadline requirement made her *over* tired.	Do not add *ly* to such words as much or over.
The ground *lessors* position was subordinated to the first mortgage.	The ground *lessor's* position was subordinated to the first mortgage.	Watch out for singular and plural use of apostrophes in possessives.
I *mean to* comply with the subpoena.	I *intend to* comply with the subpoena.	Slang
One of the most beautiful settings is in Lausanne.	Lausanne has a most beautiful setting.	*One of the most* is greatly overworked.
An *exhausting* search of sales was made.	An *exhaustive* search of sales was made.	I've seen no physical collapses as a result of a sales search.
The appraiser *arrived at an estimate* of the market value.	The appraiser *estimated* the market value or *concluded that...*	Use the active voice.
Being that the mortgage came due...	*Because* or *since* the mortgage came due...	To introduce clauses of reason, purpose, or result, use since or because.
Taxwise, the decision to appeal was correct.	*Based on tax considerations,* the decision to appeal was correct.	A colloquialism; avoid adding *wise* to nouns.
I'd like *for him* to use the Inwood Tables.	*I'd like him to...* or *I 'd prefer* he use the Inwood Tables.	*For him* is incorrect. The words to or for are never expressed when a word functions as an indirect object.
The multistory buildings *comprise* a unique complex.	The multistory buildings *compose* a unique complex.	*Comprise* is to embrace, contain. *Compose* is to make up or constitute.
He was a production-*oriented* developer.	He was primarily interested in development.	Hackneyed expression
He is an appraiser *who* is ambitious for office.	The appraiser is ambitious for office. or He is an appraiser ambitious for office.	*Who* is unnecessary to the syntax.
The question *as to* whether the layout should be altered...	The question whether the layout should be altered...	Omit needless words.
This is a subject property that has no real estate market.	The subject property has no real estate market.	
Owing *to the fact that* rehabilitation was not feasible...	*Since* rehabilitation was not feasible... or *Because* rehabilitation was not feasible	*To the fact that* is awkward and excess verbiage.
The lender calls your attention *to the fact that...*	The lender notifies you... or The lender informs you...	
All the MAIs were *not* present.	*Not* all the MAIs were present.	Modifiers preferably should be next to the word they modify.
The appraiser *only* found two sales.	The appraiser found *only* two sales.	
Advise the client by telephone in London that the purchase has been completed for only $5.00.	For only $5.00, you can advise the client in London by telephone that the purchase has been completed.	Keep related words and phrases together.
Like I said in the comparable sales analysis,...	*As* I said in the comparable sales analysis,...	Never use *like* before a phrase or clause; a historically illiterate use.
It all boils down to, or it all comes down to...	The result is, in the end,,...	Slang

Appendix E

Excerpt from *Writing Appraisal Reports*

The following is an excerpt from the book *Writing Appraisal Reports* by William C. Himstreet, originally published by the American Institute of Real Estate Appraisers in 1974.

Chapter III

On Using the Right Words

The process of communication involves the development of a message at the transmitting source, the transmission of the message, the reception of the message by the receiver, and the interpretation of the message by the receiving party. In communication theory, the development of the message is called "encoding." The interpretation of the message is called "decoding."

Encoding - Transmitting - Receiving - Decoding

Communication can be disrupted or fail in any of the four basic steps. In oral communication, for example, encoding takes place in the speaker's mind, transmitting occurs primarily through his voice, receiving is effected through the listener's hearing apparatus, and decoding takes place in the listener's mind.

If we have a limited vocabulary or select misleading words, the encoding is poor. Noise or other distractions could disrupt transmission and reception. Poor decoding can occur when the listener's interpretation of words is different from the speaker's.

People think and speak many times as fast as they write. As a result, transmission may differ tremendously from thoughts. And unlike oral communication, when a written message arrives at its destination, the sender is not present to assist in the decoding process. He cannot restate things in other words if the reader does not understand as can be done in face-to-face communication. Thus, written communication becomes far more difficult than other forms.

Rely on Simple Words

Simple, common words are more useful than long, complicated ones because the common word is more likely to be understood, it takes less time to write and read, and it calls less attention to writing style.

Compare the words in the left column with their more common, simple equivalents in the right column:

interrogate	ask
consummate	fulfill, complete
approximately	about
utilize	use
cognizant	aware
modification	change
compensate	pay
ameliorate	ease, improve
initiate	begin

If something will "mitigate the condition," do all people understand that "mitigate" means to ease the condition and to cause it to become less severe. Chances are good that a great many people would interpret the phrase to mean just the opposite—to become more severe.

The test to apply in word selection is: "Will the reader understand the meaning?" Technical jargon from various professions is particularly confusing to outsiders, so in reports prepared for nonprofessionals, the professional defines unusual terms or seeks easily understood synonyms. The word "frog" has over twenty meanings in American usage, some very specific and meaningful to people in certain business or parts of the country. In many cases, it could be replaced by a more meaningful word or phrase. Therefore, the admonition to seek the short, simple word is not a universal rule. Very often, the long word is far more meaningful.

Avoid Insincere, Emotionally Charged Words

Because the appraisal represents the most objective treatment the appraiser can apply to the estimation of value, his report should be written in objective language. Here are some words that we have a strong inclination to use frequently, yet are not objective and may lead to various interpretations by readers:

good	amazingly
bad	perfect
beautiful	
superior	
wonderful	
marvelous	
tremendous	
absolutely	
exactly	

Use "Weasel" Words Carefullv

Much has been said about the use of "weasel" words in reports. The word "weasel" as used here comes from its implication that one can weasel his way out of something.

When your data are being analyzed, you believe they lead to a certain conclusion. In stating the conclusion, you are pretty much restricted to saying one of the following:

The data prove
The data indicate
The data suggest
The data point toward

Although this section uses data as a plural word, modern usage permits it to be used either as singular or plural. Words such as *indicate, suggest,* and *point* are "weasel" words. *Prove,* of course, isn't a weasel word at all. It should be used only when the data really *prove* something. The others should be used to suggest to the reader how strongly one is willing to stand behind his findings.

Avoid Worn-Out Expressions

Expressions that are used over and over again in business soon lose their impact and risk a negative reaction.

6

When someone pays for a service, he expects to receive more than a set of over-used cliches. Here are some to consider with their modern equivalents:

Worn-Out	*Modern*
According to our records	Simply omit the phrase and continue.
Pursuant to your request; Per your request	As you requested
At an early date	Soon, promptly, or the exact date
At this time, at the present at this writing	Now
Attached please find	Attached is
Enclosed herewith	Enclosed
I have your letter	Omit. It's obvious.
Please do not hesitate	Please
Please contact me	Please let me know
Hereto, herewith, hereby, above mentioned, same, hereinafter	All are legal terms. Omit or state in layman's language.
Of recent date	Use the specific date
Wish to say, would like to say	If you wish to or would like to, why not just go ahead and say it.
Under separate cover	State how you are sending the material.
The undersigned	Me or I

As an example of what can be done with word selection leading to elimination of worn-out expressions, note the differences in the following pairs of sentences:

A. Pursuant to your request, I enclose herewith the report on the ABC property.
   The report you requested on the ABC property is enclosed.
B. If I can be of further assistance, please do not hesitate to contact me.
   If I can be of further help, please let me know.
C. I want to take this opportunity to thank you for giving me your assistance.
   Thank you for your help.
D. We hope you will avail yourself of the opportunity to use our services in the future.
   We look forward to serving you again
E. This will acknowledge receipt of your letter of June 10.
   Thank you for your letter of June 10.
F. Enclosed herewith please find a check in the amount of $10.
   A check for $10 is enclosed.

Use Words Economically

Although the previous section dealt with the elimination of worn-out words or the substitution of modern equivalents, writing can be made even more concise by avoiding redundancies. A redundant expression is one containing a word which unnecessarily repeats the idea expressed in another word. Here are some examples with the desirable expression on the right:

approximately about	approximately *or* about
consensus of opinion	consensus *or* opinion
period of time	period *or* time
whether or not	whether
important essentials	essentials
basic fundamentals	basics *or* fundamentals
exact same	same
full and complete	full *or* complete
personal opinion	opinion
refer back to	refer to
true facts	facts *or* truth
each and every	each *or* every

Most redundancies could use one or two words to express the same idea. Here are other common expressions that can be presented in fewer words even though they are not redundancies:

as of this date	now, yet, still
at the present time	now
a total of $450	$450
be kind enough	please, kindly
during the time while we	while we
in the neighborhood of	about
in reference to	about
in order to	to
for the purpose of	to
subsequent to	after
under date of	of
due to the fact that	because, due to, since
in view of the fact that	since
substantial segment of the population	many people
not in a position to	unable to
provide for the establishment of	establish
by means of	by
with the exception of	except, except for
in the event of	if
in the vicinity of	near, about
in the amount of	for
at the present time	now
along the lines of	like
for the purpose of	to
in view of the fact that	since, because
inasmuch as	because
from the standpoint of	for, to
in the near future	soon
at the cost of	for
for the reason that	because
the method by which	how
despite the fact that	although
in view of the above	therefore, so

in addition to	and, besides
give consideration to	consider
provide for the addition of	add

Other word economies can be effected by omitting words or ideas that can be implied or that are obvious without saying. For example:

> The property boundaries were checked and found to be accurate.

If they were found to be accurate, the boundaries were obviously checked. The checking, then can be implied as in:

> The property boundaries are accurate. (The property boundaries were found to be accurate.)

Frequently we overlook the effective use of adjectives and adverbs as word economy devices. Notice how the change of word form permits economy in the following pairs of sentences:

1. The site is located in a section of the shopping district, and it is a corner parcel.
   The corner-parcel site is in a shopping district.
2. He wrote a report that was up to date.
   He wrote an up-to-date report.
3. The forecast was prepared on a long-range basis.
   It was a long-range forecast.
4. Omit the expressions which have no use.
   Omit useless expressions.
5. The items were arranged in order of rank.
   The items were arranged in rank order.
6. We found twelve offices that were vacant.
   We found twelve vacant offices.

Use Specific Words

Because words are subject to a variety of interpretations, clearer understanding may be achieved by using specifics rather than generalities. For example:

1. The area has a moderate average temperature.
   The area has an average temperature of 64°.
2. Income on investment is good.
   Income on investment averages 12%.
3. The lease expires soon.
   The lease expires on December 31.

The choice of words has much to do with concise writing. People who can express themselves in fewer words than others are admired and usually acquire reputations as being those who "come right to the point." In effect, then, concise use of language reflects clear thinking. Such books as Stuart Chase's, ***The Power of Words***, deal extensively with the role of words in communication.

Chapter IV

On Good Composition

Most adults have vocabularies of 4,000 to 6,000 words. In the expression of a simple idea, the mind sorts through these thousands of words and selects and places some of them in sequence before directing the vocal or writing apparatus to transmit them.

The mind operating at random could select *any* words among the 4,000 to 6,000 and the possible combinations would run into the millions. Putting the right words into the correct sequence multiplies the millions of combinations many times more. Thus the gift of language is a process that is overwhelmingly complex.

People abuse language and create communication problems by taking this gift for granted and by failing to work to improve language skills.

Sentence Length

A good rule to follow in writing is to limit a sentence to one idea. Short sentences, like short words, are easy to read, but because a sentence is a group of words expressing an idea, it must be long enough to do the job. Most business writing authorities recommend an *average* length of 16 to 25 words. Some sentences may use only one or two words, such as "Stop!" or "I do," and others may use 40 to 50 words to express the idea. The important thing is that the average sentence length be in the desired range. The appraiser can check his own writing against this criterion by occasionally averaging the length of five or six consecutive sentences. If the average is much above 25, the reading level may be difficult. If the average is below 16, the level may be so simple that the typical adult reader will lose interest.

An average sentence length of 16 to 25 words indicates writing at a reading difficulty level between the eighth and twelfth grade (the typical adult reading levels). Most magazines and newspapers are written at that level of reading difficulty. An old set of income tax instructions illustrates a sentence written at about the sixtieth grade level of reading difficulty:

> In the case of individuals other than farmers, if 80% of the tax determined without regard to credits for taxes withheld on tax free government bonds and for income tax withheld on wages, exceeds the estimated tax increased by such credits, and in the case of farmers, if 66 2/3% of the tax, determined without regard to such credits exceeds the estimated tax, increased by such credits, there shall be added to the tax an amount equal to such excess or equal to 6 percent of the amount by which the tax so determined exceeds the estimated tax, so increased, whichever is the lesser.

The reading difficulty could be reduced by treating farmers in a separate sentence. Further clarity could be achieved, of course, by starting over. Essentially, the sentence says that 80% of the tax should have been paid by the filing date. If not, the taxpayer is subject to a 6% penalty on the difference between 80% and the amount already paid.

Sentence Construction

The natural order of a sentence is (1) subject, (2) predicate, (3) object, and (4) modifiers. The most readable construction is normally a subject followed by a verb, followed by additional words that are necessary for the thought.

The subject of the sentence receives the reader's greatest attention. What the subject is or does is the second item of interest. Thus, in formulating sentences, primary focus should be upon these two parts. Very often, however, the reader is not considered. In the following sentence, typical of those found in many appraisal reports, the first subject and verb are not the ones of most importance to the client:

> This analysis indicated a market value of $47,000 for the property.

Analysis is the subject and *indicated* is the verb. Neither word is as important to the reader as is the value of the property. An improved sentence would be:

> A market value of $47,000 was indicated by this analysis.

In the second sentence *market value* became the subject; in the first sentence "market value" was the *object*. The sentence was revised by simply reversing the subject and object.

An *active* verb denotes action, and all verbs are active except those derived from "to be" such as *is, was, were, have been*. Active verbs are supposed to make writing more interesting, and as a bonus, they often make sentences shorter. The three sentences below state the same thing:

1. It was estimated that 2,000 were in attendance at the open house.
2. About 2,000 attended the open house.
3. The open house was attended by about 2,000.

Sentence 1 has the passive *was* as the verb, but the subject, *it* really doesn't refer to anything. In Sentence 2, the subject is 2,000—much more significant—and the active verb *attended* shows people doing something. In Sentence 3, the subject is *open house*, followed by the passive *was*, and *2,000* is the object. Most sentences can be recast similarly to make the most important thing to the reader the subject.

First person voice is a grammatical term used to describe a style of writing in which the person doing the writing or speaking is the subject. Third person describes the style when the subject is the person or thing being written or spoken about.

Because professional reports should sound as objective as possible, pronouns such as *I* and *we*, are avoided. Instead of, "I analyzed recent sales prices on three nearby comparable properties," a preferred form would be: "The appraiser analyzed recent sales prices . . ." Some appraisers might hold that this construction sounds too stiff and formal. Other ways are available to avoid the use of *I:*

Using the pronoun: I analyzed recent sales prices on three nearby comparable properties.

Using the substitute: The appraiser analyzed recent sales . . .

Recasting the sentence: Recent sales prices on three nearby comparable properties were analyzed.

or

An analysis was made of recent sales . . .

The recast sentences avoided *I* and the substitute for *I,* but also incorporated the passive *were or was.* To incorporate an active verb, i.e., get along without the passives, and say something about what the analysis showed, one might write:

> An analysis of sales prices of three nearby comparable properties showed an average price of $27.50 per square foot.

In this revision, *analysis* is the subject, the active verb is *showed,* and the object is the price. Thus, "the *analysis showed $27.50,*" puts the core of the sentence into three items. The rest of the words are modifying terms to improve clarity. In addition, including a finding makes one sentence accomplish what would otherwise require two. Neither *I* nor *the appraiser* was necessary.

Sentence construction principles to be drawn from the previous discussion are:

1. An average sentence length of 16 to 25 words is desirable.
2. The natural sequence of subject, predicate, object is preferable for most sentences.
3. Use active verbs, whenever possible, to retain the reader's interest.
4. Use passive or active voice and first or third person to best advantage in writing to the reader's interests.

Varying Sentence Structure

Limiting sentences to one idea and at the same time keeping them short can lead to a report that is monotonous and choppy. Good writers vary sentence structure to avoid such shortcomings, sometimes through use of *compound* sentences, composed of two or more independent clauses. That is, compound sentences consist of two sentences joined by a conjunction or by special punctuation. For example:

> The site contains just over 20,000 square feet, but it would not be suitable by itself for construction of a major office building.

In the sentence, two independent thoughts have been joined by the conjunction *but.* A comma should precede the conjunction. Closely related ideas should be joined in compound sentences occasionally, particularly if the sentence will not be excessively long.

A *complex* sentence is one containing an independent clause and a dependent one, as in the following:

> Although it contains over 20,000 square feet, the site would not be suitable by itself for construction of a major office building.

In this example, the clause, "Although it contains over 20,000 square feet," is dependent on the rest of the sentence for its meaning. *Although* is a valuable word for beginning sentences with contrary ideas. For instance, "Although only two comparable property sales were found, the market approach was given heaviest consideration."

A variation of the *compound* and *complex* sentences is the sentence with a single subject and two verbs:

> The site contains just over 20,000 square feet but would not be suitable by itself for construction of a major office building.

Transitional words and phrases connect a sentence or paragraph to the rest of the composition. Some words and phrases which can be used at the beginning of sentences to add variety and to show the relationship of the idea to one preceding it include:

however	in addition
therefore	additionally
nevertheless	also
on the other hand	furthermore
at the same time	consequently

A sentence may even begin with *and,* but only rarely! Places where connectives will help may be detected by reading the written product aloud.

Developing Paragraphs

A paragraph is a group of sentences developing an idea. In general, a paragraph consists of a topic sentence, supporting details, and a summary or transitional sentence. The typical reader prefers short paragraphs, and short paragraphs can assist in report interpretation. As a general rule, a paragraph longer than six lines increases reading difficulty. In double-spaced typewritten material, paragraphs can be longer because they look less crowded whereas in publications such as this one, paragraphing will probably approximate the proper English rules. In any case, the way paragraphs are developed affects reader understanding.

Not all paragraphs begin with a topic sentence, as the following examples illustrate:

A. The building trend in the area may be described as improving. The Federal office building was built in 1962, Macy's department store in 1964, and the American savings and loan headquarters in 1967. In 1970 the Town and Country high-rise apartment development was completed, as were the Prudential, Commonwealth, Mutual Life, and Tishman office buildings.

B. Among newer construction, the Federal office building was built in 1962, Macy's in 1964, and the American savings and loan headquarters in 1967. The

10

Town and Country high-rise apartment development, and the Prudential, Commonwealth, Mutual Life, and Tishman buildings were all completed in 1970. The building trend in the area may be described as improving.

Paragraph A begins with the topic sentence, supported by the details following. The paragraph is said to be organized deductively, i.e., presenting the general statement first and following with the details. Paragraph B, inductive organization, presents the detailed data first and concludes with the topic statement which essentially summarizes what has been said.

For most report writing, the deductive plan is preferred. It saves the reader time by telling him what the remainder of the paragraph is all about. The inductive plan is a good one to follow when proving a point, because it follows more closely the process the appraiser followed in arriving at a conclusion.

Putting Paragraphs Together

Arranging paragraphs for the finished composition is really not difficult, with a good outline to serve as a guide and appropriate content for each item in the outline.

If some paragraphs are quite long, general remarks may be appropriate both at the beginning and at the end, i.e., both topic and summary sentences may be helpful. Connectives will provide transition between sentences and transition between major sections of the report will be accomplished by subheadings that inform the reader that he is coming to something new or different.

Making Important Ideas Stand Out

Readers pay more attention to the subject of the sentence and to the topic sentences of paragraphs than to other parts of the composition. Therefore several ways to assure that important ideas stand out are the following:

1. Use important ideas as subjects and stress those ideas in topic sentences.
2. Use specific language. Rather than "several buildings have recently been completed," name them and the dates.
3. Use a single-sentence paragraph or even a single line to illustrate an important thought.
4. Use active verbs to bring the reader into the action.
5. Say very directly, "This is important," through a leading phrase such as:

   Most important . . .
   Primarily . . .
   Significantly . . .
6. Organize findings to put important ideas first. All too often the report writer believes his report should be like a movie script and build up to a smashing climax. On the contrary, most readers of reports are selective and read what they want to read.

Using Talking Headings

Typical report headings such as "Introduction," "Findings," "Conclusion" are useful to break the report into parts, but they are not descriptive or active. Each, of course, names the following section, but none tells anything about the significance of the section. Compare these two headings:

The Neighborhood
The Neighborhood Is Growing

If the area is actually growing, telling the reader so in the heading would lead him to expect to find evidence of the growth in your report. A "talking" heading is a favor to the reader, who will appreciate the effort to make the report alive and interesting.

Chapter V

Writing Techniques

Some finer points concerning writing techniques are worth reviewing.

Avoiding Expletives

An expletive, something added to fill out a sentence, frequently can be avoided, leading to a better piece of writing. Note the following sentence:

> There are nine other major buildings in the block.

The sentence is quite clear and meaningful, but the subject of the sentence is "*there*." No one has ever seen, felt, or heard of a "there." The better construction would be:

> Nine other major buildings are in the block.

The subject is "buildings," as it should be. The tendency to use expletives is common, but for some the use can become a habit which contributes to lackluster, ambiguous writing.

Related to the "there" type writer is the "It is believed . . ." writer, as in:

> It was assumed that current public transportation facilities would remain.

In this sentence, "It" is the subject. Unfortunately, "It" is a pronoun, and in this case, it had no antecedent to tell what is referred to. The sentence would be better written this way:

> Continuation of current public transportation facilities was assumed.

Sentences beginning, "there are," and "it is," are not descriptive when the pronouns don't refer to anything. By reorganizing the thought, the real subject may be found and used.

Writing Clear Definitions

Basic to effective report writing is a definition of those terms which might be unfamiliar to the reader. Definitions are easy to write if the three parts of a definition are understood—the *term* being defined, the *family* to which the term belongs, and the *differentiation* that separates the term from other members of the family. In the following definition, *United States* is the term, *country* is the family, and the *geographic location* forms the differentiation:

> The United States is a country bordered on the south by Mexico and on the north by Canada.

Modifying terms could be added to expand the definition as in:

> The United States is a western hemisphere republic . . .

In appraisal reports, *market value* generally warrants definition because it is a member of the family of appraisal terms and carries with it a distinctive differentiation.

Using Tabulations

The tabulation technique enables the report writer to enumerate items which might otherwise contribute to long sentences and focuses the reader's attention on each item. For example:

> Depreciation may be one or all of three kinds: Physical deterioration or the physical wearing out of the property; functional obsolescence or lack of desirability in terms of layout, style, and design as compared with a new property serving the same function; economic obsolescence resulting in a loss of value from causes outside the property itself.

Tabulate each of the three items, and the result is:

> Depreciation may be one or all of three kinds:
> 1. Physical deterioration or the physical wearing out of the property.
> 2. Functional obsolescence or lack of desirability in terms of layout, style, and design . . .
> 3. Economic obsolescence resulting in a loss . . .

The numbering of items improves the concept of three kinds and makes each easier to understand.

Using Parallel Construction

To express ideas of the same relative importance, state them in similar form. This technique, called parallel construction, simplifies relationships. The following sentence violates the principle of parallel construction:

> We are going to the mountains to go hunting, hike, and to swim.

Revised:

> We are going to the mountains to hunt, to hike, and to swim.
>
> We are going to the mountains to hunt, hike, and swim.
>
> We are going to the mountains to go hunting, hiking, and swimming.

The revised sentences place the three activities in parallel terms. The following sentence also violates parallel construction:

> The purposes of this appraisal were to estimate the market value of the property and determining the basis for underwriting a loan.

Revised:

> The purposes of this appraisal were *to estimate* the market value of the property and *to determine* the basis for underwriting a loan.

In the revised version each of the purposes begins with the same kind of phrase. Typically, errors in parallel construction occur in long lists of tabulated items. To check the parallel construction of lists, read the first

12

two or three words in each item. The ones not parallel will become readily apparent.

Using Proper Tense

A difference between passive voice and verb tense in report writing might take the following form:

It was assumed . . .

or

It is assumed . . .

Very simply, because the appraiser made the assumption during analysis and before sitting down to write, the past tense, *was*, is correct.

Anything the appraiser did prior to writing is past—so past tense is correct. Anything to which the report calls attention, as in "the data shows," is present tense. On the other hand, if the reader is informed that later in the report he *will* see certain information, the future tense should be used. A reader also may be reminded that a previous page *showed* something, calling for the past tense. Anything prior to writing is past, anything during the writing is present, and anything anticipated is future.

Using Accurate Pronouns

One of the leading demons contributing to lack of clarity in reports is the faulty pronoun reference. Use of *those, their, these, its, above-mentioned* and similar pronouns may mislead the reader as to which previous noun the pronoun refers.

For example, "Procedures have been changed. These are the cause of . . ." requires a noun after *these* to assure clearness. The second sentence might read, "*These changes* are the cause of . . ." thus assuring accurate pronoun reference, and increasing understanding.

If a pronoun reference is not clear, repeat the noun even if it seems repetitious.

Don't Rely on Headings for Meaning

A report should be understandable even with all headings and subheadings removed. Thus, the first few words after a heading ordinarily will be repetitious of the heading, as they are *not* in this example:

Cost Data

This was gathered . . .

If the heading were removed, the next sentence would not be clear because *this* had no antecedent. Therefore, write the sentence as though the heading were not included:

Cost Data

Cost data was gathered . . .

Using Documentation

Because appraisal reports are typically original work, formal documentation in the form of footnotes and bibliography references is not critical. However, for legal purposes, the appraiser is responsible for identifying sources of information. To be unable to recall a source of information can be embarrassing when asked to do so in court. Because appraisals are often made many months before the appraiser is called on to testify, the need for documentation in appraisal reports is even greater.

One good way to document a report is to attach a schedule of interviews and dates as an addendum to the report. An appraiser's own conclusion or opinion about the appraisal may be qualified by using words such as *in my opinion*. This opinion is, of course, the nearest thing to fact, because the appraiser is recognized as a professional in appraising, just as a doctor, lawyer, and Certified Public Accountant are considered authoritative in their fields.

Three types of statements only partially based on facts may be made in reports. First, *opinions* are statements based on a combination of the professional's experience and whatever data is available.

Judgments are statements about the good or bad of something. To compare the appraised property with a nearby property and make a statement such as "This property is better than . . . ", the statement should be preceded with "in my judgment." To judge good or bad is to go beyond the limits of data. A scientist may discover a relationship between smoking and lung diseases by stating the frequency with which smokers incur lung ailments compared with nonsmokers. But when he says smoking is bad, he is stating his judgment, and should say so.

An *inference* is similar to an opinion and a judgment because it is a statement about the unknown based on the known. An appraiser uses all the evidence at his command in arriving at a conclusion, and to go beyond a conclusion to predict what will happen in the future is an inference. Such a statement should be prefaced with a phrase such as "This data infers" or "The inference may be made . . ." to qualify the prediction.

Similarly, the source of data about neighboring properties should be identified in language such as, "The following data, gathered from managers of four nearby comparable properties, shows . . ."

Two methods of citing documents as sources of information are generally used. The first, of course, is the typical footnote at the bottom of the page, simply placing the number, slightly raised above the line of writing following the sentence containing the cited information. The identification of the document—author, title, publisher, and date—is placed at the bottom of the page. If a page number from the document is cited because of a quote or paraphrase, the page number should follow the date, as in:

[1]William C. Himstreet and Wayne M. Baty, *Business Communications,* Third Edition, Wadsworth Publishing Company (Belmont, California), 1969. page 203.

The second method is to place the number in parentheses (1) after the cited material and to identify the documented items in numeric order on a separate page in the addenda. This arrangement does away with the problem of arranging a page so the footnote will fit at the bottom.

Appendix F

Common Grammar and Style Pitfalls in Appraisal Reports

The following examples have been taken from actual appraisal reports and are intended to illustrate common grammar and style errors.

Example 1

Original Text

The tenant originally had three consecutive ten year renewal terms. The tenant is currently in its' second renewal.

Issues

- Technically, the *tenant* did not have renewal terms. The *lease* contained the renewals.
- When words or numbers are used to modify another word, a hyphen should be used (ten-year renewal terms).
- The use of *its'* is not proper; this is not a word. The form of *it* that shows possession is *its* (no apostrophe). Note that another common use of the word *it* is *it's*. This is the contraction form meaning "it is."

Example 2

Original Text

The subject is located in an established location and serves the local population living in its immediate trade area. It has good physical characteristics that would allow it to compete adequately in the local marketplace.

Issues

- In the first sentence, the use of multiple variations of the word *local* is repetitive.
- In the second sentence, the term *good* is vague and should be replaced with a more descriptive adjective. A phrase such as "located on a high-traffic arterial in a desirable, affluent neighborhood" is preferable.
- Also in the second sentence, including the word *would* places the sentence in the conditional tense, which is unnecessary. Removing *would* gives the sentence a more active tone.

Example 3

Original Text

With few exceptions, this area is fully developed. Overall, the commercial real estate market in this area can be characterized as being stable. In summary, the subject's neighborhood is characterized as an established area in Plainville. This area will likely continue to be vital as economic forces improve in the region. On balance, we are optimistic with our outlook for the immediate area.

Issues

- The use of the word *area* five times in one paragraph is excessive. Synonyms should be used, or the sentences should be restructured.
- Similarly, the use of *characterized* in two consecutive sentences is unnecessarily repetitive. Using synonyms or restructuring the sentences can help the writer avoid needless repetition of words.
- The second sentence is an example of excessive wordiness. This should be replaced with something more succinct, such as "Overall, the commercial real estate market in this area is stable."

Example 4

Original Text

The Rutland Mall occupies a large tract of land on the southwest corner of Route 79 and Route 10. The subject property is located within the mall property on an internal street known as Ring Road. This is accessible off Route 79. Route 79 is the primary north-south corridor serving this area of Plum County. The subject property is situated approximately four miles south of the Metro Expressway and Eisenhower Parkway, and one mile north of the Southern Expressway.

Route 79 is one of the busiest roadways in the region, as it is the focal point of an established office subdistrict, a vast industrial district, and a significant retail district. At the subject's location, Route 79 is a six-lane roadway controlled by traffic lights. This is a connecting road between the south and north regions of the county that runs parallel to the Plum County/Orange County border. Route 10 is an east-west roadway providing linkage between Metro City and Farmington. This is a very busy road, and it is a divided highway, providing two lanes of traffic in each direction. The subject property has good access and visibility from a regional standpoint.

Issues

- Words such as *vast* that connote extremes or are emotionally charged should be avoided. (Other examples of such words are *astonishing, ideal, tremendous,* and *fabulous*). Use of less "flowery" adjectives such as *sizable* or *substantial* is preferred. Even better, an estimate of the actual size of the district allows the reader to judge its significance more directly.
- Many of the sentences are brief and result in a "choppy" paragraph flow. Combining the ideas presented using conjunctions or other means would improve this paragraph.
- The paragraph is very long, which is not appealing to readers. It should be broken down into multiple paragraphs structured around individual concepts, as shown in the following improved version.

Improved Text

The Rutland Mall occupies a large tract of land on the southwest corner of Route 79 and Route 10. The subject property is located within the mall property, on an internal street known as Ring Road. Given the site's elevation and proximity to Routes 79 and 10, the subject is highly visible from these two high-traffic arterials.

Access to the property is provided by Route 79, a primary north-south arterial in this section of Plum County. Industrial and commercial uses dominate this corridor. Commercial uses include various low- and mid-rise office and retail structures, and over 10,000,000 square feet of industrial uses are concentrated in the area.

Route 10 is a major east-west divided highway that supports two lanes of traffic in each direction between Metro City and Farmington. Metro Expressway and Eisenhower Parkway (four miles north of the subject) and Southern Expressway (one mile south) are other major thoroughfares in the area.

Example 5

Original Text

The highway network in Rand County provides easy access to Grandville. The Central Parkway is located just east of Grandville, and the Northern and Southern Expressways are respectively four to five miles north and south of Grandville. The primary north/south roadways in the subject's immediate area include Merilon Avenue, John August Boulevard, and Clinton Avenue. The primary east/west roadways include Stanley Avenue, Greenwood Turnpike, and New City Road.

The subject is located within a defined industrial-business district within Grandville. It has good access and is easily accessible from the local streets.

Issues

- The use of the town's name (Grandville) with such frequency is excessive. The sentences should be restructured to eliminate the need for repeating the name, or "the town" can be used once the name is initially provided.
- In the last sentence, two variations of the word *access* is needlessly repetitive.

Example 6

Original Text

We have been provided by Goldman Properties, Inc., with the terms of the ground lease with the Port Authority of New City, which was amended and restated on July 16, 2001. Annual ground rent and PILOT payments to the Port Authority are calculated based on base rent and an amount equal to the applicable percentage of the amount of Gross Revenues for such full or partial year.

Issues

- The first sentence is written in the passive voice. To recast this sentence in the active voice, the subject of the sentence needs to be performing the action: "Goldman Properties, Inc., provided the terms of the ground lease..."
- The first sentence runs on and should be separated into two sentences. In general, sentences averaging 16 to 25 words are recommended. An improved rewording of this sentence (including recasting it in the active voice) is: "Goldman Properties, Inc., provided the terms of the ground lease with the Port Authority of New City. The lease was amended and restated on July 16, 2001."

- Capitalizing *gross revenues* is inappropriate since this is not a proper noun.
- The second sentence is confusing, and it is not made clear to the reader exactly how the rent is calculated.

Example 7

Original Text

The major elements of comparison used to value the subject site include the property rights conveyed, the financial terms incorporated into the transaction, the conditions or motivations surrounding the sale, changes in market conditions since the sale, the location of the real estate, and the property's utility and physical characteristics.

Issues

Including a list of items within the body text makes it difficult for the reader to identify and comprehend the individual components. For items that are not necessarily in a sequence, the use of indented bullets is a preferred method of presentation, as shown in the following rewrite.

Improved Text

The major elements of comparison used to value the subject site include:

- The property rights conveyed
- The financial terms incorporated into the transaction
- The conditions or motivations surrounding the sale
- Changes in market conditions since the sale
- The location of the real estate
- The property's utility and physical characteristics

Example 8

Original Text

By analyzing sales that qualify as arm's-length transactions between willing and knowledgeable buyers and sellers, we can identify value and price trends. The basic steps of this approach are:

1. Research recent, relevant property sales and current offerings in the competitive area;
2. Select and analyze properties that are similar to the subject property, analyzing changes in economic conditions that may have occurred between the sale date and the date of value, and other physical, functional, or locational factors;

3. Identify sales that include favorable financing and calculate the cash-equivalent price;
4. Reduce the sale prices to a common unit of comparison, such as price per square foot of rentable area, effective gross income multiplier, or net income per square foot;
5. Make appropriate comparative adjustments to the prices of the comparable properties to relate them to the subject property; and
6. Interpret the adjusted sales data and draw a logical value conclusion.

Issues

The use of a list is desirable when several items are being discussed that belong in a specific sequence. In this instance, however, the report's visual appeal is compromised by the lack of indentation. The attractiveness of the sequence is improved by setting it apart from the body text as follows in the improved version.

Improved Text

By analyzing sales that qualify as arm's-length transactions between willing and knowledgeable buyers and sellers, we can identify value and price trends. The basic steps of this approach are:

1. Research recent, relevant property sales and current offerings in the competitive area;
2. Select and analyze properties that are similar to the subject property, analyzing changes in economic conditions that may have occurred between the sale date and the date of value as well as other physical, functional, or locational factors;
3. Identify sales that include favorable financing and calculate the cash-equivalent price;
4. Reduce the sale prices to a common unit of comparison such as price per square foot of rentable area, effective gross income multiplier, or net income per square foot;
5. Make appropriate comparative adjustments to the prices of the comparable properties to relate them to the subject property; and
6. Interpret the adjusted sales data and draw a logical value conclusion.

Example 9

Original Text

Currently, the overall Adams County residential lot market is supply-sided, with supply outweighing demand in the subject's market as available inventory increases as a cooling has occurred as the subject's market corrects from a high demand in early- to mid-2005.

Issues

- Care must be taken to avoid confusing the reader when using jargon, industry-specific phrases, and market-specific terminology. In this instance, it appears that the writer is conveying that excess supply is apparent. It is better to state that oversupply exists than to use a term (*supply-sided*) that can be misinterpreted.
- The use of the word *subject's* twice in the same sentence is repetitive.
- This is a run-on sentence containing several independent thoughts and unnecessary repetition of the word *as*. An improved rewriting follows in the improved text.

Improved Text

The Adams County residential lot market is currently oversupplied. Demand decreased beginning in mid- to late-2005, when numerous subdivisions entered the market.

Example 10

Original Text

The XYZ Corporation (the major tenant) is seeking to reduce their space in the building by 20,000 square feet.

Issues

The proper pronoun must be selected when referring to single or collective nouns. In this instance, *its* should be used in place of *their*.

Example 11

Original Text

This is the sale of multiple parcels of land with frontage on Town Center Road, Stevenson Avenue, and Ventura Highway. This was an off-market transaction.

Issues

While it is acceptable to use certain industry-specific terms in documents such as appraisal reports, it is critical that the meaning of any such jargon be clearly understood and widely used within the industry. In this instance, *off-market* may be used by some, but it would not necessarily be widely recognized or understood by all readers of an appraisal report. If the author's intent is to convey that the property was not publicly or broadly marketed, it is better to state that directly. The author should also inform the reader about the impact of this issue on the transaction.

Example 12

Original Text

The sale was verified with Linda Yantek of Estate Development Company, the seller, on May 21, 2009. Verification with the broker Dan Fine occurred on 5/27/09.

Issues

The date-reference methods are not used consistently, resulting in a sloppy appearance. In addition, it is best to write out the month portion of the date. Using other formats (such as 05/27/09) can lead to misinterpretations depending on the different ordering conventions that prevail in different countries.

Example 13

Original Text

Sales 1–3 are older structures that were not in good condition at the time of sale. The prices indicated by these transactions are at the low end of the comparable range.

Issues

The dash used in the first sentence is intended to replace the word *through* to indicate a range. In general, the use of this symbol to replace the word *to* or *through* is discouraged, since it can sometimes be misinterpreted as a minus sign. Given the potential for miscommunication, writers should spell out *to* and *through* in appraisal reports.

Example 14

Original Text

The gross leasable area of the shopping center is 35,000 sf. The lease was signed on Dec. 9, 2007.

Issues

The use of abbreviations in this example, while not necessarily misleading to the reader, conveys a less-than-professional appearance.

Failure to spell out square feet and similar terms is not proper and should be avoided.

Abbreviations should rarely be used in formally written documents like appraisal reports. It is acceptable to use abbreviations for commonly used and understood words and acronyms such as Mrs., Dr., CPA, or NASDAQ. Abbreviations can also be applied for long terms or names that will be used repeatedly throughout the document, such as USPAP, provided that the abbreviation is properly identified the first time it is used within the document. In most other instances, abbreviations should be used sparingly to avoid confusing the reader and/or compromising the professionalism of the report.

Example 15

Original Text

We modeled all leases in accordance with the lease terms provided by the ownership. None of the tenants are currently in default, and we assume that they will fulfill the obligations of their leases.

Issues

In this case, *none* refers to "not one." As a result, it takes the singular verb, or *is*. This example should read as follows in the improved version.

Improved Text

We modeled all leases in accordance with the lease terms provided by the ownership. None of the tenants is currently in default, and we assume that they will fulfill the obligations of their leases.

Appendix G

Sample Quality Control Audit Checklist

Quality Control Audit Checklist

Auditor Name: __________

Audit Date(s): __________

File No.: __________

Property Name: __________

Property Address: __________

Appraisal Office: __________

Primary Appraiser Name: __________

Other Report Signer(s): __________

QC Reviewer: __________

				Internal Use Only		
Content Items	**Rating**	**Corrective Action?**	**Comments**	**Weighting**	**Wtd. Score**	**Max. Score**
1. Letter of Transmittal						
a. Client, date(s) of value, extraordinary assumptions, hypothetical conditions identified				1	0	0
b. Client title field completed				1	0	0
c. Client file number completed				1	0	0
2. Extraordinary Assumptions & Hypothetical Conditions						
a. Extended lease-up properly addressed				3	0	0
b. Retrospective value properly addressed				3	0	0
c. Proposed construction properly addressed				2	0	0
d. Proposed lease(s) properly addressed				2	0	0
e. Other issues properly addressed				1	0	0
3. Summary of Salient Facts						
a. Data placed in all standard fields				1	0	0
b. Significant assignment/property factors identified				1	0	0
c. Sales history noted and related to value estimate				2	0	0
d. Leasing/occupancy status of subject noted				1	0	0
4. Introduction						
a. Scope matches appraisal problem				1	0	0
b. Sales history/disposition section adequately identifies any sales/significant changes (renovation, leasing status, etc.)				2	0	0
c. Subject sale/contract/listing properly analyzed and related to value conclusion				3	0	0

Content Items	Rating	Corrective Action?	Comments	Internal Use Only Weighting	Wtd. Score	Max. Score
5. Regional & Local Area Analysis						
a. Data up to date; conclusions match data in tables				1	0	0
b. All information relevant to subject property tied together				1	0	0
c. New/competing developments, access, major properties, special/adverse hazards, & changes in area discussed				1	0	0
6. Market Analysis						
a. Conclusion is logical and supported by market data				2	0	0
b. All information relevant to subject property tied together				2	0	0
c. Subject's position within the market or submarket explained; marketability/feasibility discussed				2	0	0
7. Site Description						
a. Physical factors (visibility, topography, etc.) identified				2	0	0
b. No redundant data; title report reviewed				1	0	0
8. Improvements Description						
a. Bldg. use types, amenities adequately described; recent capital expenditures identified				2	0	0
b. Adequate property history (sales, listings, tenancy changes, renovations, etc.)				2	0	0
c. Capital expenditures and/or deferred maintenance issues discussed and tied in with the approaches to value				2	0	0
d. Layout description paints clear picture for the reader				1	0	0
e. Effective age vs. actual age is logical				1	0	0
f. Ample graphics (current photos, site plans, etc.) included for reader's understanding				2	0	0
8. Real Property Taxes & Assessments						
a. Local assessment and billing process provided				1	0	0
b. Any under- or over-assessment on subject discussed				2	0	0
c. Whether a change in assessment warranted and/or likely and whether tax adjustment included in appraisal explained				2	0	0
d. Partial assessment addressed				2	0	0
e. Delinquent taxes addressed				2	0	0
9. Zoning						
a. Permitted uses and zoning requirements identified				2	0	0
b. Subject's conformity with zoning and any impact on marketability or value discussed				2	0	0
10. Highest & Best Use						
a. Conclusion logical given market analysis, zoning write-up, property description, etc.				1	0	0
b. Financial feasibility supported by value estimate, other conclusions in the report				2	0	0
c. If conclusion is "hold for future development," supported with proper market data				2	0	0
d. If conclusion is "continued use," discussion of "as is" value relative to site as vacant included				2	0	0

Content Items	Rating	Corrective Action?	Comments	Weighting	Wtd. Score	Max. Score
				Internal Use Only		
11. Valuation Approaches						
a. Appropriate approaches used, based on scope of work				3	0	0
b. Proper explanation included for any excluded approaches				3	0	0
12. Land Valuation						
a. Proper unit(s) of comparison (per square foot, per unit, etc.) applied				2	0	0
b. Misspellings, formatting, and other errors minimal in comparable sales summaries				2	0	0
c. Proper/reasonable adjustments applied in grid				3	0	0
d. Narrative matches adjustment grid				2	0	0
e. Proper support for per-unit conclusion (not just stating range)				3	0	0
f. Overall adjustments reasonable and suggest true comparability (gross adjustments not too high)				2	0	0
g. Market participant interviews and listings included				2	0	0
13. Cost Approach						
a. Ent. profit and depreciation properly developed given property description, market analysis data				2	0	0
b. External obsolescence properly considered				2	0	0
c. If proposed or new, developer's costs and appraiser's estimate compared				2	0	0
14. Sales Comparison Approach						
a. Proper unit(s) of comparison (per square foot, per unit, etc.) applied				2	0	0
b. Misspellings, formatting, and other errors minimal in comparable sales summaries				2	0	0
c. Proper/reasonable adjustments applied in grid				3	0	0
d. Narrative matches adjustment grid				2	0	0
e. Proper support for per-unit conclusion (not just stated range)				3	0	0
f. Overall adjustments reasonable and suggest true comparability (gross adjustments not too high)				2	0	0
g. Market participant interviews and listings included				2	0	0
15. Income Capitalization Approach						
a. Subject lease(s) properly analyzed (tenant profile, term, space type, etc.)				3	0	0
b. Market rent supported by current subject actual/asking rents, adequate comps., analysis leads reader conclusion				3	0	0
c. Misspellings, formatting, and other errors minimal in comparable rent summaries				2	0	0
d. Confidentiality considered when identifying comparable rentals, expenses				2	0	0
e. Absorption properly substantiated				2	0	0
f. Subject expenses properly analyzed; any variations from historicals in forecast explained				3	0	0
g. Initial *OAR* and *IRR* selections logical given comp. sales/survey data; narrative leads reader to conclusion				3	0	0
h. Residual *OAR* relates properly to the implied going-in *OAR* (not selected *OAR* in direct capitalization method)				3	0	0

Content Items	Rating	Corrective Action?	Comments	Internal Use Only Weighting	Wtd. Score	Max. Score
16. Reconciliation & Final Value Opinion						
a. Various strengths/weaknesses of approaches explained				2	0	0
b. Conclusion to any recent sales or listings of the subject explained				3	0	0
c. Spread among the approaches used is reasonable				2	0	0
17. Addenda						
a. Actual contents match contents page				1	0	0
b. Addenda items legible, add value to the analysis				1	0	0
18. General						
a. Narrative and supporting data lead the reader to the value conclusion				3	0	0
b. Ample maps, pictures, etc. included; comps. properly placed on maps; photos properly labeled				2	0	0
c. Copyright, sourcing, and use permission properly identified				2	0	0
d. Attention to detail (absence of typos, math errors, etc.) adheres to the highest standards				3	0	0
e. Depth of analysis appropriate for report type				3	0	0
f. Grammar and style professional and aligned with standards				2	0	0
g. Sufficient QC review detail applied to identify problems				2	0	0
h. License numbers and states valid; appraiser and all signatories are certified within the subject state				1	0	0
i. Blank pages, headers, and footers				2	0	0
j. Tables sized properly to ensure legibility and attractive appearance				2	0	0
k. Report matches what is requested in engagement letter				2	0	0
					0	0
Overall Rating					#DIV/0!	

Timing

- Due date
- Actual delivery date
- No. days late
- Communication w/client for any lateness

Corrective Actions Required:

1. ______________________________
2. ______________________________
3. ______________________________

* Ratings:

3: Above standard

2: Meets standard

1: Below standard

0: Not applicable

Bibliography

Aisuke, Daisuke, Mariko Sanchanata, and Yoshio Takahashi. "Toyota Faces Fallout over Recall." *The Wall Street Journal* (February 1, 2010).

The American Customer Satisfaction Index. Scores by Industry. http://www.theacsi.org/index.php?option=com_content&task=view&id=18&Itemid=33/.

Antony, Jiju. "Pros and Cons of Six Sigma: An Academic Perspective." *Improvement and Innovation.com* (January 7, 2008). http://www.improvementandinnovation.com/features/articles/pros-and-cons-six-sigma-academic-perspective?page=3/.

The Appraisal of Real Estate. 13th ed. Chicago: The Appraisal Institute, 2008.

Besterfield, Dale H. *Quality Control.* Upper Saddle River, NJ: Prentice-Hall, 2001.

Deming, W.E. *Quality, Productivity, and Competitive Position.* Cambridge, MA: Massachusetts Institute of Technology, Center for Advanced Engineering Study, 1982.

Dubay, William H. *The Principles of Readability.* Costa Mesa, CA: Impact Information, 2004.

Eckes, George. *The Six Sigma Revolution.* New York: John Wiley & Sons, 2001.

Evans, James R., and William M. Lindsay. *The Management and Control of Quality.* Cincinnati: South-Western College Publishing, 1999.

Garner, Bryan A. *Garner's Modern American Usage.* 3rd ed. Oxford University Press, 2009.

George, Michael L. *Lean Six Sigma for Service.* New York: McGraw-Hill, 2003.

Gitlow, Howard S., PhD, David M. Levine, PhD, and Edward A. Popovich, PhD. *Design for Six Sigma for Green Belts and Champions.* Upper Saddle River, NJ: Prentice Hall, 2006.

Gray, W. S., and B. E. Leary. *What Makes a Book Readable?* Chicago: University of Chicago Press, 1935.

"GSEs to Enhance Appraisal Data Collection." *Appraiser News Online* 11, no. 9/10 (May 26, 2010).

Harry, Mikel, PhD, and Richard Schroeder. *Six Sigma: The Breakthrough Management Strategy Revolutionizing the World's Top Corporations.* New York: Doubleday, 2000.

Himstreet, William C. *Writing Appraisal Reports.* Chicago: American Institute of Real Estate Appraisers, 1974.

Ishikawa, Kaoru. *Introduction to Quality Control.* Tokyo: 3A Corporation, 1989.

Johnson, L. Marvin. *Quality Assurance Program Evaluation.* West Covina, CA: L. Marvin Johnson, 1990.

Johnson, Michael D., and Anders Gustafsson. *Improving Customer Satisfaction, Loyalty, and Profit.* San Francisco: Jossey-Bass, 2000.

Juran, J. M. *Juran on Leadership for Quality.* New York: The Free Press, 1989.

_____. *Juran's Quality Control Handbook.* New York: McGraw-Hill, 1988 and 1999.

_____. "Managing for Quality." *Journal for Quality and Participation* 11, no. 1 (January/February 1988): 8-12.

Kano, Noriaki, Nobuhiku Seraku, Fumio Takahashi, and Shinichi Tsuji. "Attractive Quality and Must-Be Quality." *Journal of the Japanese Society for Quality*: 2, 14.

Karlgaard, Rich. "Four Styles of Leadership." *Forbes* (November 2, 2009).

______. "Recovery's Seven Secrets." *Forbes* (June 7, 2010).

Keiningham, Timothy L., and Terry Vavra. *The Customer Delight Principle: Exceeding Customers' Expectations for Bottom-Line Success.* New York: McGraw-Hill, 2001.

Kotler, Philip, and Kevin Lane Keller. *Marketing Management.* 13th ed. Upper Saddle River, NJ: Prentice Hall, 2009.

Linné, Mark R., and John Cirincione. "Open Data Standards: Why You Should Care," *Valuation* (4th Quarter 2009).

Marks, Michael Lee. "In With the New." *The Wall Street Journal* (May 24, 2010): Section R.

McNamara, Carter, PhD. "Basics of Conducting Focus Groups." Free Management Library. http://www.managementhelp.org/evaluatn/focusgrp.htm/.

Michel, Stefan, David Bowen, and Robert Johnston. "Making the Most of Customer Complaints." *The Wall Street Journal* (September 22, 2008). http://online.wsj.com/article/SB122160026028144779.html?mod=todays_us_the_journal_r/.

MindTools. "Active Listening." http://www.mindtools.com/CommSkll/ActiveListening.htm.

Mlodinow, Leonard. "A Hint of Hype, A Taste of Illusion." *The Wall Street Journal* (November 14-15, 2010): Section W.

Murley, Peter. *Handbook of Customer Service.* Cheltenham, UK: Gower Publishing Limited, 1997.

National Center for Education Statistics, US Department of Education, Office of Educational Research and Improvement. "Adult Literacy in America." December 1993. http://www.nald.ca/fulltext/Report2/rep15-01.htm/.

Nelson, Bob, PhD. "Everything You Thought You Knew about Recognition is Wrong." *Workforce Management* (January 2004). http://www.workforce.com/archive/feature/23/61/87/index.php.

Parsowith, B. Scott. *Fundamentals of Quality Auditing.* Milwaukee: ASQC Quality Press, 1995.

Powell, Gabriel. "Step-by-Step Guide to Designing InDesign Templates." *Adobe Press* (March 14, 2008). http://www.adobepress.com/articles/article.asp?p=1181454/.

Pyzdek, Thomas. *The Six Sigma Handbook.* New York: McGraw-Hill, 2003.

Rattermann, Mark R. *Using Residential Appraisal Report Forms: URAR, Form 2055, and the Market Conditions Form.* Chicago: Appraisal Institute, 2009.

Sanchanata, Mariko, and Yoshio Takahashi. "Toyota's Recall May Top $5 Billion." *The Wall Street Journal* (March 10, 2010): Section B.

Shirouzu, Norihiko. "Inside Toyota, Executives Trade Blame over Debacle." *The Wall Street Journal* (April 14, 2010): Section A.

Strunk, William, Jr., and E. B. White. *The Elements of Style.* 4th ed. Longman, 1999.

Takahashi, Yoshio. “Toyoda Apologizes to Holders.” *The Wall Street Journal* (June 25, 2010): Section B.

Tompkins, Neville C. “Employee Satisfaction Leads to Customer Service-Employee Relations.” *HR Magazine* (November 1992). http://findarticles.com/p/articles/mi_m3495/is_n11_v37/ai_13603614/.

Uniform Standards of Professional Appraisal Practice. 2010-2011 ed. Washington, DC: The Appraisal Foundation, 2010.

Williams, Mary A., Thomas Bertels, and Harvey Dreshin. *Six Sigma Pocket Guide.* Lexington, MA: Rath & Strong, 2004.

The Writing Center, University of North Carolina at Chapel Hill. “Editing and Proofreading,” 2009. http://www.unc.edu/depts/wcweb/handouts/proofread.html/.